ENCYCLOPEDIA OF LANGUAGE AND EDUCATION

Encyclopedia of Language and Education

VOLUME 4: SECOND LANGUAGE EDUCATION

The volume titles of this encyclopedia are listed at the end of this volume.

Encyclopedia of Language and Education

Volume 4

SECOND LANGUAGE EDUCATION

Edited by

G. RICHARD TUCKER

Department of Modern Languages
Carnegie Mellon University
Pittsburgh, USA

and

DAVID CORSON

The Ontario Institute for Studies in Education
University of Toronto
Canada

KLUWER ACADEMIC PUBLISHERS

DORDRECHT / BOSTON / LONDON

Library of Congress Cataloging-in-Publication Data

Second language education / edited by G. Richard Tucker and David
    Corson.
        p.   cm. -- (Encyclopedia of language and education ; v. 4)
    Includes bibliographical references and index.
    ISBN 0-7923-4640-8 (alk. paper). -- ISBN 0-7923-4596-7 (set : alk.
paper)
    1. Language and languages--Study and teaching. 2. Second language
acquisition.   I. Tucker, G. Richard. II. Corson, David.
    III. Series.
    P53.S3914 1997
    418'.007--dc21   97-30203

ISBN 0-7923-4931-8 (PB)   ISBN 0-7923-4640-8 (HB)
ISBN 0-7923-4936-9 (HB-SET)   ISBN 0-7923-4596-7 (HB-SET)

Published by Kluwer Academic Publishers,
P.O. Box 17, 3300 AA Dordrecht, The Netherlands

Sold and distributed in the U.S.A. and Canada
by Kluwer Academic Publishers,
101 Philip Drive, Norwell, MA 02061, U.S.A.

In all other countries, sold and distributed
by Kluwer Academic Publishers Group,
P.O. Box 322, 3300 AH Dordrecht, The Netherlands

Printed in the Netherlands (on acid-free paper)

TABLE OF CONTENTS

VOLUME 4: SECOND LANGUAGE EDUCATION

GENERAL EDITOR'S INTRODUCTION

ENCYCLOPEDIA OF LANGUAGE AND EDUCATION

This is one of eight volumes of the Encyclopedia of Language and Education published by Kluwer Academic. The publication of this work signals the maturity of the field of 'language and education' as an international and interdisciplinary field of significance and cohesion. These volumes confirm that 'language and education' is much more than the preserve of any single discipline. In designing these volumes, we have tried to recognise the diversity of the field in our selection of contributors and in our choice of topics. The contributors come from every continent and from more than 40 countries. Their reviews discuss language and education issues affecting every country in the world.

We have also tried to recognise the diverse interdisciplinary nature of 'language and education' in the selection of the editorial personnel themselves. The major academic interests of the volume editors confirm this. As principal volume editor for Volume 1, Ruth Wodak has interests in critical linguistics, sociology of language, and language policy. For Volume 2, Viv Edwards has interests in policy and practice in multilingual classrooms and the sociology of language. For Volume 3, Bronwyn Davies has interests in the social psychology of language, the sociology of language, and interdisciplinary studies. For Volume 4, Richard Tucker has interests in language theory, applied linguistics, and the implementation and evaluation of innovative language education programs. For Volume 5, Jim Cummins has interests in the psychology of language and in critical linguistics. For Volume 6, Leo van Lier has interests in applied linguistics and in language theory. For Volume 7, Caroline Clapham has interests in research into second language acquisition and language measurement. And for Volume 8, Nancy Hornberger has interests in anthropological linguistics and in language policy. Finally, as general editor, I have interests in the philosophy and sociology of language, language policy, critical linguistics, and interdisciplinary studies. But the thing that unites us all, including all the contributors to this work, is an interest in the practice and theory of education itself.

People working in the applied and theoretical areas of education and language are often asked questions like the following: 'what is the latest research on such and such a problem?' or 'what do we know about such

G. R. Tucker and D. Corson (eds), Encyclopedia of Language and Education,
Volume 4: Second Language Education, vii–ix.
© *1997 Kluwer Academic Publishers. Printed in the Netherlands.*

and such an issue?' Questions like these are asked by many people: by policy makers and practitioners in education; by novice researchers; by publishers trying to relate to an issue; and above all by undergraduate and postgraduate students in the language disciplines. Each of the reviews that appears in this volume tries to anticipate and answer some of the more commonly asked questions about language and education. Taken together, the eight volumes of this Encyclopedia provide answers to more than 200 major questions of this type, and hundreds of subsidiary questions as well.

Each volume of the Encyclopedia of Language and Education deals with a single, substantial subject in the language and education field. The volume titles and their contents appear elsewhere in the pages of this work. Each book-length volume provides more than 20 state-of-the-art topical reviews of the literature. Taken together, these reviews attempt a complete coverage of the subject of the volume. Each review is written by one or more experts in the topic, or in a few cases by teams assembled by experts. As a collection, the Encyclopedia spans the range of subjects and topics normally falling within the scope of 'language and education'. Each volume, edited by an international expert in the subject of the volume, was designed and developed in close collaboration with the general editor of the Encyclopedia, who is a co-editor of each volume as well as general editor of the whole work.

The Encyclopedia has been planned as a necessary reference set for any university or college library that serves a faculty or school of education. Libraries serving academic departments in any of the language disciplines, especially applied linguistics, would also find this a valuable resource. It also seems very relevant to the needs of educational bureaucracies, policy agencies, and public libraries, particularly those serving multicultural or multilingual communities.

The Encyclopedia aims to speak to a prospective readership that is multinational, and to do so as unambiguously as possible. Because each book-size volume deals with a discrete and important subject in language and education, these state-of-the-art volumes also offer authoritative course textbooks in the areas suggested by their titles. This means that libraries will also catalogue these book-size individual volumes in relevant sections of their general collections. To meet this range of uses, the Encyclopedia is published in a hardback edition offering the durability needed for reference collections, and in a future student edition. The hardback edition is also available for single-volume purchase.

Each state-of-the-art review has about 3000 words of text and most follow a similar structure. A list of references to key works cited in each review supplements the information and authoritative opinion that the review contains. Many contributors survey early developments in their topic, major contributions, work in progress, problems and difficulties, and future directions for research and practice. The aim of the reviews, and of the Encyclopedia as a whole, is to give readers access to the international literature and research on each topic.

David Corson
General Editor Encyclopedia of Language and Education
Ontario Institute for Studies in Education of the University of Toronto
Canada

INTRODUCTION

The present volume brings together a unique collection of reviews which examine diverse facets of second language learning and teaching. The collection is, I believe, particularly timely given the rapidly expanding number of individuals for whom education in a second or later-learned language is a commonplace occurrence. The use of a second or later learned language in education may be attributed to, or be a reflection of, numerous factors such as the linguistic heterogeneity of a country or region (e.g., Luxembourg or Singapore); specific social or religious attitudes (e.g., the addition of Sanskrit to mark Hinduism or Pali to mark Buddhism); or the desire to promote national identity (e.g., in India, Nigeria, the Philippines). In addition, innovative language education programs are often implemented to promote proficiency in international language(s) of wider communication together with proficiency in national and regional languages. The composite portrait of language education policies and practices throughout the world is exceedingly complex – and simultaneously fascinating.

In Eritrea, for instance, an educated person will likely have attended some portion of schooling taught via Tigrigna *and* Arabic *and* English – and developed proficiency in reading these languages which are written using three different scripts (Ge'ez, Arabic, and Roman)! In Papua New Guinea, on the other hand, a country which has a population of approximately 3,000,000, linguists have described more than 870 mutually unintelligible languages. Here it is common for a child to grow up speaking one local indigenous language at home, another in the market place, adding Tok Pisin to her repertoire as a lingua franca, and English if she continues her formal schooling. Analogous situations recur in many parts of the world such as India which has declared 15 of its approximately 1,650 indigenous languages to be "official"; or Guatemala, or Nigeria, or South Africa – to name but a few countries in which multilingualism predominates, and in which students are frequently exposed to numerous languages as they move from their homes into their communities and eventually through the formal educational system.

The 22 contributions to the present volume examine in some detail diverse aspects of second language education ranging from a focus on the basic contributions of linguistic theory and research to our understanding of second language learning and teaching on the one hand to a series of reviews of innovative language education practices in selected regions of the world on the other.

G. R. Tucker and D. Corson (eds), Encyclopedia of Language and Education,
Volume 4: Second Language Education, xi–xv.
© *1997 Kluwer Academic Publishers. Printed in the Netherlands.*

For purposes of the present volume, second language education has been defined operationally to encompass education which occurs in those settings and situations in which a dominant language is offered as a second language (e.g., ESL in England or the United States whether as a subject of study or vehicle through which other material is studied), as well as those cases in which an official, but not necessarily dominant, language is mandated (e.g., French or English in certain parts of the Middle East or the Mahgreb). The contributions also focus mainly, albeit not exclusively, on second language education for school-aged learners.

THEMATIC ORGANIZATION OF VOLUME

Although each of the 22 contributions stands alone and can profitably be consulted for specific information, the volume is also organized thematically with a progression of five interrelated sections. The initial contributions by Shirai and Schachter focus on *theoretical underpinnings* and examine the ways in which work in generative linguistics has indirectly influenced second language teaching by influencing second language acquisition research which in turn generated implications for syllabus design, textbook preparation and even choice of program model. The next set of four contributions by Oxford, Gardner, Singleton and de Bot examine diverse aspects of *individual learner characteristics* as they impinge upon and affect second language learning and retention in disparate formal and non-formal settings throughout the world. The third set of contributions by Allwright, Crandall, Hamayan, Burnaby and Gunnarsson review issues related to the *delivery of instruction*. Collectively, they identify, describe and raise critical questions about the characteristics of programs and approaches which help individuals to learn second languages as well as those which help them to make the transition to academic instruction via the second language. The fourth set of papers by Widdowson, Jung and Shohamy examine aspects of *teacher preparation*. Papers consider issues ranging from the ways in which views about the purposes and the content of teacher education programs have changed over the past several decades to a consideration of the implications of technology-enhanced learning for future teachers and students. The last section comprises an examination of *innovative language education programs* in seven purposefully selected regions of the world (Christian & Rhodes for North America; Kettemann for Europe; Medgyes for Central and Eastern Europe; Abu Absi for the Middle East and North Africa; Rodseth for southern Africa; Pakir for Southeast Asia; and Watts for the South Pacific). These regions were selected because of their inherent interest as well as the general accessibility of documentation. The paper by Paulston frames and sets the stage for an examination of a variety of policy and programmatic issues within the context of effects of prolonged contact of ethnic groups within modern nation states. In short, the individual papers will, I hope, be read profitably either in isolation or collectively as a volume treating a range of interrelated phenomena.

From this latter perspective, there are a number of important cross-cutting themes which seem to underpin many of the reviews and indeed much of the work by members of the language education profession. I propose to identify and comment briefly on each of these themes; and then to conclude by alluding to two relatively neglected areas which I believe warrant future concern. The five cross-cutting themes include: continuing attention to the interplay of theory, research and educational practice; a growing prominence of innovative practice throughout the world typified by programs integrating language and content instruction; a critical need for additional attention to teacher development – both preservice and in-service; a growing concern that the effective spread of languages such as English and French as second languages will inevitably result in the further loss or erosion of endangered languages; and a growing realization that potentially effective educational innovations may not be sustainable in many settings. The two relatively neglected areas which may well receive increased attention during the coming decade are further discussion of the role of cultural content in the development of materials and curricula, and the paucity of work, whether in areas of assessment, curriculum or program, in languages other than English.

MAJOR CROSS-CUTTING THEMES

Several of the contributors to this volume (e.g., Allwright, Christian & Rhodes, Crandall, Hamayan, Schachter, Shirai and Widdowson) have called attention to the continuing interplay of theory, practice and edu-cational research. Christian and Rhodes, for example, note that during the past decade converging social forces in the U. S. have demanded an improvement in traditional programs of second language teaching and learning which has led to additional basic and applied research culminat-ing in the broader implementation of innovative second language programs characterized by the integration of language and content. Likewise Cran-dall notes the important interplay of research and practice in the search for appropriate models of instruction or programs to help children learn a second language and make an effective transition to academic instruction via the second language. Hamayan, as well, calls attention to the strong linkages among theory, research and practice in the continuing search to better understand the special needs of individuals from minority back-grounds who must acquire facility in a second language for educational or occupational purposes and who are living in circumstances of poverty, trauma, social or political persecution.

As basic and applied research continues to inform educational practice,

I was struck by the number of disparate settings in which quite different and situationally appropriate innovative educational programs are being implemented which are characterized by the integration of language and content instruction. Numerous contributors (e.g., Christian & Rhodes, Kettemann, Medgyes, Pakir, Rodseth and Watts) either describe exciting programs such as those in some of the so-called small countries of the South Pacific (e.g., Tonga or Kiribati) or note that programs seeking to enhance the integration of language across the curriculum will expand in the near future as in southern Africa. Within this context of worldwide concern for the implementation of innovative programs to better meet the educational needs of an expanding body of learners comes an almost universal recognition that the number of trained teachers is simply too small. Thus, almost all of the contributors who describe innovative programs also call for additional attention to teacher development (e. g., Abu Absi, Christian & Rhodes, Kettemann, Medgyes, Pakir, Rodseth and Watts). As Crandall and Widdowson both note, there is a need for additional teachers and also in many cases for a reconceptualization of traditional programs of language teacher education. In this vein, Allwright chronicles a major shift in the focus of work in classroom-oriented research with a return to the reflective teacher as an object of central concern.

Despite the exciting interplay of theory, practice and research which has led to the implementation of numbers of innovative second language programs throughout the world, numerous contributors (e.g., Paulston, Rodseth and Watts) express the fear that the continuing spread of languages such as English and French as languages of wider communication will inevitably result in the further loss of presently endangered languages. Thus, they argue that the development of facility in a second language must not occur at the expense of the heritage language – a theme examined in greater detail in Volume 1 and to some extent in Volume 5. Finally, several of the contributors (e.g., Medgyes, Pakir and Watts) observe that effective educational innovations may not be sustainable in many settings. Pakir cautions, for example, that creative curriculum development does not always lead to implementation of successful program innovation while Medgyes points out that a heavy reliance on bilateral assistance in numerous settings has resulted in disappointment when the short term assistance is terminated and many newly developed programs cannot be sustained with local resources. Relatively little attention was devoted to this topic in the present volume, but clearly this is one which warrants additional attention.

Two other areas stand out as relatively neglected ones which may well receive increased attention during the coming decade: the lack of focus on innovative development, whether in areas of assessment, curriculum or program, in languages other than English – a need discussed, for example, by Shohamy (see also Volume 7 of this series); and further discussion of the role of cultural content in the development of materials and curricula – work specifically called for by Abu Absi and Pakir. Clearly both of these topics are candidates for future work in decades to come.

CONCLUDING OBSERVATIONS: INDICATORS OF THE VITALITY OF THE FIELD

I have been struck during the past several years by the salient indicators of the vitality of this field. There are numerous regularly appearing journals (e.g., *Language and Education*, *Journal of Multilingual and Multicultural Development*, *Language Learning*) or series uniquely devoted to publication of work in the area; there are regular fora (e.g., the conferences of the Association Internationale de Linguistique Appliqué, American Association for Applied Linguistics; National Association for Bilingual Education) devoted to facilitating communication among researchers, practitioners and policy makers; and many new monographs on diverse aspects of this topic which appear with regular frequency. Clearly, the continuing demographic, social and political changes that have been described by various contributors to this volume make it increasingly likely that those concerned with diverse aspects of second language education will find continuing support for and interest in their work during the decade ahead.

G. Richard Tucker
Carnegie Mellon University, USA

Section 1

Theoretical Underpinnings

YASUHIRO SHIRAI

LINGUISTIC THEORY & RESEARCH: IMPLICATIONS FOR SECOND LANGUAGE TEACHING

Linguistic theory and research have always had some influence on second language teaching to varying degrees. This review first discusses how different types of linguistic theory – structural, generative, and functional linguistics – have influenced second language teaching, and then discusses some current second language acquisition research that has important implications for second language teaching.

EARLY DEVELOPMENTS

The period when linguistics had the strongest influence on second/foreign language teaching was the 1950's and early 1960's, when the audio-lingual approach, which is based on structuralist linguistics (and behaviorist psychology), was the most influential teaching method. Based on the structural linguistic tenet that 'languages can differ without limit' and the behaviorist learning theory of habit formation, second language learning was considered to be essentially creating a new habit (the target language) by suppressing the old habit (the mother tongue). Learning difficulty, therefore, was believed to stem mainly from the difference between the first language (L1) and the second language (L2). The Contrastive Analysis Hypothesis was a major tool in this approach: it was thought that by comparing the learner's L1 and the target language, the areas of difficulty could be predicted, which in turn would make the teaching of linguistic structure more efficient. Techniques emphasized in the audio-lingual approach were structural oral drills which aimed at having learners acquire the structural properties of the target language. By means of oral drills such as substitution, conversion, and mimicry memorization, learners were expected to develop the habits of the L2 structure, and at the same time overcome interference from habits from the L1 (Lado, 1957).

Although the audio-lingual method continued to be in vogue in the 1960's, in the field of linguistics Chomsky's generative transformational grammar had begun to change the scene dramatically. Structural linguistics as well as behaviorist psychology had focused only on the analysis of 'observable behavior', claiming that postulating non-observable constructs was unscientific. Chomsky's generative transformational grammar, however, not only proposed a more adequate model of description by using non-observable constructs such as 'deep structure,' and 'transformation',

G. R. Tucker and D. Corson (eds), Encyclopedia of Language and Education,
Volume 4: Second Language Education, 1–9.
© *1997 Kluwer Academic Publishers. Printed in the Netherlands.*

but it also addressed deeper questions, such as why language has the form it has, and how humans acquire it. During the 1960's, Chomsky's generative transformational grammar gained the status of orthodoxy in theoretical linguistics (see Newmeyer, 1986 for a detailed account). It was also instrumental in the fall of behaviorist psychology, and the rise of cognitive psychology, which is more mentalistic.

With the demise of structural linguistics and behaviorist psychology, audio-lingualism lost its theoretical backbone. Furthermore, various empirical studies which tested the Contrastive Analysis Hypothesis (e.g., Whitman & Jackson, 1972) did not support it. In addition, it was shown that not all errors made by learners are based on L1 interference; some errors are the result of creative processes of hypothesis testing (intra-lingual errors, Richards 1971). Losing both its theoretical and empirical validity, audio-lingualism lost its legitimacy by the late 1960's.

MAJOR CONTRIBUTIONS

Unlike structural linguistics, Chomsky's generative theory of language did not have much to say about second language teaching (Chomsky, 1966). Generative linguistics has therefore not influenced teaching methodology directly. However, it did influence second language teaching indirectly through the work of second language acquisition researchers inspired by the spirit of generative linguistics. At the same time, there were also other theoretical frameworks of linguistics, namely those of a more social and functional orientation, that influenced second language teaching as well as research on second language acquisition.

Currently, two schools of communicative approaches are considered to be good sources of models of second language teaching: the Input Model (e.g., the Natural Approach) and the Input-interaction Model (e.g., Communicative Language Teaching).

Although there have been earlier proponents of input (i.e., comprehension-based) models of L2 teaching (e.g., Postovsky, 1977), Krashen is the most well-known advocate of this approach. Based on his own synthesis of second language acquisition (SLA) research, he postulated that second language acquisition occurs when the learner comprehends the language input in a low-anxiety, high-motivation situation, and proposed that the teacher's role is to provide students with just such an environment in the classroom. He also claimed that conscious grammar teaching/learning is effective only in monitoring (i.e., checking) grammatical correctness, not in the acquisition of L2 *per se* (Krashen & Terrell, 1983). Krashen's theory appears to be based on three major areas of research: (1) Chomsky's generative linguistics (2) research on the effectiveness of different L2 teaching methods, and (3) research on affective factors (motivation, anxiety, personality, etc.). The influence of generative linguistics is indirect. First,

Krashen borrowed Chomsky's notion of the Language Acquisition Device (LAD), though only at a metaphorical level. He claimed that given linguistic input that is comprehensible, the LAD of L2 learners will work just like that of children acquiring L1. Second, Krashen's theory is based heavily on research on morpheme acquisition order, which claims there is a universal order that cannot be altered by instruction. These morpheme studies are strongly influenced by generative linguistics. As discussed earlier, the predominant view of the 1950's and 1960's was that learners' errors result mostly from L1 interference, but Chomsky, in invalidating behaviorist psychology and structural linguistics, emphasized instead the universal aspects of language and language acquisition. Inspired by Chomsky's ideas, second language researchers began to investigate the learners' acquisition process. Studies on morpheme acquisition point to some universal tendencies in second language acquisition, which in turn inspired Krashen's model of second language acquisition (Dulay, Burt & Krashen, 1982). It should be noted, however, that Krashen's theory of second language acquisition has been questioned by other researchers (see, for example, McLaughlin, 1987, Gregg, 1984), even though his teaching method is generally regarded as effective.

Communicative Language Teaching (CLT; sometimes called the Communicative Approach), on the other hand, developed independently from Krashen's Natural Approach. It originated in a project undertaken by the Council of Europe, whose primary goal was to construct a teaching methodology to teach foreign languages to meet the increasing need for communication in a second language in the rapidly internationalizing Europe (see, for example, van Ek & Alexander, 1975). The outcome was the Notional Functional Syllabus, which emphasized the teaching of communicative functions of language (e.g., requesting, apologizing, disagreeing) rather than of linguistic structures. To teach communicative abilities using this syllabus, a number of teaching principles/techniques (e.g., information-gap activities, use of authentic language) were proposed which have now grown into the present day CLT.

CLT has its theoretical underpinnings in Speech Act Theory, Functional Grammar and sociolinguistics (Munby 1978). Speech Act Theory was developed by philosophers such as John Austin, John Searle, and Paul Grice. Austin (1962) pointed out that when people say something, they are not only uttering the sentence, but are also engaging in some pragmatic act such as requesting, warning, promising, instructing, etc., and he developed a theory of how such 'speech acts' are performed. This led to the 'functions' used in CLT.

Systemic Functional Grammar (Halliday, 1978) is also radically different from Chomskyan formal linguistics. Whereas Chomsky emphasizes the concept of modularity (i.e., the autonomy of different modules of linguistic competence, such as independence of syntax from semantics or pragmatics), and whereas Chomsky further assumes that linguistics should focus on the study of competence (i.e., abstract knowledge representation in the idealized native speaker's mind) and disregard performance (i.e., actual use of language), Halliday argues that the study of 'functions' of language is important in itself, and that the nature of language should be explained in functional terms. Naturally, Halliday's ideas are quite compatible with the needs of CLT, whose focus is to help learners acquire the ability to use a second language in a communicative setting. Halliday's theoretical constructs, including the interpersonal functions of language, were thus translated and used in actual L2 teaching syllabuses, and were also used as important constructs in language testing (Bachman, 1990).

Hymes (1972) proposed the notion of Communicative Competence which is generally considered today as the L2 ability to be attained in CLT. Coming from a background of sociolinguistics which investigates language in actual use, Hymes considered Chomsky's notion of linguistic competence too narrow, and asserted that a theory of language competence should include knowledge concerning the rules of language use, such as rules about social appropriateness. The notion of communicative competence was further refined and expanded by Canale and Swain (1980) in relation to second language teaching and testing, and their paper has since been a reference point for any discussion of Communicative Competence.

WORK IN PROGRESS

The communicative approaches discussed above do not have much to say about instruction in 'grammatical competence', which includes knowledge of phonology, morphology, syntax, and vocabulary. These approaches emphasize 'learning by doing' and claim that such linguistic competence will be acquired during the process of communicative activities that focus on meaning/function. At present, this may be the most practical approach since there is not enough research done regarding how linguistic competence is (and should be) acquired by L2 learners. However, research in second language acquisition has shed some light on the process of how linguistic competence is acquired.

Interest in linguistic universals and markedness has spurred some second language acquisition research that may be relevant to how some linguistic structures should be taught. Markedness is a term which originated in the Prague school of functional linguistics. In its original formulation, markedness was a binary feature (i.e., marked vs. unmarked). For example, the singular form of a noun (*book*) is unmarked, and the plural form (*books*) is marked. The unmarked form is formally more basic, and the marked form is more complex. Subsequent research on typological universals has extended the scope of markedness to include a hierarchy of markedness; that is, something is more (or less) marked than another. Often discussed in second language acquisition research is the Noun Phrase Accessibility Hierarchy (Keenan & Comrie, 1977). The claim is that relativization of subject NPs (e.g., *the girl who came*) is more basic (unmarked) than that of object NPs (e.g., *the girl who I like*), because any language that can relativize object NPs can also relativize subject NPs. The hierarchy of markedness claimed was:

Subject > Direct Object > Indirect Object > Object of Preposition > Genitive > Object of Comparison

Therefore, if a language can relativize, say, genitives (e.g., *the girl whose father I like*) it can relativize any NP to the left of Genitive in the hierarchy. This relationship holds for frequency within a language as well. Keenan (1975) shows that the above hierarchy corresponds to the text count frequency in English, subject relative being most frequent, direct object relative second, and so forth.

This hierarchy has been used to predict the difficulty L2 learners face in acquiring relative clauses. Gass (1979) has shown that learners have more difficulty acquiring relatives lower on the hierarchy (i.e., to the right) than those on the left, such as Subject. This leads to the general claim that unmarked items are acquired more easily than marked items.

The markedness principle also applies to the area of semantics. Kellerman (e.g., 1978) has shown that psycholinguistic markedness of lexical items with multiple meanings (i.e., polysemy) is an important factor in lexical development in L2. He concludes that learners tend to believe that the basic (unmarked) meanings of a word in their L1 are translatable into the L2 (e.g., *break a cup*) whereas more marked meanings (e.g., *break a record*) are not. Tanaka and Abe (1985) and Ijaz (1986) further showed that unmarked meanings of L2 lexical items are easier to acquire than marked meanings.

Gass and Ard (1984) extended the markedness principle in semantics to the acquisition of the tense-aspect system. They showed that the unmarked, prototypical meanings are easier to acquire than marked meanings. For example, the progressive form (be + V-ing) is easier when it denotes action in progress (*he is smoking now*) than planned future (*he is leaving tomorrow*). Andersen and Shirai (1994) discuss acquisition of tense-aspect morphology in various languages, and argue that learners start with unmarked, prototypical cases and only later do they acquire full potential of the morphology, including more marked use. All in all, various linguistic categories are acquired starting from the basic, unmarked member of the category, with the marked members being acquired later. In SLA research, several reasons for this acquisitional pattern have been proposed. For example, it may be that unmarked items are universally easier, for processing reasons (and possibly for innate reasons as well). Also, unmarked items tend to be more frequent in the native speaker's normal language input.

Finally, unmarked items tend to be taught early, and/or learners get more exposure to them in classroom.

The teacher's (or textbook writer's) intuition is normally to present a basic item when the learner is exposed to a new linguistic item. Studies on simplified input have shown that native speakers tend to restrict their input in talking to non-native speakers, and only use what they perceive to be basic (prototypical, unmarked) examples. It appears, as Hatch (1983) suggests, that native speakers feel more comfortable using basic meaning of a word (e.g., *break the cup*) rather than more marked meaning (e.g., *break a record*) since they tend to assume that the learner would know the basic meaning of polysemous words. An ESL teacher, in introducing the progressive aspect, would not start with a marked use such as *He's leaving tomorrow*, but with the more prototypical meaning (e.g., *He's running*). Indeed this has always been one of the basic premises in L2 teaching – so basic that not much has been said about it.

There is a possibility that this assumption should be questioned on two counts, both of which concern the issue of how to teach marked items within a particular linguistic domain. First, there is the problem of how to go beyond the unmarked items, and get the students to acquire marked ones. Bardovi-Harlig and Reynolds (1995) show that past tense marking by classroom learners of English tends to be restricted to unmarked use (i.e., past tense with punctual verbs such as *finish*, to denote completive events). They discuss possible teaching techniques (e.g., focused noticing) to expand learners' restricted past tense to be more native-like. Note, however, that it might be possible to avoid this situation by consciously presenting various marked uses, not just the unmarked uses, of a linguistic category right from the beginning.

Second, it may be more effective (for some grammatical items at least) to train learners on marked items first. It has been shown (e.g., Eckman, Bell & Nelson, 1988) that instruction on the items lower on the NP Accessibility Hierarchy also has an effect on the items higher on the hierarchy, but not vice versa. In other words, if the learner is trained on the less basic (i.e., more marked) structure, then the effect of the instruction will 'project' to the more basic (i.e., unmarked) structure. Similar results are obtained in Zobl's study of personal pronouns in English as L2 (Zobl, 1983).

PROBLEMS AND DIFFICULTIES

The research on markedness in SLA presents interesting possibilities in syllabus design and textbook writing. For example, if the findings on relative clauses are reliable, learners should be trained on object relatives first rather than more basic (less marked) subject relatives since subject relatives are supposed to come free if the learner acquires object relatives. However, the idea of presenting less basic items first does not work all the time. Research on L2 German word order rules has shown that learners do *not* acquire a particular rule unless they are already at the stage where they are 'ready' for it (Teachability Hypothesis, Pienemann 1984). Linguistic features that exhibit such rigid acquisitional sequences that cannot be altered have been called 'developmental', whereas those that can be influenced by motivation, instruction, etc. are referred to as 'variational' (Meisel et al., 1981; Pienemann et al., 1993). Pienemann and others have established, through longitudinal observation and experimental studies of L2 German, that some linguistic items (e.g., adverbial fronting) cannot be learned until the learner reaches a particular stage in development, whereas other items (e.g., copula) can be acquired regardless of the stage at which the learner is. The latter (i.e., variational items) can be amenable to instruction (i.e., teachable at any stage).

It is not clear, however, how such findings can be related to the principle of 'projection' discussed above, where the acquisition of marked items triggers that of unmarked items. Furthermore, such projection has been observed so far only in two areas – relative clauses and possessive pronouns in English.

FUTURE DIRECTIONS

Future research should address the issue of which linguistic features are 'developmental', 'variational' and/or 'projectional'. For linguistic items that are developmental, which can only be acquired in rigid sequence, L2 instruction may as well avoid situations where learners are required to use such structures before they are ready. For variational items, which can be learned at any point in the learner's development, we do not need to worry much about when to introduce them, except for practical considerations. For projectional items, for which the acquisition of marked items facilitates the acquisition of unmarked items, more marked items should be taught in addition to the most basic or unmarked items, even though this goes against the intuition of most teachers, who normally introduce basic, unmarked items first. Needless to say, there is a long way to go before such empirically motivated instructional programs will be in place, but second language acquisition research should at least start to uncover these areas if it is to have a constructive impact on second language teaching. With principles grounded in solid empirical research, communicative approaches currently in place will be much improved.

Another area for future research is the issue of input vs. output in communicative approaches. Krashen emphasizes the importance of not requiring learners to speak until they are ready. The issue of whether L2 teaching should place more emphasis on comprehension or whether it should put emphasis on production as well as input is an important one, and further research is needed to resolve this question. Research on related issues is under way both from the Input Model perspective (Van Patten & Cadierno, 1993), and from the Input-interaction Model perspective (Swain & Lapkin, 1995). Finally, it should be noted that generatively-oriented second language researchers, despite Chomsky's (1966) skepticism about applying linguistics to language teaching, have begun exploring the role of instruction within the generative linguistic framework, and are addressing important issues, such as the role of negative and positive evidence (e.g., explicit grammar instruction; White, 1991; see also Schachter's review in this volume). Regardless of theoretical orientation, future research in second language acquisition will need to specify optimal use of input, output, error correction, explicit grammar instruction in second language teaching.

Cornell University, USA

REFERENCES

Andersen, R. W. & Shirai, Y.: 1994, 'Discourse motivations for some cognitive acquisition principles', *Studies in Second Language Acquisition* 16, 133–156.
Austin, J.: 1962, *How to Do Things with Words*, Harvard University Press, Cambridge MA.
Bachman, L.: 1990, *Fundamental Considerations in Language Testing*, Oxford University Press, Oxford.
Bardovi-Harlig, K. & Reynolds, D. W.: 1995, 'The role of lexical aspect in the acquisition of tense and aspect', *TESOL Quarterly* 29, 107–131.
Canale, M. & Swain, M.: 1980, 'Theoretical bases of communicative approaches to second language teaching and testing', *Applied Linguistics* 1, 1–47.
Chomsky, N.: 1966, 'Linguistic theory', in R.C. Mead (ed.), *Reports of the Working Committee*, Northeast Conference on the Teaching of Foreign Languages, New York.
Dulay, H., Burt, M. & Krashen, S.: 1982, *Language Two*, Oxford University Press, New York.
Eckman, F.R., Bell, L. & Nelson, D.: 1988, 'On the generalization of relative clause instruction in the acquisition of English as a second language', *Applied Linguistics* 9, 1–20.
Gass, S.: 1979, 'Language transfer and universal grammatical relations', *Language Learning* 29, 327–344.
Gass, S & Ard, J.: 1984, 'Second language acquisition and the ontology of language universals', in W.E. Rutherford (ed.), *Language Universals and Second Language Acquisition*, 33–68.
Gregg, K.R.: 1984, 'Krashen's monitor and Occam's Razor', *Applied Linguistics* 5, 79–100.
Halliday, M.A.K.: 1978, *Language as a Social Semiotic*, Edward Arnold, London.
Hatch, E.: 1983, 'Simplified input and second language acquisition', in R.W. Andersen (ed.), *Pidginization and Creolization as Language Acquisition*, Newbury House, Rowley, MA, 64–86.
Hymes, D.: 1972, 'On communicative competence', in J.B. Pride & J. Holmes (eds.), *Sociolinguistics*, Penguin Books, Harmondsworth, UK.
Ijaz, I. H.: 1986, 'Linguistic and cognitive determinants of lexical acquisition in a second language', *Language Learning* 36, 401–451.

Keenan, E.: 1975, 'Variation in universal grammar', in R. Fasold & R. Shuy (eds.), *Analyzing Variation in Language*, Georgetown University Press, Washington, DC, 136–148.

Keenan, E., & Comrie, B.: 1977, 'Noun phrase accessibility and universal grammar', *Linguistic Inquiry* 8, 63–99.

Kellerman, E.: 1978, 'Giving learners a break: Native language intuitions as a source of predictions about transferability', *Working Papers on Bilingualism* 15, 59–92.

Krashen, S.D. & Terrell, T.D.: 1983. *The Natural Approach: Language Acquisition in the Classroom*, Pergamon, Oxford.

Lado, R.: 1957, *Linguistics Across Cultures*, University of Michigan Press, Ann Arbor, MI.

Meisel, J.M., Clahsen, H. & Pienemann, M.: 1981, 'On determining developmental stages in natural second language acquisition', *Studies in Second Language Acquisition* 3, 109–135.

McLaughlin, B.: 1987, *Theories of Second Language Learning*, Edward Arnold, London.

Munby, J.: 1978, *Communicative Syllabus Design*, Cambridge University Press, Cambridge.

Newmeyer, F.J.: 1986, *Linguistic Theory in America* (second edition), Academic Press, San Diego CA.

Pienemann, M.: 1984, 'Psychological constraints on the teachability of languages', *Studies in Second Language Acquisition* 6, 186–212.

Pienemann, M., Johnston, M. & Meisel, J.: 1993, 'The multidimensional model, linguistic profiling, and related issues: A reply to Hudson', *Studies in Second Language Acquisition* 15, 495–503.

Postovsky, V.: 1977. 'Why not start speaking later?', in M. Burt, H. Dulay & M. Finocchiaro (eds.), *Viewpoints on English as a Second Language*, Regents, New York, 17–26.

Richards, J.C.: 1971, 'Noncontrastive approach to error analysis', *English Language Teaching Journal* 25, 204–219.

Swain, M. & Lapkin, S.: 1995, 'Problems in output and the cognitive process they generate: A step towards second language learning', *Applied Linguistics* 16, 371–391.

Tanaka, S. & Abe, H.: 1985, 'Conditions on interlingual semantic transfer', in P. Larson, E.L. Judd, & D.S. Messerschmitt (eds.), *On TESOL '84: A Brave New World for TESOL*, TESOL, Washington, DC., 101–120.

van Ek, J.A. & Alexander, L.G.: 1975, *The Threshold Level English*, Pergamon Press, Oxford.

Van Patten, B. & Cadierno, T.: 1993, 'Explicit instruction and input processing', *Studies in Second Language Acquisition* 15, 225–243.

White, L.: 1991, 'Adverb placement in second language acquisition: Some effects of positive and negative evidence in the classroom', *Second Language Research* 7, 133–161.

Whitman, R. & Jackson, K. L.: 1972, 'The unpredictability of contrastive analysis', *Language Learning* 22, 29–41.

Zobl, H.: 1983, 'Grammars in search of input and intake', in S.M. Gass & C.G. Madden (eds.), *Input in Second Language Acquisition*, Newbury House, Rowley MA, 329–344.

JACQUELYN SCHACHTER

LINGUISTIC THEORY AND RESEARCH: IMPLICATIONS FOR SECOND LANGUAGE LEARNING

Many of the issues of great interest to theoreticians in language and language acquisition are also of great interest to classroom professionals. Yet
there is insufficient communication between these two groups, valuable
though that always is for both groups. And the literature in each area is
dense with terminology that prevents easy access to the facts of interest and
to the claims espoused. In this introduction I propose to delineate three
issues of great importance in both areas and to do so in language plain
enough so that the reader may find it interesting and intriguing enough to
attempt to dip into the literature of another field, in spite of its attendant
difficulties.

One of the most intriguing questions to date is whether or not one can
maintain that there is a sensitive (critical) period for language learning – a
period during which children are especially sensitized to linguistic input,
a period before which and after which language learning is considerably
more difficult and ultimate success is not guaranteed. It has been claimed
(cf. Lenneberg, 1967) that there is such a period for language, between
the ages of two and puberty; but those who argue against this position
are as numerous as those who argue for it (cf. Singleton's paper, this
volume). The practical consequences of certain knowledge on this issue
are not difficult to envision. This knowledge could guide educational
policy makers on the most appropriate times to begin foreign or second
language education in the school systems. And it could guide classroom
behavior of teachers concerned with the manner of presentation of the
language to young students.

Related to the sensitive period issue is the question regarding the extent
to which post-adolescent learners can and do learn the components of a
language (the phonology, the syntax, etc.) implicitly, and the associated
question on the value of explicit teaching of linguistic form. One of the
things we know about adult knowledge of their L1 is that it is largely
unconscious knowledge, and furthermore, implicitly gained knowledge
(Chomsky, 1986). There is general agreement that parents do not aid their
children's language learning by formulating rules or generalizations about
a language and then teaching them to their children (Gleitman & Wanner,

G.R. Tucker and D. Corson (eds), Encyclopedia of Language and Education,
Volume 4: Second Language Education, 11–19.
© *1997 Kluwer Academic Publishers. Printed in the Netherlands.*

1982). However, there is no such agreement on the value of such activities in the case of the post-adolescent adult.

Associated with the issues surrounding explicit language teaching, although by no means limited to such teaching, is the issue involving the provision of negative feedback on learner error production in the L2. When a learner of English says "Where I can find post office?", does it do any good to correct her? Are there more or less effective ways to provide negative feedback? Does indirect feedback have any pedagogical value? What about the written language?

A SENSITIVE PERIOD FOR LANGUAGE?

An early proponent of the notion that there was a biological basis for language acquisition, Lenneberg (1967) argued for a sensitive period between the ages of two and 13, partly on the basis of studies of children who received brain lesions (typically in Broca's and Wernicke's areas in the left hemisphere) affecting their ability to speak and understand, and their subsequent ability to recover their linguistic capacities. He found that those whose lesions occurred before puberty recovered fully but that those whose impairment took place after puberty were never able to fully recover linguistically. He also claimed as evidence the well known phenomenon that the early teens were the time of a considerable drop off in the abilities of adolescents to learn a second language.

Lesion studies continue (Dronkers & Pinker In press), but they have an inherent disadvantage for researchers in that the lesions are where they are, not necessarily precisely where an investigator would place them in order to get answers to specific questions on the location and function of certain brain structures. Because of the attendant problems associated with lesion studies, a number of researchers have turned to the study of late learners of American Sign Language (ASL), a natural language in all regards, with visual words rather than aural ones (Poizner, Klima, & Bellugi, 1987). These are people born congenitally deaf but who are normal in all other regards. Often, these people have hearing parents and so are not exposed to ASL as a first language until they go into boarding schools for the deaf, where they pick up ASL from other children. Studies of these late learners of ASL show certain deficits (Newport, 1984, Mayberry & Eichen, 1991) not seen in those who were exposed to ASL from birth.

The issue of a sensitive period has been viewed a little differently for L2 acquisition. In this case we assume normal L1 activation, and ask if there are periods during which L2 acquisition is facilitated by heightened sensitivity of the L2 learner to some aspects of the linguistic input. There are two basic positions on this question. One is that there is no sensitive period for language acquisition and that once one has activated the mechanisms and knowledge base necessary for L1 acquisition they remain forever available for L2 acquisition (Flynn & Martohardjono, 1992). The most convincing argument in favor of this claim is that the developmental paths of L1 and L2 look much the same. There are set developmental orders of acquisition of a given L2 regardless of the learner's L1 and the error types look to be common to both L1 and L2 learners. Another argument is that a small number of people appear to reach native speaker ability in an L2, even though first exposure to the L2 was in adulthood. Yet another argument is based on parsimony: why posit two mechanisms for language acquisition, one for child L1, one for adult L2?

The contrasting position is that there is in fact a sensitive period for language acquisition for both L1 and L2, and that once a learner has passed it, L2 acquisition is going to be less successful (Schachter, 1996). Clearly, the strongest argument supporting this position is that adults have so much difficulty learning an L2 and almost never reach the level of completeness that would let them pass as a native speaker of the L2. Moreover, an adult can learn to communicate in a related L2 much faster and with less effort than in an unrelated L2. A French speaker can learn Italian with relative ease, but Mandarin Chinese only with great difficulty.

There are a number of recent studies supporting the sensitive period concept. Johnson and Newport (1989, 1991) studied immigrant Chinese speakers of English whose age of acquisition varied from three to adulthood on a variety of surface features and one underlying principle of English, subjacency. They found a linear decline in proficiency associated with higher ages of arrival in the U.S. in tests of both the surface features and subjacency. Weber Fox and Neville (In press) studied areas of brain activation during the processing of sentences with semantic anomalies and sentences with syntactic anomalies in Chinese immigrants who varied in age of arrival, viz. 1–3, 4–6, 7–10, 11–13, over 16. They found comparable brain wave activity for semantic anomalies for all groups, but on the syntactic tests, they found progressively altered presence and distribution of brain wave activities for those individuals whose first exposure to English was later than the normal exposure for natives. In fact, in contrast to the responses of the earlier bilinguals, the responses of the late learning group showed no hemispheric specialization for any of the sentence types tested, results that are clearly compatible with a sensitive period hypothesis.

The notion that phonological/syntactic and semantic/pragmatic knowledge might be differentially affected by a sensitive period for language has gained some support in recent years. Long (1990) in reviewing the sensitive period literature has claimed, for instance, that the sensitive period for phonology ends at about six, with that for syntax ending at about 15. Lee and Schachter (1996) have even argued for multiple sensitive periods within a single component of language, syntax.

EXPLICIT AND IMPLICIT LEARNING

It is generally agreed that classroom instruction makes a difference in adult second language acquisition when contrasted with naturalistic exposure. However, the role of explicit grammar, particularly in instruction on the acquisition of the syntax of a language, is a topic that has been hotly debated. Krashen (1985) asserts that explicit knowledge of a language does not facilitate acquisition. Schmidt (1992) argues, in contrast, that nothing in the L2 can be acquired, including syntax, unless it is "noticed", which for Schmidt ranges in meaning from *attending* to learning explicit rules.

There has prevailed in the SLA literature a great deal of terminological fuzziness involved in the use of the terms *explicit* and *implicit* teaching and learning. But by means of a terminological distinction borrowed from the psychology literature, this fuzziness can be clarified. In the psychological literature, the term attention is usually taken to be consistent with William James's (1890) definition as "the taking possession by the mind, in clear and vivid form, of one out of what seem several simultaneously possible objects or trains of thought." Awareness, in contrast, has a very specific meaning (cf. Curran & Keele 1993): that an individual is able to detect and verbalize the pattern that she has learned. Given these definitions, we can restate Krashen's and Schmidt's claims as follows: Krashen claims acquisition occurs without attention (to form) whereas Schmidt claims that acquisition must occur with attention and may occur with both attention and awareness.

Who is right in this debate? Krashen cites, among other things, the successes of the Canadian French immersion programs. But as we have seen above, these successes may be due more to the fact that the children in these programs were within the sensitive period for language learning. And the question remains, what about adults?

Several recent studies have tackled this question squarely, using controlled presentations via computers, some using artificial languages, some natural languages. Tomasello and Herron (1989) tested the so-called Garden Path method whereby learners are led to make errors by being presented with a pattern which does not hold for all cases in the exercise. When the exceptions are presented, the learner makes the error, and at that point is given the rule and an example of how the rule works. Tomasello and Herron claim that the garden path method was better than the control method (the standard presentation of a rule before practice). However, their test involved only one token per type and is therefore suspect. Doughty (1991) taught relative clauses to three groups: ROG = rule oriented group, MOG=meaning oriented group, COG = control group. The ROG group received explicit instruction on the formation of the relative clauses; the MOG group received clarification of the content of the relative clauses as well as the sentences in which they occurred. The COG group received the same amount of exposure to the relative clauses as did the experimental groups but no teaching effort. On the formation of relative clauses, both experimental groups improved more than did the control, but no significant differences were found between the explicit and implicit experimental groups. Schachter, Rounds, Wright and Smith (1996) looked at the development of complex wh-questions in intermediate learners of English. They had four groups: Rule, Focus, Dual-Task, Control; the Rule and Focus groups' attention was directed to form, the Dual-Task group's attention was directed to meaning; the Rule group had explicit grammar presentation, the others did not. All experimental groups did better than the control. The explicit Rule group, however, did no better than the implicit Focus group, supporting the results of the Doughty study.

DeKeyser(1995), using a miniature artificial language, predicted that explicit teaching would be better for simple categorial rules and that implicit teaching would be better for prototype rules. The results showed that the first hypothesis was correct, but not the second. Robinson (1996) tested two kinds of explicit and two kinds of implicit presentation of form. His results are complex, but he claims that they support the hypothesis that explicit learning of complex rules is possible if the rules are made salient, and that implicit learning of complex rules is not more effective than explicit learning of them.

NEGATIVE FEEDBACK

One of the frequent questions teachers ask is whether correction of learner errors in the L2 does any good. In the linguistic literature, direct correction is included in negative feedback, along with confirmation checks, clarification requests, and failures to understand. In the study of L1 acquisition, it is fairly well established that, with the exception of vocabulary correction (That's not a doggie; that's a cow), negative feedback is not often available to the child and not attended to when it is offered (Brown & Hanlon, 1970; Braine, 1981).

This still leaves open the question of the value of negative feedback in older child L2 and adult L2 learning. After all, we know from other domains that these groups of learners can take advantage of negative feedback presented to them (cf. Karmiloff-Smith, 1992; Wason & Johnson-Laird, 1977). The studies focused on this issue can be roughly divided into descriptive and experimental categories. The descriptive studies in general present situations in which teachers (particularly in immersion classrooms) rarely correct for form, but do correct for content (cf. Chaudron, 1986). Studies with child-child and adult-adult interactions show only a small percentage of learner errors being corrected (Oliver, 1995 is an exception), and only a small percentage of these being taken up by the learners. It is clear from these studies that the goal of both native speakers and learners is communication, and with that goal in mind, negative feedback is difficult for learners to incorporate.

The experimental studies present a more mixed picture. Studies such as these are extremely difficult to devise and carry out. In a well-designed study Carroll and Swain (1993) tested for dative alternation with four experimental groups (each with a different kind of feedback) and a control group (with no feedback). But the whole experiment, from beginning to end, took place within a week and not much learning took place. Sasaki (1996) also had a well designed test, but the native speaker controls did not behave as expected, thus throwing into doubt the results with nonnatives. More recently, DeKeyser (1995) and Robinson (1996) have experimented with artificial languages, computerized lessons and feedback; their results are complex but only partially support the use of negative feedback.

LIKELY FUTURE DIRECTIONS IN RESEARCH AND PRACTICE

Clearly, much more needs to be discovered about the three critical areas discussed above: sensitive periods for L2 language learning, the relative values of implicit and explicit language teaching to L2 learners, and the value of providing negative feedback when learners make errors.

From an evaluative perspective, what seems most salient about the sensitive period research is that it is demonstrated to exist. Nonetheless, it does not appear to apply equally to all components of language. The lexicon can be learned throughout life; and the studies show that pragmatic knowledge (including discourse structures) is immune to sensitive period effects. It is when we come to the learning of phonology, morphology and syntax, what might be called the core of the language, that we find the most distinctive effects. This alone should impel educational policy makers to argue for early immersion-type exposure to an L2 within the school system. These conclusions do not, of course, entail the abandonment of the L1, but rather the integration of both the L1 and the L2 into the school curriculum. Many interesting programs are doing just that.

Of course, the use of immersion-type language presentation to young children and older children precludes a decision on the value of explicit grammar presentation since in many of these programs language per se is not taught. But in the area of adult language learning, the debate on implicit versus explicit grammar teaching rages on, in large part because the research studies are in conflict. What appears to be a hopeful sign is presented in the Doughty and Schachter et al. studies. Having a similar design they demonstrate that both implicit and explicit learning of (probably difficult) categorial rules takes place, and that the explicit presentation gives no advantage to learners in those conditions over learners in attentional but not rule-based conditions. Nevertheless, other studies provide a cautionary note to those who may want to generalize this result beyond the boundaries of the research labs. DeKeyser, Robinson, Ellis and others divide rules differently–categorial and prototypical, easy and hard, and here the picture becomes murkier, with little consensus among studies. At present, until a clearer picture emerges, it is probably more prudent to base pedagogical decisions on the assumption that both implicit and explicit teaching to adults aids in language learning, and to follow the research studies as they appear.

The work on negative feedback can be summed as follows: The descriptive studies show that native speakers (including teachers) correct relatively few learner errors and of those few, learners indicate uptake on even fewer. And the experimental studies, small in number, often have design flaws of such importance that their results cannot be trusted. Good studies can be designed, as some of those described show, and no doubt more will be carried out in the near future. On this issue, one should also suspect that there will be no easy answers on the value of negative data. It is not difficult to imagine that for some kinds of language phenomena, say semantically weak grammatical phenomena (cf. gender agreement in Spanish, third person singular marker in English) massive amounts of negative data may be required, whereas for other kinds of phenomena (cf. relative clause formation in any language) negative feedback will do no good whatsoever. One should look for interesting developments in this area.

University of Oregon, USA

REFERENCES

Braine, M.D.S.: 1971, 'On two types of models of the internalization of grammars', D. Slobin, (ed.), *The Ontogenesis of Grammar*, Academic Press, New York, 1971, 153–188.

Brown, R. & Hanlon, C.: 1970, 'Derivational complexity and order of acquisition in child speech', J.R. Hayes, (ed.), *Cognition and the Development of Language*, John Wiley and Sons, New York, 11–54.

Carroll, S. & Swain, M.: 1993, 'Explicit and implicit negative feedback: An empirical study of the learning of linguistic generalizations', *Studies in Second Language Acquisition* 15, 357–386.

Chaudron, C.: 1987, 'A descriptive model of discourse in the corrective treatment of learners' errors', *Language Learning* 27, 29–46.

Chomsky, N.: 1986, *Knowledge of Language*, Praeger, New York.

Curran, T. & Keele, S.W.: 1993, 'Attentional and nonattentional forms of sequence learning', *Journal of Experimental Psychology: Learning, Memory, and Cognition* 19, 189–202.

DeKeyser, R.: 1995, 'Learning L2 grammar rules: An experiment with a miniature linguistic system', *Studies in Second Language Acquisition* 17, 379–410.

Doughty, C.: 1991, 'Second language instruction does make a difference: Evidence from an empirical study of SL relativization', *Studies in Second Language Acquisition* 13, 431–469.

Dronkers, N. & Pinker, S.: In press, 'Language and the Aphasias', in E. Kandel, J. Schwartz, and T. Jeffries (eds.), *Principles in Neural Science*, 4th edition.

Ellis, N.: 1994, *Implicit and Explicit Learning of Languages*, Academic Press, London.

Flynn, S. & Martohardjono, G.: 1992, 'Evidence against a critical period hypothesis: Syntax'. Paper delivered at the annual meeting of the American Association of Applied Linguistics, Seattle, Washington.

Gleitman, L.R. & Wanner, E.: 1982, 'The logic of language acquisition', in Wanner & Gleitman (eds.), *Language Acquisition: The state of the art*, Cambridge University Press, Cambridge, 3–50.

James, W.: c1892, *Psychology*, H. Holt & Co., New York.

Johnson, J. & Newport, E.: 1989, 'Critical period effects in second language learning: The influence of maturational state on the acquisition of English as a second language', *Cognitive Psychology* 21, 60–99.

Johnson, J. & Newport, E.: 1991, 'Critical period effects on universal properties of language: The status of subjacency in the acquisition of a second language', *Cognition* 39, 158–215.

Karmiloff-Smith, A.: 1992, *Beyond Modularity: A Developmental Perspective on Cognitive Science*, MIT Press, Cambridge, MA, 65–90.

Krashen, S.: 1985, *The Input Hypothesis: Issues and implications*. Pergamon, Oxford.

Lee, D. & Schachter, J.: 1996, 'Sensitive period effects in binding theory'. Unpublished paper.

Lenneberg, E.: 1967, *Biological Foundations of Language*. New York: Wiley & Sons.

Long, M.: 1990, 'Maturational constraints on language development', *Studies in Second Language Acquisition* 12(3), 251–286.

Mayberry, R.I. & Eichen, E. B.: 1991, 'The long-lasting advantage of learning sign language in childhood: Another look at the critical period in language acquisition', *Journal of Memory and Language* 30, 486–512.

Neville, H., Coffey, S.A., Lawson, D.A., Fischer, A., Emmorey, K., & Bellugi, U.: 1984, 'Neural systems mediating American Sign Language: Effects of sensory experience and age of acquisition', unpublished paper.

Newport, E.: 1984, 'Constraints on learning: Studies in the acquisition of ASL', *Papers and Reports on Child Language Development 23*, 1–22.

Oliver, R.: 1995, 'Negative feedback in child NS-NNS conversation', *Studies in second language acquisition* 17, 459–482.

Poizner, H., Klima, E., & Bellugi, U.: 1987, *What the Hands Reveal about the Brain*, MIT Press, Cambridge, MA.

Robinson, P.: 1996, 'Learning simple and complex L2 rules under implicit, incidental, rule-search, and instructed conditions', *Studies in Second Language Acquisition* 18, 27–67.

Sasaki, Y.: 1996, 'Processing and learning of Japanese double- object and causative sentences: An error-feedback paradigm', Unpublished paper.

Schachter, J.: 1996, 'Maturation and the issue of Universal Grammar in L2 acquisition', in W. Ritchie and T.K. Bhatia (eds.), *Handbook of Language Acquisition*, vol. 2, Academic Press, New York.

Schachter, J., Rounds, P.L., Wright, S., & Smith, T.: 1996, 'Comparing conditions for learning syntactic patterns: Attentional, nonattentional, and aware', University of Oregon Institute of Cognitive and Decision Sciences Technical Report No. 96-08.

Schmidt, R.: 1992, 'Psychological mechanisms underlying second language fluency', *Studies in Second Language Acquisition* 14, 357–385.

Tomasello, M. & Herronn C.: 1989, 'Feedback for language transfer errors: The garden path technique', *Studies in Second Language Acquisition* 11, 385–395.

Wason, P.C. & Johnson-Laird, P.N.: 1977, *Psychology of Reasoning*, B.T. Batsford Ltd., London, Chapters 13 & 16.

Weber-Fox, C.M. and Neville, H.J.: In Press, 'Maturational constraints on functional specializations for language processing: ERP and behavioral evidence in bilingual speakers'.

Section 2

Focus on the Learner

REBECCA L. OXFORD

CONDITIONS FOR SECOND LANGUAGE (L2) LEARNING

The purpose is to discuss "conditions for learning a second language," or "L2 learning conditions." *Language* is viewed as: (a) systematic, generative, and used for communication; (b) a set of arbitrary symbols (primarily vocal but also may be visual) that have conventionalized meanings; (c) used in a speech community or culture; and (d) acquired by all people in certain universal ways though with minor variations (Brown, 1994a, p. 5). *L2 learning* refers to the learning of another language once a first language (L1) has been learned (Spolsky, 1988). *Learning conditions* are the factors, either internal or external, influencing learning (Spolsky, 1988). Thus, L2 learning conditions are the inner or outer influences on the conscious, active gaining of communication capacities in a post-L1 language.

EARLY DEVELOPMENTS

The idea of specifying conditions for learning originated with Robert Gagné, who first published a book on this theme in 1965 and later amplified the theme in successive editions. Gagné (1977) focused on conditions for five main learning outcomes or capabilities: (a) intellectual skills, including discrimination, concrete concept, defined concept, rule, and higher-order rule; (b) strategy use; (c) verbal information; (d) motor skill; and (e) attitude. For each learning outcome, Gagné, like Spolsky later on, proposed two sets of learning conditions: internal and external. Here's an illustration. For learning a concrete concept such as "underneath," the individual must be able to discriminate (an internal condition for learning). In the learning situation, the learner must be exposed to the dimension of "underneath" as an instance along with a non-instance and must be given several contiguous examples in order to generalize (external conditions for learning). Gagné presented these conditions in an information-processing mode (conscious learning leading to automaticity) salted with behaviorism.

Gagné's general information-processing theories contrast with L2 information-processing theories. Gagné paid great attention not only to cognitive learning outcomes (intellectual skills, verbal information) and strategic learning outcomes, but also to affective learning outcomes and motor learning outcomes, whereas L2 information-processing theorists limited their L2 learning outcomes to cognitive and strategic. For in-

G.R. Tucker and D. Corson (eds), Encyclopedia of Language and Education,
Volume 4: Second Language Education, 23–31.
© *1997 Kluwer Academic Publishers. Printed in the Netherlands.*

stance, O'Malley & Chamot (1990) – though their concepts about strategies were in general highly valuable – presented socioaffective outcomes
almost as an afterthought, representing them as a minor subtype of strategic outcomes. They paid scant attention to motor/physiological outcomes
such as using appropriate kinesics (body language, physical distance), dif-
ferentiating accent patterns via the hearing mechanism, identifying and
processing non-L1 sounds, and transforming phonetic input to graphemic
output.

MAJOR CONTRIBUTIONS

Spolsky (1988) created the most elaborate set of L2 learning conditions.
He listed 74 conditions divided into eight groups: linguistic outcomes, psycholinguistic conditions, individual differences in ability and personality,
linguistic issues, social context of L2 learning, attitudes and motivation,
learning opportunities, and optimal conditions for formal L2 learning. This
section on major contributions is devoted to a review of Spolsky's list of
conditions.

Conditions 1–19 centered on *linguistic outcomes*, summarized in *Condition 20*: Prefer to say that someone knows an L2 if one or more criteria
are met, e.g.: (a) an underlying knowledge or skills, (b) analyzed or unan-
alyzed, (c) implicit or explicit, (d) of individual structural items (sounds,
lexis, structures) (e) that integrate into larger systemic units, (f) such as
functional skills (g) for specified purposes (academic, communication) (h)
or as overall proficiency, (i) productive or receptive, (j) with a specified
degree of accuracy and fluency (l) and with a specified approximation to
native speaker usage (m) of one or more specified varieties of language.

Conditions 21–26 concerned *psycholinguistics*: The individual has already learned the L1, physiological barriers blocking L1 learning will
block L2 learning, native-like pronunciation is developed when one starts
L2 learning early, abstraction/analysis skills aid formal classroom L2 learning, childlike openness aids informal L2 learning, and social dependence
enhances L2 learning. *Conditions 27–33* focused on *individual differences
in ability and personality*: IQ correlates with formal L2 learning but not
with informal L2 learning, sound discrimination aids L2 speaking and listening, a good memory helps vocabulary learning, grammatical sensitivity
enhances speed in controlling grammatical and pragmatic L2 structure,
learning occurs best when the opportunity matches the learner's preference for sensory learning style (visual, auditory, kinesthetic, or tactile) or
mode (group or individual), the learner's expectations and learning style
help control the selection of L2 learning strategies, and language anxiety
interferes with L2 learning.

Conditions 34–41 centered on *linguistic issues:* The closer the L1 to the
L2 in terms of Universal Grammar rules, the more quickly the learner will

learn the L2. *Conditions 42–49* dealt with the *social context of L2 learning:* Desire to learn the L2 is affected by the number of L2 speakers present, L2 standardization (in a formal learning situation), L2 vitality (in an informal learning situation), the "officialness" of the L2, the L2's modern value or "great tradition" value, and the L2's communicative and culturally integrative value (vs. the desire to maintain one's own linguistic/cultural identity). *Conditions 50–56* concerned *attitudes and motivations of the L2 learner:* Aptitude, time on task, motivation, attitude, and perceived language value affect the speed and quality of L2 learning.

Conditions 57–73 addressed *learning opportunities:* Opportunities are provided for analysis, synthesis, contextualized embedding, comparing one's own knowledge with native-speaker knowledge, communicating with fluent others and drilling; and L2 learning takes place in an open area (informal) or a classroom (formal), with language ranging from un-controlled through simplified (such as foreigner talk). *Condition 74* was the capstone, summarizing the *optimal conditions for formal L2 learning:* Multiple opportunities are available for observing and practicing the L2, and the more these match other relevant conditions (the learner, the goals, the situation), the more efficient the L2 learning is.

Spolsky's L2 learning conditions were based partially on Jackendorff's (1983) preference model. Some conditions are *necessary,* some are *typical,* and some are *graded* (the more of something, the greater the likelihood of L2 learning progress). A condition can be both *typical* and *graded* or both *necessary* and *graded,* but it cannot be both *necessary* and *typical.* Gagné's earlier framework tended to imply the necessity of all the conditions he listed, whereas Spolsky's framework allowed greater flexibility. Spolsky's list is valuable because it is so comprehensive. One advantage of Spolsky's contribution – the list-like format – is also a disadvantage, in that this format does not always allow the amount of integration one might wish across conditions. Spolsky did a herculean job organizing his complex list, but integrating each condition with the other conditions to which it might reasonably be related would have required many additional volumes. Taxonomization is a perhaps unavoidable disadvantage of all lists of L2 learning conditions; see examples of such lists below.

OTHER IMPORTANT CONTRIBUTIONS AND WORK IN PROGRESS

Before Spolsky, some researchers had already ventured into the realm of L2 learning conditions. Strevens' (1985) six postulates could be considered L2 learning conditions:

- L2 presentation mode affects comprehension and therefore learning.

- L2 progress is influenced by previous experience, language abilities, volition (motivation), and features of general language learning.

- Language is comprehended and learned not as diverse, atomistic items but as a flux of data.

- L2 learning is initially just receptive but also becomes productive.

- Gaining a practical L2 command requires multiple presentations and practice opportunities.

- Informed L2 teaching demands a wide range of techniques.

Ellis (1985) listed a number of learning-condition-like hypotheses about second language acquisition (SLA), summarized here:

- SLA follows a natural sequence but shows some variations in specific order, rate, and proficiency level.

- Situational factors indirectly determine rate and proficiency level but not order and sequence. Thus, classroom SLA and natural SLA follow the same general routes.

- The learner's interlanguage is dynamic, variable, and yet systematic and consists of formulaic speech and creative utterances.

- Interlanguage variability is influenced by situational factors, by the learner's procedural (strategic) knowledge, and by Universal Grammar, which makes some rules easier to learn than others for a given learner.

- Interactively adjusted discourse input helps determine sequence, order, and rate.

- Affective differences determine rate and proficiency level but not sequence or order.

- The nature of the L1 (e.g., markedness) influences order but not sequence.

Four years after Spolsky's contributions, the Association for Supervision and Curriculum Development asked L2 experts (Byrnes, Larson, Met, Osgood, Oxford, & Phillips, 1992) to create a set of principles or conditions for L2 learning. Possibly the Association felt the need to produce a list that was shorter and simpler than Spolsky's list of 74 conditions. The Association's 11 principles were:

- L2 learning should emulate authentic language use.

- The goal of L2 learning is performance with language.

- L2 learning is not additively sequential but is recursive and paced differently at various stages.

- The L2 develops in a series of approximations to native-like norms; therefore, interlanguage-based "errors" occur.

- Comprehension abilities precede and exceed productive abilities.

- L2 use requires an understanding of the cultural context.

- L2 instruction takes into account individual learning styles and strategies, anxiety levels, motivations, and teaching strategies.

- L2 use is facilitated when students actively engage in meaningful, authentic, and purposeful language learning tasks.

- Assessment reflects instructional goals and is performance-oriented.

- Technology and textbook materials support but do not determine L2 learning goals.

- Teachers are proficient in the L2, are experienced in the culture, and have expertise specific to the language.

Narratively presented, rather than list-like, discussions of L2 learning conditions were offered by Scarcella & Oxford (1992) and Lightbown & Spada (1993). However, Brown (1994b) returned to the list format by presenting 12 principles or conditions divided into three groups: cognitive, affective, and linguistic. *Cognitive:* (a) Efficient L2 learning involves a timely movement of the control of a few language forms into the automatic processing of a relatively unlimited number of language forms. (b) Meaningful L2 learning leads toward better long-term retention than rote learning. (c) People's actions are driven by the anticipation of reward. (d) The most powerful rewards are intrinsic (self-provided). (e) L2 mastery depends largely on use of learning strategies. *Affective*: (f) As one learns an L2, one develops a second identity or language ego. (g) Self-confidence influences L2 development. (h) L2 learners must take risks. (i) L2 teaching involves teaching customs, values, and ways of thinking or feeling. (j) Cultural adaptation affects L2 learning and vice versa. *Linguistic:* (k) The L1 both facilitates and interferes with L2 learning. (l) Interlanguage is systematic or quasi-systematic. (m) L2 classroom instruction must be communicative, attending to both use and usage, both fluency and accuracy, authentic language, and students' eventual need to apply the language in new contexts.

Ehrman's (1996) book on understanding L2 difficulties included adult case studies, whose focus was individual differences in learning styles, learning strategies, motivation, anxiety, personality factors, and ego boundaries. Ehrman showed the interaction of such factors to external, situational, and methodological issues and explained how conditions for L2 learning could be improved, particularly for students experiencing learning difficulties. The book did not provide a finite list of L2 learning conditions but instead generally explored psycholinguistic and person-related conditions, more so than linguistic or social conditions. A very interesting contribution was the chapter on learning disabilities.

Major work in progress has concentrated on one or more of the principles or conditions noted above, although not usually all of them at once. A prominent issue in L2 learning disability research is whether anxiety is a cause of L2 learning problems (MacIntyre, 1995) or whether anxiety is merely an unfortunate consequence of such problems (Sparks & Ganschow, 1991). Significant research is occurring in L2 learning strategies (Cohen, 1990; Oxford, 1996b), learning styles (Reid, 1995), and affective aspects of communication (MacIntyre, 1995), all of which are placed by the researchers in a broad context of the learner, the learning situation, and the overall social setting.

Motivation as a condition for L2 learning is undergoing a significant theoretical expansion (Crookes & Schmidt, 1991; Dornyei, 1990, 1994; Oxford, 1996a). The well known social psychological framework (Gardner, 1985) is now expanding to a broader theory with additional components: (a) intrinsic and extrinsic motivation; (b) goal setting; (c) cognitions such as attribution theory, learned helplessness, self-efficacy, and self-confidence; (d) need for achievement; and (e) course-specific, teacher-specific, and group-specific motivational elements (Dornyei, 1994).

PROBLEMS AND DIFFICULTIES

One difficulty is the erroneous but lingering mindset that just one or two conditions influence L2 learning success or failure. This is exemplified by Sparks & Ganschow's (1991) repeated citing that poor auditory processing is the basis of virtually all L2 learning disabilities. With olympian amounts of evidence supporting the multifactorial, multiconditional nature of L2 learning (Brown, 1994b; Lightbown & Spada, 1993; Scarcella & Oxford, 1992; Spolsky, 1988), it is unreasonable to highlight a single "explanatory" condition.

Non-researchers might find it difficult to know how to integrate and use the diverse sets of L2 learning conditions. The condition lists are of varying lengths and different levels of detail, making them somewhat confusing to practitioners. Each list is a taxonomy of sorts, and these taxonomies do not fit together neatly.

Moreover, most of the lists of L2 learning conditions have centered on either formal learning or informal learning. More information is needed about the similarities and differences between formal and informal learning. In addition, motor or physiological factors in L2 learning have been largely ignored by researchers when constructing lists of L2 learning conditions.

FUTURE DIRECTIONS

L2 learning disabilities could become part of systematic research on L2 learning conditions. Expansion beyond one or just a few simplistic cause(s) of L1 learning is essential. More learning-condition research is warranted on strategy instruction, learning styles, motivation, beliefs, L1 effects on L2 development, role shifts for teachers and learners, differences between formal and informal L2 learning, and motor/physiological L2 learning conditions (see Hamayan this volume). This research would enhance the theory of L2 learning.

Researchers could also integrate the various sets of conditions for L2 learning cited above, lists that are currently difficult to use because of their contrasting levels of detail. Using a validated, "macro" list of L2 learning conditions, researchers could also set about providing practical implications that would be useful to teachers. There are dangers inherent in moving from theory to practice and vice versa, as Spolsky (1988) warned, but the need for two-way movement between theory and practice is great. The most useful path for practitioners is probably that of formally valued eclecticism or enlightened eclecticism (Brown, 1994b; Spolsky, 1988). This version of eclecticism suggests that, because of diversity in L2 learning conditions, no single instructional method can take precedence. Moreover, the very concept of method becomes suspect when seen through the lens of L2 learning conditions, as Spolsky and Brown both suggested in the statements below.

> ... Advances in language teaching are not dependent on the imposition of fixed ideas or the promotion of fashionable formulas, but arise from the 'independent efforts of teachers in their classrooms' exploring principles and experimenting with techniques' ... [This approach] would not only provide the best set of opportunities, but would do this in a way that exploits previous knowledge, takes advantage of individual student capacities, respects learners' personalities, and benefits from positive attitudes and minimizes negative ones. (Spolsky, 1988, p. 200)

> Method, as a unified, cohesive, finite set of design features, is now given only minor attention. The profession has at last reached the point of maturity where we recognize that the complexity of language learners in multiple worldwide contexts demands an eclectic blend of tasks each tailored for a particular group of learners in a particular place, studying for particular purposes in a given amount of time. (Brown, 1994b, p. 74)

Any theoretical or practical application of information on L2 learning conditions requires solid conclusions substantiated by adequate research in a variety of settings with various languages and with many different learners who have contrasting goals, needs, abilities, and backgrounds. Although fragmentary, "small-N" studies might be valuable, it would be more helpful if smaller studies were linked with larger studies using the same (or at least complementary) research techniques, especially regarding general sampling procedures, instrumentation, data collection, and analysis. This would allow generalizations to be made more readily.

Research on L2 learning conditions should be conducted in an organized, integrated attempt to understand the conditions and the relationships among those conditions. Thoughtful interweaving of qualitative and quantitative research on L2 learning conditions could be very effective.

University of Alabama, USA

REFERENCES

Brown, H.D.: 1994a, *Principles of Language Learning and Teaching*, 3rd ed., Prentice Hall, Englewood Cliffs, NJ.
Brown, H.D.: 1994b, *Teaching by Principles*. Englewood Cliffs, NJ: Prentice Hall.
Byrnes, H., Larson, J., Met, M., Osgood, J., Oxford, R. & Phillips, J.: 1992, *Curriculum Handbook – Section 7: Second Language Learning Principles*. Association for Supervision and Curriculum Development, Alexandria, VA, 7.1–7.60.
Cohen, A.D.: 1990, *Language Learning: Insights for Learners, Teachers, and Researchers*. Heinle & Heinle, Boston.
Crookes, G. & Schmidt, R.: 1991, 'Motivation: reopening the research agenda,' *Language Learning* 41, 469–512.
Dornyei, Z.: 1990, 'Conceptualizing motivation in foreign-language learning,' *Language Learning* 40, 45–78.
Dornyei, Z.: 1994, 'Motivation and motivating in the foreign language classroom,' *Modern Language Journal* 78, 273–284.
Ehrman, M.: 1996, *Understanding Second Language Learning Difficulties*, Sage, Thousand Oaks, CA.
Ellis, R.: 1985, *Understanding Second Language Acquisition*, Oxford University Press, Oxford, UK.
Gagné, R.: 1977, *The Conditions of Learning*, 3rd ed., Holt, Rinehart, & Winston, New York.
Gardner, R.C. 1985. *Social Psychology and Second Language Learning: The Role of Attitudes and Motivation*, Edward Arnold, London, UK.
Jackendorff, R.: 1983, *Semantics and Cognition*, MIT Press, Cambridge, MA.
Lightbown, P. & Spada, N.: 1993, *How Languages Are Learned*, Oxford University Press, Oxford, UK.
MacIntyre, P.: 1995, 'On seeing the forest and the trees: A rejoinder to sparks and Ganschow,' *Modern Language Journal* 79, 245–248.
O'Malley, J.M., & Chamot, A.U.: 1990, *Learning Strategies in Second Language Acquisition*, Cambridge University Press, Cambridge, UK.
Oxford, R.L.: 1996a, *Language Learning Motivation: Pathways to the New Century*, University of Hawaii Press, Honolulu.
Oxford, R.L. (ed.): 1996b, *Language Learning Strategies Around the World: Crosscultural Perspectives*, University of Hawaii Press, Honolulu.
Reid, J. (ed.): 1995, *Learning Styles in the ESL/EFL Classroom*, Heinle & Heinle, Boston.

Scarcella, R. & Oxford, R.L.: 1992, *The Tapestry of Language Learning: The Individual in the Communicative Classroom*, Heinle & Heinle, Boston.

Sparks, R.L. & Ganschow, L.: 1991, 'Foreign language learning differences: Affective or native language aptitude differences?,' *Modern Language Journal* 75, 3–16.

Spolsky, B.: 1988, *Conditions for Second Language Learning*, Oxford University Press, Oxford, UK.

Strevens, P.: 1985, 'Language learning and language teaching: Towards an integrated theory,' Forum lecture, LSA-TESOL Institute.

R.C. GARDNER

INDIVIDUAL DIFFERENCES AND SECOND LANGUAGE LEARNING

Despite the fact that sometimes circumstances appear very similar, there are often wide variations in the level of proficiency attained in a second language, even by students in the same class. Some students become fairly skilled in a relatively short time while others appear to barely grasp the rudiments of the target language. These differences in proficiency occur even though most individuals learn their own language quite successfully with no apparent effort. Over the years, there has been considerable research conducted to determine reasons for these differences, and many characteristics of individuals have been hypothesized to play a role in accounting for this diversity. These characteristics have included a number of general factors such as age, gender, and various personality attributes, as well as a host of variables that are more directly specific to the task of learning another language. This contribution directs attention to five classes of these latter variables that are currently seen to be of major importance. One reason for this, other than space limitations, is that these variables can be linked theoretically as well as empirically to individual differences in second language achievement. Relationships between achievement and variables such as age, gender and personality characteristics are either equivocal or cannot be linked theoretically with achievement without recourse to their involvement with the other more language-specific variables.

The five classes of variables include Language Aptitude, Attitudes, Motivation, Language Anxiety and Language Learning Strategies. Clearly, other variables could be added to this list, but these seem to be among the most frequently investigated and discussed in the research literature. In preparation for writing this contribution, a computer survey was conducted of three data bases, *Linguistics and Language Behavior Abstracts*, *ERIC*, and *Psyclit* to determine the research conducted on eight different factors that have been shown to correlate with measures of second language proficiency. These were Anxiety, Aptitude, Attitudes, Field Independence, Intelligence, Language Learning Strategies, Motivation, and Self-confidence. Abstracts were identified for publications since 1985, focusing attention on these eight factors in the context of foreign and/or second language learning, and 1480 abstracts were obtained. When redundancies were eliminated due to appearance of the same abstract in more than one data base, this number was reduced to 1247, representing 1041 different articles.

G.R. Tucker and D. Corson (eds), Encyclopedia of Language and Education,
Volume 4: Second Language Education, 33–42.
© *1997 Kluwer Academic Publishers. Printed in the Netherlands.*

This research activity is distributed unevenly over the various topics. The most frequently investigated topic was Attitudes, with 509 different articles appearing since 1985. The other counts were Language Learning Strategies (276), Motivation (227), Language Aptitude (107), Intelligence (49), Anxiety (47), Field Independence (17), and Self-Confidence (15). Examination of the abstracts suggested that the category 'Attitudes' is often used in the data bases to include affective variables in general, and that often attitudes are studied as aspects or correlates of motivation. For this reason, these two categories, Attitudes and Motivation, are treated together here. Moreover, the category 'Intelligence' frequently included studies involving artificial intelligence in the context of language learning, rather than studies focusing on individual differences in intelligence. Thus, this category was omitted in this presentation. Finally, because the frequency of studies of Field Independence and Self-Confidence was so low, it was felt best not to include these as separate categories either.

In the following overview, each of the four categories of variables will be considered in terms of history, and major contributions and current research. In a subsequent section, problems and difficulties, and future directions will be considered in general terms since the issues involved seem to be appropriate to all the categories.

LANGUAGE APTITUDE

History. Language Aptitude is a term that has been used to identify those ability characteristics that influence how well individuals can learn a second language. Initially, research was concerned with the role that intelligence played in second language learning, but in the early 1920's, researchers became dissatisfied with the prediction attainable with measures of intelligence, and instead focused their attention on special prognosis tests (Henmon, 1929). In this period there were a number of such tests published, such as the *Foreign Language Prognosis Test* (Symonds, 1930). These tests made use of sample language learning tasks, translation tests, measures of verbal ability, and the like in order to predict achievement, with little regard for explaining why these measures did predict achievement.

Major Contributions and Current Research. The modern day era began in 1959 when Carroll and Sapon published the Modern Language Aptitude Test (MLAT) that attempted to measure abilities that seemed to be involved in language learning. This test developed from a series of studies that investigated the factor structure of verbal ability measures hypothesized to be related to achievement in a second language. Based on this research, Carroll & Sapon (1959) proposed that achievement in a second language was influenced by four different abilities, each of which was measured by the MLAT. These were *phonetic coding, grammatical sensitivity, rote memory*, and *inductive language learning ability*. Since that time, there have been other measures of language aptitude developed, including an elementary form of the MLAT, but the general rationale underlying these measures is not different from that used in the development of the MLAT or the earlier prognosis tests. A recent overview of approaches to the concept of language aptitude is provided in an edited book by Parry & Stansfield (1990).

Currently, there appears to be relatively little research concerned with refining measures of language learning abilities, and according to the survey of research publications described above, interest in this type of research has declined since 1988. Some research has been conducted on factors that might account for individual differences in language ability. Thus, although Carroll (1967) found no evidence to indicate that second language training had any effect on language aptitude, Skehan (1986) demonstrated that individual differences in language aptitude could be traced back to differences in first language development and linguistic experiences.

ATTITUDES AND MOTIVATION

The concepts of Attitudes and Motivation are often treated together in the area of second language learning, which might be considered quite meaningful since attitudes have motivational properties, and motivation has attitudinal implications. In the area of language learning, however, it is possible to consider a number of attitudinal variables such as attitudes toward groups and/or individuals who speak the language, toward languages in general, toward the learning situation, and/or toward the teacher, etc. In much the same way, motivation can be considered in terms of effort, affect, desire, needs, goals (e.g., types) or attributions.

History. The history of interest in attitudes and motivation in language learning can be traced to Arsenian (1945) who raised questions concerning the role of attitudes toward the other language group, to Nida (1956) who hypothesized that one individual's difficulty with learning a second language originated in earlier experiences concerning languages and identity, and to Lambert (1955) who proposed that extreme levels of proficiency could be due to favourable attitudes toward the other community. Each of these publications might be seen as the origin of the concept of an integrative motive (see below), though Kelly (1969) argues that the history of motivation is long, proposing that the concept of integrative motivation can be traced back to St. Augustine.

Other conceptualizations of motivation have also been proposed. One of the first modern discussions of motivation in second language learning was presented by Marckwardt (1948) in the first article in the inaugural issue of

Language Learning. In this article, he proposed that there were five motives for learning a second language, three practical and two non-utilitarian. The three practical motives were assimilation of an ethnic minority, the promotion of trade and commerce, and scientific and technical usefulness. The two non-utilitarian motives were self-cultural development and maintenance of ethnic identity of a linguistic minority. He did not attempt to order these motives in terms of importance, preferring to consider them each as possible factors depending upon the individual.

Major Contributions and Current Research. One of the earliest investigations of attitudes in second language acquisition was conducted by Jordan (1941) who developed Thurstone scales of attitudes toward five school subjects, French, mathematics, English, history, and geography. He found that scores on all tests correlated significantly with their corresponding measures of achievement. The correlation between attitudes toward learning French and achievement was 0.26 ($n = 231$) and was the second highest of the correlations obtained.

Gardner & Lambert (1959) conducted a factor analysis of measures of language aptitude, verbal skills, attitudes, motivation, audience anxiety, and achievement, and obtained two factors related to achievement. One was identified as a linguistic aptitude factor, the other as a motivation factor, which included not only measures of motivation but also attitudes toward the other language community, and an interest in learning the language for integrative reasons. This linking of motivation with favorable attitudes toward the other community and a desire to learn the language in order to foster emotional ties with that community has come to be labelled an integrative motive (Gardner, 1985).

Considerable research has since been concerned with investigating the nature of this motivation further, and the Attitude/Motivation Test Battery (AMTB) (Gardner, 1985) was developed to measure various components and supports of motivation. In this research, it has been recognized that motivation is an important factor in second language acquisition, and that integrative motivation is one important component. Other factors, however, can also influence motivation. One such factor is a need for achievement linked directly to language learning (Dörnyei, 1990).

One important development is the appearance of a number of models of second language acquisition that include motivational concepts as a major part of them. Some of these models are more general than others, often considering a number of individual difference variables in addition to motivation, while others are more circumscribed. Three such models are the social context model (Clément, 1980), the socio-educational model of second language acquisition (Gardner, 1985), and the monitor model (Krashen, 1981).

One of the developments of the research initiated by Gardner & Lambert (1959) and Lambert (1967) was a focus on two different orientations in language study, viz., integrative and instrumental orientations. Some research has been directed towards determining which of these orientations or motivations may be more conducive to second language achievement, or determining that perhaps one is more likely to eventuate in achievement in some contexts, and the other in others. Such research has led to calls for expanding the horizons of motivational research (see, for example, Crookes & Schmidt, 1991), and a lively debate on the best way to characterize motivation appeared in the 1994–95 issues of the *Modern Language Journal*. One attempt to expand the concept (Tremblay & Gardner, 1995) resulted in the conclusion that alternative ways of conceiving motivation could be incorporated into the socio-educational model of second language acquisition without any loss of generality.

LANGUAGE ANXIETY

History. The history of research on anxiety in second language acquisition is relatively short. Measures of audience anxiety were included in some of the earlier studies of individual differences in second language learning (e.g., Gardner & Lambert, 1959; Tarampi, Lambert & Tucker, 1968), while general measures such as test anxiety and manifest anxiety were the major focus in other research (e.g., Chastain, 1975). Generally, the results were equivocal, and a review of some of the research to that time prompted Scovel (1978) to conclude that anxiety could have both a facilitating and debilitating effect on second language acquisition. Subsequent research has indicated, however, that any effects that are obtained tend to be debilitating.

Major Contributions and Current Research. A number of tests of language anxiety have been developed. Measures of French Class Anxiety and French Use Anxiety are subscales of the AMTB (Gardner, 1985). Horwitz, Horwitz & Cope (1986) developed the Foreign Language Class Anxiety scale, claiming that such anxiety is a composite of communication apprehension, social evaluation and test anxiety. MacIntyre and Gardner (1994) developed measures of French Anxiety that focused on anxiety associated with input, processing and output. They demonstrated that anxiety aroused at any of these three stages could have an effect at that stage. They argued that such findings had implications for any procedures concerned with reducing the effects of language anxiety.

Clément (1980) proposed a different view of language anxiety. Rather than focusing on the negative component, he posited that achievement in a second language was dependent on feelings of self-confidence with the language, and such self-confidence was seen to be negatively related to language anxiety. Clément & Kruidenier (1985) demonstrated that a measure of Self-Confidence with English (as a second language) was in fact linked directly with language anxiety.

Major developments in language anxiety research include the demonstration that language anxiety is relatively independent of general anxiety and that it appears to develop from negative experiences while learning the language (MacIntyre & Gardner, 1989). Horwitz, Horwitz & Cope (1986) conceptualize language anxiety '. . . as a distinct complex of self-perceptions, beliefs, feelings, and behaviors related to classroom language learning arising from the uniqueness of the language learning process' (p. 128). That is, anxiety includes both negative affect that could impair learning, and beliefs and expectations about proficiency that could impair performance.

LANGUAGE LEARNING STRATEGIES

History. Language learning strategies can refer to approaches and procedures that individuals use to help them learn a language, or to techniques that teachers propose to promote successful language acquisition. We shall direct attention to the former. Early research on such strategies tended to focus on different approaches used by successful and unsuccessful students, and made use of interviews, questionnaires, or diaries to identify them (cf., Naiman, Fröhlich, Stern & Todesco, 1978; Stern, 1975). Examples of the strategies identified included such diverse behaviors as willing to guess, desire to communicate, active participation, searching for meaning, etc. As can be seen, these cover a wide range of approaches.

Major Contributions and Current Research. Research on language learning strategies has focused on a broad range of attributes. Thus, Reiss (1985) investigated seven strategies, guessing, motivation to communicate, attending to form, practising, monitoring, attending to meaning, and using mnemonics. A popular test of strategies has been proposed by Oxford (1990). The Strategies Inventory for Language Learning (SILL) consists of 80 items for English speaking students learning a new language, and 50 items for speakers of other languages learning English. Both versions provide indices of the use of six strategies, remembering more effectively, using mental processes, compensating for missing knowledge, organizing and evaluating learning, managing emotions, and learning with others. Research has demonstrated that individual differences in the effective use of strategies is associated with proficiency in a second language (Oxford, 1990), and that the use of strategies is influenced by such factors as motivation to learn the language, personality, and the like (Politzer, 1983).

PROBLEMS AND DIFFICULTIES

Each of these individual difference variables have been shown to relate to achievement in a second language, and there has been sufficient replication of the findings in various contexts to conclude that they are somehow implicated. The few studies that fail to replicate the major findings may indicate simply that other factors such as contextual considerations, measurement operations and/or errors, or sampling errors are operating to overshadow relationships. These studies should not be ignored, of course, since a careful analysis of the factors responsible for the discrepant results will help to clarify the conditions under which such relationships exist. Attention must be paid, however, to the careful identification and measurement of the individual difference variables involved.

One difficulty with all of this research is that it deals with individual differences. Consequently any research is correlational and any causal interpretation is equivocal at best. This leads to a large number of different interpretations of comparable data (cf., the models discussed earlier), and disagreements concerning underlying processes. Unfortunately, such disagreements cannot be reconciled, and the only thing that will favor one model over another is its ability to incorporate larger amounts of data or permit generalizations that are not possible from other models. This will involve much more structure than currently exists in any of the existing models, and will require formal mathematical modelling. One possible solution to the problem might be to use causal modelling approaches to assess the adequacy of various models. Causal modelling (see Pedhazur & Schmelkin, 1991, for a clear presentation of this procedure) is a technique that permits a researcher to assess how well the relationships among a set of data conform to a model in which individual difference variables are hypothesized to be causes and/or effects of other variables. The procedure requires careful attention to detail in defining the underlying constructs, and though it cannot demonstrate causation unequivocally, it is a useful first step in this direction. Currently, research has not been conducted that will permit contrasts of competing models, but with extended use of this procedure, it should be possible to do so eventually.

FUTURE DIRECTIONS

Future directions in research should be concerned with the assessment of attributes, and with identifying the major dimensions underlying the variables. Concern with assessment is required to ensure that the measures of the attributes are not confounded by other factors. Thus, there should be more research concerned with reliability and validity of assessments. Reliability should be assessed in terms of both internal consistency and stability. If internal consistency reliabilities are low, attention should be directed toward more careful analysis of the nature of the concepts, and their relation to the items used to assess them. If test/retest reliabilities are low, it should be determined whether this is due to difficulties with the assessment procedure or fluctuations in the attribute being assessed. Not all attributes associated with learning another language will necessarily be stable over time, given the intricacies and adjustments involved in learning another language.

Validity should be investigated from a number of perspectives. Presently, much of the research is concerned primarily with predictive and concurrent validity in that correlations are reported between measures of proficiency or related variables and the measures of the attributes of interest. More attention should be devoted, however, to construct validity. Understanding will profit from a clearer picture of the relationship between the attribute in question and other variables with which it should be related (convergent validity) as well as those with which it should not (discriminant validity).

In a related vein, more attention should be directed toward the dimensionality of the various individual difference variables involved. It is clear, for example, that the variables discussed here, language aptitude, attitudes and motivation, anxiety, and language learning strategies, are all implicated in language learning, but none of them operates in isolation. Moreover, from their description, it is clear that some of them have elements in common, and it would be beneficial to determine how the various variables relate to one another and how they operate in unison to influence individual differences in second language acquisition. Finally, the time is ripe for a meta analysis of the roles played by the individual difference variables in acquiring a second language. Meta analysis (see Durlak, 1994, for a nice discussion of this technique) is a procedure that involves bringing together, in a formal manner, the findings from a number of related studies, and determining the consistency in the results. Such research should focus not only on the relationships of these variables to achievement, but also on the relationships of these variables to each other and to other variables associated with the acquisition of a second language. Such research is necessary to permit the more formal modelling that is now due.

University of Western Ontario
Canada

REFERENCES

Arsenian, S.: 1945, 'Bilingualism in the post-war world', *Psychological Bulletin* 42, 65–86.
Carroll, J.B.: 1967, *The Foreign Language Attainments of Language Majors in the Senior Years: A Survey Conducted in U.S. Colleges and Universities*, Harvard University Press, Cambridge MA.

Carroll, J.B., & Sapon, S.M.: 1959, *Modern Language Aptitude Test: MLAT*, Psychological Corporation, New York.

Chastain, K.: 1975, 'Affective and ability factors in second language acquisition', *Language Learning* 25, 153–161.

Clément, R.: 1980, 'Ethnicity, contact and communicative competence in a second language', in H. Giles, W.P. Robinson & P.M. Smith (eds.), *Language: Social Psychological Perspectives*. Pergamon Press, Oxford, 147–154.

Clément, R., & Kruidenier, B.G.: 1985, 'Aptitude, attitude and motivation in second language proficiency: A test of Clément's model', *Journal of Language and Social Psychology* 4, 21–37.

Crookes, G., & Schmidt, R.W.: 1991, 'Motivation: Reopening the research agenda', *Language Learning* 41, 469–512.

Dörnyei, Z.: 1990, 'Conceptualizing motivation in foreign language learning', *Language Learning* 40, 45–78.

Durlak, J.A.: 1994, 'Understanding meta analysis', in L.G. Grimm & P.R. Yarnold (eds.), *Reading and Understanding Multivariate Statistics*, American Psychological Association, Washington DC, 319–352.

Gardner, R.C.: 1985, *Social Psychology and Second Language Learning: The Role of Attitudes and Motivation*, Edward Arnold, London.

Gardner, R.C., & Lambert, W.E.: 1959, 'Motivational variables in second language acquisition', *Canadian Journal of Psychology* 13, 266–272.

Henmon, V.A.C.: 1929, 'Prognosis tests in the modern foreign languages', in V.A.C. Henmon (ed.), *Prognosis Tests in the Modern Foreign Languages*, MacMillan, New York, 3–31.

Horwitz, E.K., Horwitz, M.B., & Cope, J.: 1986, 'Foreign language classroom anxiety', *The Modern Language Journal* 70, 125–132.

Jordan, D.: 1941, 'The attitudes of central school pupils to certain school subjects and the correlation between attitude and attainment', *British Journal of Educational Psychology* 11, 28–44.

Kelly, L.G.: 1969, *Twenty-five Centuries of Language Teaching: 500 BC-1969*, Newbury House, Rowley, MA.

Krashen, S.D.: 1981, *Second Language Acquisition and Second Language Learning*, Pergamon, New York.

Lambert, W.E.: 1955, 'Measurement of the linguistic dominance of bilinguals', *Journal of Abnormal and Social Psychology* 50, 197–200.

Lambert, W.E.: 1967, 'A social psychology of bilingualism', *Journal of Social Issues* 23, 91–109.

MacIntyre, P.D., & Gardner, R.C.: 1989, 'Anxiety and second language learning: Toward a theoretical clarification', *Language Learning* 39, 251–275.

MacIntyre, P.D., & Gardner, R.C.: 1994, 'The subtle effects of language anxiety on cognitive processing in the second language', *Language Learning* 44, 283–305.

Marckwardt, A.H.: 1948, 'Motives for the study of modern languages', *Language Learning* 1, 3–99. (Reprinted in *Language Learning* 38 (1988), 161–169.)

Naiman, N., Fröhlich, M., Stern, H.H. & Todesco, A.: 1978, *The Good Language Learner*, Research in Education Series No. 7, Ontario Institute for Studies in Education, Toronto, Ontario.

Nida, E.A.: 1956, 'Motivation in second-language learning', *Language Learning* 7, 11–16.

Oxford, R.: 1990, *Language Learning Strategies: What Every Teacher Should Know*. Newbury House, New York.

Parry, T.S., & Stansfield, C.W. (eds.): 1990, *Language Aptitude Reconsidered*. Prentice Hall, Englewood Cliffs, NJ.

Pedhazur, E.J. & Schmelkin, L.P.: 1991, *Measurement, Design, and Analysis: An Integrated Approach*, Lawrence Erlbaum, Hillsdale NJ.

Politzer, R.L.: 1983, 'An exploratory study of self-reported language learning behaviors and their relation to achievement', *Studies in Second Language Acquisition* 6, 54–68.

Reiss, M.A.: 1985, 'The good language learner: another look', *Canadian Modern Language Review* 41, 511–523.

Scovel, T.: 1978, 'The effect of affect on foreign language learning: A review of the anxiety research', *Language Learning* 28, 129–142.

Skehan, P.: 1986, 'Cluster analysis and the identification of learner types', in V. Cook (ed.), *Experimental Approaches to Second Language Acquisition*, Pergamon, Oxford, 81–94.

Stern, H.H.: 1975, 'What can we learn from a good language learner?', *Canadian Modern Language Review* 31, 304–318.

Symonds, P.M.: 1930, *Foreign Language Prognosis Test*, Teachers College Press, Columbia University.

Tarampi, A.S., Lambert, W.E., and Tucker, G.R.: 1968, 'Audience Sensitivity and Oral Skill in a Second Language', *Philippine Journal for Language Teaching* 6, 27–33.

Tremblay, P.F., & Gardner, R.C.: 1995, 'Expanding the motivation construct in language learning', *The Modern Language Journal* 79, 505–518.

DAVID SINGLETON

AGE AND SECOND LANGUAGE LEARNING

The question of whether the age at which individuals begin to be exposed to
a second/foreign language (henceforth L2) plays a role in L2 development
has long been a theme of discussion amongst researchers, educators and
indeed learners (for reviews see Long, 1990; Singleton, 1989, 1995). The
reasons for this interest in the age issue relate not only to theoretical
issues such as whether a putative innate language faculty continues to
function beyond a particular maturational point (see, e.g., Martohardjono
and Flynn, 1995; Schachter: this volume), but also to very practical issues
such as when L2 instruction should begin in school – which has recently
become again a major subject of debate in many countries (see, e.g.,
C.M.I.E.B./C.L.A./Ville de Besançon, 1992).

EARLY DEVELOPMENTS

A good deal of what was written about the age factor and L2 learning in
the earlier part of the century was anecdotal. For example, Tomb (1925)
wrote of the 'common experience' in the days of the British Raj of hearing
English children in Bengal fluently conversing in English, Bengali, Santali
and Hindustani, while their parents could muster just enough Hindustani
to issue orders to their servants. Stengel (1939), for his part, developed a
highly sophisticated Freudian analysis of the influence of age on L2 learning, but, again, his notions about children's language learning were based
on nothing more rigorous than impressionistic observation. Science appeared to come into the picture in the 1950s, when the neurologist Penfield
(Penfield & Roberts, 1959) became involved in the discussion, advocating
early exposure to L2s on purportedly neurophysiological grounds. However, as Dechert (1995) points out, Penfield's views on this matter came out
of his own history, in particular his experience of immersing his children in
German and French, rather than out of his work as a scientist. Lenneberg's
contribution (Lenneberg, 1967) can also be criticized for its impressionistic approach to the L2 question. Lenneberg saw the human capacity for
language acquisition as constrained by a 'critical period' beginning at age
two and ending around puberty, this period coinciding with the lateraliza-
tion process – the specialization of the dominant hemisphere of the brain
(usually the left) for language functions. Part of his argument in favour
of the critical period (1967: 176) was that after puberty the learning of
L2s required 'labored effort' and foreign accents could not be 'overcome

G.R. Tucker and D. Corson (eds), Encyclopedia of Language and Education,
Volume 4: Second Language Education, 43–50.
© *1997 Kluwer Academic Publishers. Printed in the Netherlands.*

easily'. While Lenneberg supported his arguments in relation to maturational aspects of L1 development with a range of neurological evidence
(some of which has since been re-interpreted), he offered no evidence
of any kind in respect of his claims regarding post-pubertal L2 learning,
relying instead simply on an implicit appeal to popular assumptions.

MAJOR CONTRIBUTIONS

Much of the research which has actually looked at learning outcomes has
been tied to the evaluation of early L2 instruction in schools. Thus, for
example, the age question was an important theme of Burstall, Jamieson,
Cohen and Hargreaves's (1974) report on a project that introduced French
into selected primary schools in England and Wales for pupils from the
age of eight during the period 1964–1974. After monitoring the progress
of some 17,000 pupils from the project over five years of secondary school
French, comparing it with the progress of pupils who had not received
primary-level instruction in French, Burstall *et al.* concluded that there
was a progressive diminution of any advantage conferred by early exposure
to French. Smaller-scale studies conducted in other countries (e.g., Oller
& Nagato, 1974; Stankowski Gratton, 1980) produced similar findings.

Studies involving subjects who have acquired an L2 'naturalistically',
on the other hand, yield a converse pattern. Subjects with several years'
naturalistic exposure to their L2 whose first encounter with the L2 dates
back to early childhood are found, on the whole, to outperform those whose
L2 experience began in later years; whereas naturalistic studies of subjects
with more limited exposure to the L2 show older beginners outperform-
ing younger ones. An example of an investigation involving naturalistic
subjects with long exposure to the L2 is Hyltenstam's (1992) study of
the long-term L2 attainment of immigrants in Sweden who had arrived at
various stages during their childhood and whose period of residence in the
country exceeded three years. The numbers of errors produced in Swedish
by subjects who had arrived in Sweden after age 7 were consistently in
a higher range than that of native speaker controls, whereas the range of
numbers of errors produced by earlier arrivals overlapped with those of
both the other groups (see also, e.g., Oyama, 1976; Patkowski, 1980).
Among studies involving subjects with shorter-term experience of an L2
in an L2 environment, a representative example is Ervin-Tripp's (1974)
investigation of 31 English-speaking children ranging in age from four to
nine years who had been naturalistically exposed to French in Switzerland
for up to nine months. The older children in this study tended to outperform the younger ones across the board. Another shorter-term study,
Snow and Hoefnagel-Höhle's (1978) investigation of naturalistic learners
of Dutch of various ages newly resident in the Netherlands, actually seems

to provide direct evidence of younger naturalistic learners catching up with older learners over a period of about a year.

Krashen, Long and Scarcella's (1979) influential review interprets the evidence on age and L2 learning as follows: while older beginners generally outperform their juniors – at least in some respects – in the initial stages of learning, in terms of long-term outcomes, broadly speaking, the earlier exposure to the L2 begins the better. This may now be considered the 'consensus view'. Because of evidence such as that of the Burstall et al. study, Krashen et al. restrict their version of the 'younger = better in the long run' position to naturalistic L2 acquisition. However, before concluding that maturational factors interact differently with formal instructional learning from the way in which they interact with naturalistic acquisition, one should perhaps bear in mind Stern's (1976) criticism of the Burstall et al. study (applicable to all similar studies), which pointed to the likely blurring effect of mixing experimental and control groups in the same classes at secondary level. Also, one needs to recognize that a period of experiencing an L2 in an L2 environment typically delivers vastly more exposure to the L2 than an equivalent period of formal second-language instruction. Accordingly, if the amount-of-exposure variable is held constant, the notions of 'initial advantage' and 'eventual effects' become associable in most formal contexts with considerably longer real-time periods than in naturalistic situations (cf. Singleton 1989: p. 236). It is noteworthy in this connection that the results of studies of L2 *immersion* programmes, where a formal context is combined with massive amounts of exposure, 'favor ... early programs over delayed and, in most cases, late programs' (Holobow, Genesee & Lambert, 1991: p. 180).

WORK IN PROGRESS

Important strands of current research relating to the age factor in L2 learning include: (i) investigations of learners who succeed in 'beating the Critical Period' (ii) very fine-grained experimental studies of phonetic production and perception in learners whose L2 exposure begins at different maturational points, and (iii) work on processing strategies used by L2 learners at different ages.

With regard to (i), one can cite, for example the work of Ioup (e.g., 1995) and Bongaerts (e.g., Bongaerts, van Summeren, Planken & Schils, 1996). Ioup has been conducting a detailed study of two subjects who learned Arabic as a second language in their adult years in an Arabic-speaking environment, one on the basis of extensive formal instruction and the other in an entirely untutored fashion. She has compared the respective performances of her two subjects on a range of tasks – speech production, accent identification, translation, grammaticality judgment and interpretation of anaphora – with native speaker performances and with each other, and has established that both learners are attaining levels of performance close to native norms. Ioup considers the hypothesis that for those few second language learners who are able to achieve native-like proficiency formal instruction may not be a prerequisite. However, she treats this hypothesis with caution, observing that her untutored subject in fact engaged in a certain amount of self-tuition and made continual use of corrective feedback. Bongaerts et al., for their part, have been focusing more narrowly on the question of accent acquisition. In two successive small-scale experiments they have demonstrated that 'excellent' learners of English with Dutch L1 backgrounds who began learning English in a formal instructional setting after age 12 are able to attain English pronunciation scores – assigned by English native speaker raters – that fall within the same range as those attained by native-speaker controls. One possibility considered by Bongaerts et al. is that the close typological relationship between Dutch and English may have played a role in the outcome of their experiments (cf. also Kellerman, 1995), and, with this in mind they are now looking into the L2 accent acquisition of Dutch learners of French.

With regard to (ii), the age-related experimental phonetic studies, these have for many years been particularly associated with the name of Flege. Much of Flege's current work (e.g., Flege, 1996) is focusing on the effects of rate of speech on the production and perception of new phonetic categories among 'early bilinguals' (whose exposure to the L2 began in very early childhood) and 'late bilinguals' (whose exposure to the L2 began in adulthood). Flege refers to evidence of sometimes striking differences among late Spanish/English bilinguals in terms of segmental production and perception. After examining variation in Voice Onset Time (VOT) associated with the production by such bilinguals of English stops and with their rating of stimulus segments as (good to poor) examples of English stops, he concludes that differences between early and late bilinguals may be due in part to whether or not they succeed in establishing English phonetic categories which they have not previously encountered in Spanish. It transpires that the differences between those who do and those who do not establish the new categories are especially discernible in terms of degrees of recalibration of VOT values for different speaking rates. While the vast majority of Flege's early bilinguals show signs of having established the new category, only a minority of his late bilinguals seem to have achieved this, which clearly points to an age factor; on the other hand, the fact that even *some* of his late bilingual subjects emerge from such very rigorous acoustic studies as succeeding in establishing the new category must constitute significant evidence against absolutist versions of the critical period hypothesis.

Concerning (iii), investigations of processing strategies in relation to age, despite the fact that, as Harley, Howard & Hart (1995, p. 44) point out, Lenneberg's original formulation of his critical period hypothesis refers not only to age-related differential success but also to the differences in the nature of the acquisition process, this latter claim has been the subject of only limited research interest. There are some signs that interest in this area may now be growing. Thus, for instance, an interesting study conducted by Liu, Bates & Li (1992) examines how age of first encounter with the L2 affects manner of processing of L2 sentences (in terms of the use of word order and animacy as cues to interpretation) by Chinese learners of English. The results of this study suggest that whereas those whose acquisition of English began after age 20 transferred Chinese processing strategies into English, those whose exposure to English began before age 13 deployed the same strategies as monolingual English speakers. Comparable findings relative to micro-level aspects of L2 speech perception strategies are reported by Cutler (e.g., 1996). Harley et al.'s own (1995) study fails to establish age-related differences in the exploitation of prosodic as opposed to syntactic cues in receptive L2 sentence processing by Cantonese-speaking learners of English, although as the researchers acknowledge, the fact that Cantonese is a tonal language may have played a role in predisposing all the learners in question to attend principally to prosody.

PROBLEMS AND DIFFICULTIES

Some of the problems that arise in investigating the age factor in L2 learning have already been alluded to. Comparisons of school-based learners with and without the benefit of early L2 instruction – such as the Burstall et al. (1974) study – are often vulnerable to criticism on the ground that the early starters are sent back to square one on reaching secondary school and therefore cannot do other than stagnate. Problems may also reside, more generally, in the methodologies used to elicit and/or to analyse data. For example, Kellerman (1995) finds what he sees as three major flaws in Johnson & Newport's (1989) widely-cited grammaticality judgment-based study: he casts doubt on the assumption that a non-native speaker assessing a sentence in grammaticality judgment tasks will necessarily focus on the same feature or features as a native speaker; he points out that in grammaticality judgment tests there may be instances where the variables of formal correctness/deviancy and functional plausibility/implausibility are fatally confounded; and he criticizes the failure to take cross-linguistic influence into account (see also above). Difficulties may also arise when studies rely on native-speaker judgments of authenticity of accent, accent rating being a complex business (see, e.g., Scovel, 1995) and sometimes rather a quirky one.

A further area of problematicity concerns the rather monolithic approach which is frequently taken towards the question of age effects. If it is the case, for instance, that innate principles, such as those envisaged by Chomskyan Universal Grammar, guide certain aspects of language acquisition, then those areas of grammar on which such innate principles bear presumably need to be distinguished from language-particular morphosyntactic elements which develop – alongside and in interaction with language-particular aspects of the lexicon – unaided by any inborn guidance system. If, as some researchers claim, such innate principles remain available throughout life and are operative during second language acquisition, it follows that those parts of L2 grammatical development which they inform ought not to be affected by the age factor, whatever may be the situation in relation to other aspects (cf. Martohardjono & Flynn, 1995).

FUTURE DIRECTIONS

At the outset of this discussion it was mentioned that interest in the age issue in relation to L2 learning has both a theoretical and a practical dimension. These two dimensions will continue to be present in age-related L2 research. Reference has been made to the fact that in the theoretical domain a major question is whether the innate principles which are assumed by some linguists to guide L1 acquisition persist as aids to L2 learning. Opinions on this issue vary, in terms of how much, if any, of a putative innate system remains accessible, at what maturational point accessibility diminishes or ceases, and whether there are acquisitional circumstances which facilitate or inhibit accessibility. This controversy is likely to attract discussion and research for some considerable time. Another earlier-mentioned theoretical issue that has begun to be looked into and which is likely to remain on the research agenda is that of the nature of L2 processing at different maturational stages. It may well be that some answers in this latter area may provide some useful input to the debate about the former. An element in research in both areas will undoubtedly be the increasingly intensive study of those 'excellent' L2 learners who seem to achieve native-like competence even though their exposure to the L2 begins in adulthood. At a more practical level, given the growing interest in early L2 instruction, there will be mounting pressure for definitive answers to be found to a range of questions about the efficacy of such instruction, questions like: How long-term are the long-term benefits, if any, of primary-level L2 instruction? What are the conditions necessary for such benefits, if they exist, to accrue? Finally, given the aging populations of many countries where L2 researchers are active, more attention – both theoretical and practical – may be paid in the future to the operation of maturational factors in L2 learning in later adulthood, middle age and senescence, building on the small amount of research that has already been conducted at this older end of the age-scale (see, e.g., Singleton 1989, pp. 89ff., 142ff. & 248ff.; see the review by Harley in Volume 8).

Trinity College
University of Dublin, Ireland

REFERENCES

Bongaerts, T., van Summeren, C., Planken, B. & Schils, E. (1996): 'Excellente tweede-talleerders en uitspraakverwerving: verdere evidentie tegen de kritische periode hy-pothese', *Gramma/TTT* 4(2), 87–102.
Burstall, C., Jamieson, M., Cohen, S. & Hargreaves, M.: 1974, *Primary French in the Balance*, NFER Publishing Company, Windsor.
C.M.I.E.B./C.L.A./Ville de Besançon: 1992, *Actes de la IVe Rencontre Internationale Langues et Cités. L'Enseignement Précoce des Langues en Europe à l'Horizon 2000: Bilan et Perspectives*, Centre Mondial d'Information sur l'Education, Besançon.
Cutler, A.: 1996, 'Listening to native and foreign speech', paper presented at the Sixth Annual Conference of the European Second Language Association, Nijmegen, March–June 1996.
Dechert, H.: 1995, 'Some critical remarks concerning Penfield's theory of second language acquisition', in D. Singleton & Z. Lengyel (eds.), *The Age Factor in Second Language Acquisition*, Multilingual Matters Ltd., Clevedon, 67–94.
Ervin-Tripp, S.: 1974, 'Is second language learning like the first?', *TESOL Quarterly* 8, 111–127.
Flege, J.: 1996, 'Inter-subject variability in late bilinguals' pronunciation of an L2', paper presented at the Annual Conference of the American Association for Applied Linguistics, Chicago, March 1996.
Harley, B, Howard, J. & Hart, D.: 1995, 'Second language processing at different ages: Do younger learners pay more attention to prosodic cues to sentence structure?', *Language Learning* 45, 43–71.
Holobow, N., Genesee, F. & Lambert, W.: 1991, 'The effectiveness of a foreign language immersion program for children from different ethnic and social class backgrounds: Report 2', *Applied Psycholinguistics* 12, 179–198.
Hyltenstam, K.: 1992, 'Non-native features of near-native speakers: On the ultimate attainment of childhood L2 learners', in R. Harris (ed.), *Cognitive Processing in Bilinguals*, Elsevier, Amsterdam, 351–368.
Ioup, G.: 1995, 'Evaluating the need for input enhancement in post-critical period language acquisition', in D. Singleton & Z. Lengyel (eds.), *The Age Factor in Second Language Acquisition*, Multilingual Matters Ltd., Clevedon, 95–123.
Johnson, J. & Newport, E.: 1989, 'Critical period effects in second language learning: The influence of maturational state on the acquisition of ESL', *Cognitive Psychology* 21, 60–99.
Kellerman, E.: 1995, 'Age before beauty: Johnson and Newport revisited', in L. Eubank, L. Selinker & M. Sharwood Smith (eds.), *The Current State of Interlanguage: Studies in Honor of William E. Rutherford*, John Benjamins, Amsterdam, 219–231.
Krashen, S., Long, M. & Scarcella, R.: 1979, 'Age, rate and eventual attainment in second language acquisition', *TESOL Quarterly* 13, 573–582.
Lenneberg, E.: 1967, *Biological Foundations of Language*, Wiley, New York.
Liu, H., Bates, E. & Li, P.: 1992, 'Sentence interpretation in bilingual speakers of English and Chinese', *Applied Psycholinguistics* 12, 451–484.

Long, M.: 1990, 'Maturational constraints on language development', *Studies in Second Language Acquisition* 12, 251–285.

Martohardjono, G. & Flynn, S.: 1995, 'Is there an age factor for universal grammar?', in D. Singleton & Z. Lengyel (eds.), *The Age Factor in Second Language Acquisition*, Multilingual Matters Ltd., Clevedon, 135–153.

Oller, J. & Nagato, N.: 1974, 'The long-term effect of FLES: An experiment', *Modern Language Journal* 58, 15–19.

Oyama, S.: 1976, 'A sensitive period for the acquisition of a non-native phonological system', *Journal of Psycholinguistic Research* 5, 261–284.

Patkowski, M.: 1980, 'The sensitive period for the acquisition of syntax in a second language', *Language Learning* 30, 449–472.

Penfield, W. and Roberts, L.: 1959, *Speech and Brain Mechanisms*, Princeton University Press, Princeton, NJ.

Scovel, T.: 1995, 'Differentiation, recognition, and identification in the discrimination of foreign accents', in J. Archibald (ed.), *Phonological Acquisition and Phonological Theory*, Lawrence Erlbaum, Hillsdale, NJ, 169–181.

Singleton, D.: 1989, *Language Acquisition: The Age Factor*, Multilingual Matters Ltd., Clevedon.

Singleton, D.: 1995, 'Introduction: A critical look at the critical period hypothesis in second language acquisition research', in D. Singleton & Z. Lengyel (eds.), *The Age Factor in Second Language Acquisition*, Multilingual Matters Ltd., Clevedon, 1–29.

Snow, C. & Hoefnagel-Höhle, M.: 1978, 'The critical period for language acquisition: Evidence from second language learning', *Child Development* 49, 1114–1128.

Stankowski Gratton, R.: 1980, 'Una Ricerca Sperimentale sull'Insegnamento del Tedesco dalla Prima Classe Elementare', *Rassegna Italiana di Linguistica Applicata* 12(3), 119–141.

Stengel, E.: 1939, 'On learning a new language', *International Journal of Psychoanalysis* 20, 471–479.

Stern, H.: 1976, 'Optimal age: Myth or reality?', *Canadian Modern Language Review* 32, 283–294.

Tomb, J.: 1925, 'On the intuitive capacity of children to understand spoken languages', *British Journal of Psychology* 16, 53–54.

KEES DE BOT

LANGUAGE ATTRITION

Although there probably has been language attrition as long as there has been language acquisition and language teaching, research on this phenomenon is mostly of a recent date. In the history of foreign language teaching, complaints about non-acquisition abound, but it is not clear from the reports to what extent what had been learnt at some point was actually lost or simply not acquired.

Language attrition is clearly a multifaceted phenomenon, which calls for cooperation between researchers from different disciplines, such as theoretical linguistics, sociolinguistics, psycholinguistics, education and cognitive psychology. In it, many of the topics discussed in recent applied linguistic work get a special focus if we agree that an improvement of language acquisition and language teaching is at the heart of applied linguistics: what languages do we teach, what aspects of those languages can be taught most effectively in class, what approaches lead to highest retention over time, how is language information stored and processed, and what can we do to improve that storage and processing. Arguments about topics like the role of input and output, interaction in the classroom, methods of instruction and study abroad, to name just a few, will have to be related to long term retention of foreign language skills.

EARLY DEVELOPMENTS

Although some work on language attrition has been done in the more remote past (Ebbinghaus's 1885 seminal work on retention of word knowledge, Kennedy, 1932 on Latin Syntax, Scherer, 1957 on German proficiency), work in this field really started in the US in the late 1970s (Lambert & Freed, 1982). The volume by Lambert & Freed was based on a conference held at the University of Pennsylvania in 1980 in which researchers from different fields were gathered to discuss the potential of research on this topic.

Since then, research on language loss has seen a rapid growth in different countries. Major publications in this field are Weltens et al. (1986), special issues of the journals Applied Psycholinguistics (1986), ITL-Review of Applied Linguistics (1989) and Studies in Second Language Acquisition (1989), Weltens (1989) and Seliger & Vago (1991).

As overviews of the literature show, there are many reports on language

G.R. Tucker and D. Corson (eds), Encyclopedia of Language and Education,
Volume 4: Second Language Education, 51–59.
© *1997 Kluwer Academic Publishers. Printed in the Netherlands.*

attrition, but until recently there is hardly any hard evidence that in particular *foreign language attrition* actually occurs. The largest study is that by Bahrick (1984) who looked at the retention of Spanish. In this cross sectional study, skills in Spanish were tested in speakers who had learned the language until 40 years prior to the time of testing, and who presented a range of proficiency levels as defined by amount of education in Spanish. Bahrick used a wide range of language proficiency tests. His data showed that there was heavy attrition in the initial periods of non-use and less attrition in subsequent years. Some of the language skills appeared to remain intact even after 25 years of non-use. This study provoked a comment by Neisser (1984) who concluded from Bahrick's data that there might be what he calls 'a critical threshold during learning' which implies that some knowledge that has been learned up to a certain level has become immune to forgetting. The idea of a critical threshold has become an important issue in later research on attrition because it may serve as an explanation for some of the later empirical findings.

MAJOR CONTRIBUTIONS

In the Lambert & Freed volume a whole range of issues related to language attrition were raised. In his contribution, Andersen (1982) presented a list of hypotheses related to linguistic aspects of attrition. One of his claims was that language contrast will play an important role: since 'shared' knowledge will be easier to retain than new knowledge he hypothezised that contrasting elements in the foreign language would be more difficult to retain than shared elements. A second linguistic hypothesis stated by Andersen is that elements that are more 'functional', 'marked' or 'frequent' are better retained.

One of the 'big' questions in attrition research is the relation between language acquisition and language forgetting. Ever since Jakobson presented his 'Regression-hypothesis', which states that attrition is a mirror-image of acquisition, researchers have tried to establish a relation between acquisition and forgetting. The main problem with the regression hypothesis is that it is not clear what underlies the orders of acquisition and forgetting, and as a consequence, finding a relation as such is not of real theoretical interest. In addition the establishment of 'order of acquisition' and accordingly 'order of forgetting' calls for longitudinal designs that have not been used widely so far. With respect to foreign language skills the regression hypothesis has been interpreted as 'those things learned best will be retained best' (see de Bot & Weltens, 1991 for a discussion of the regression hypothesis)

One of the most extensive studies on foreign language attrition so far is a study by Weltens (1989). He reports on the loss of French competence by speakers of Dutch. In his research he introduced two independent variables: level of competence achieved, defined as the number of years of school-French, and length of period of disuse. The subjects were given a number of (receptive) phonological, lexical and grammar tests, and a questionnaire which contained a number of self-assessment tests. The lexical tests were constructed in such a way that a possible influence of language contrast and frequency of occurrence could be measured independently: there were high and low frequency cognates and non-cognate words in the tests. The outcomes of this research can be summarized as follows. General receptive proficiency in French, as measured by a multiple choice cloze test, is not subject to attrition after four years of disuse, whereas receptive aspects of grammar – and, to some degree, vocabulary – clearly are. For the first factor, level of competence achieved, it was shown that attrition is independent of training level. For the second factor, period of non-use, no significant differences between groups were found for lexical aspects, while there was significant attrition for grammar in the first interval of two years. Phonological skills, and listening and reading proficiency even increased significantly over time. The self-assessment tests and the morpho-syntactic tests revealed that there was substantial attrition in the first two years which then levels off. Both language contrast and frequency played an important role: low frequency and linguistic contrast led to attrition. Weltens gave a number of possible explanations for the discrepancy between his findings and those by others who did find substantial loss. The first is that his subjects had already reached a level of proficiency which was above the critical threshold and which, to use Neisser's (1984) phrase, 'confers immunity against forgetting'. A second explanation lies in the type of skills tested. The Weltens study was concerned with receptive skills only, and it is possible that productive skills are more easily lost than receptive skills (cf. Moorcroft & Gardner 1987). A third explanation has to do with what 'period of non-use' actually means. This point will be discussed in more detail later on.

A final explanation could be that the informants tested were given so much time that they had ample opportunity to reactivate their knowledge of the language. It is quite possible that the attrition reported in self reports is in fact caused by time pressure: There is general consensus in the psychological literature on memory that all information that was stored at some point will remain in memory. What does become more difficult and more time-consuming is retrieval of information. In order to test two of these explanations, Grendel carried out two investigations on the retention of French as a foreign language in the Netherlands. In the first she investigated orthographic and semantic aspects of word knowledge in Dutch students of French by means of lexical decisions (Grendel et al., 1993). The aim of this study was to investigate both attrition of knowledge and the reactivation of that knowledge in an experimental setting in which there was considerable time pressure: the informants had to indicate as quickly as possible whether a letter string on a screen was a word in French or not. Her data suggest that disuse of French does not lead to a decrease of specific orthographic or semantic skills but to a more general slowing down of the process of lexical access, but the extent of this slowing down is probably too limited to explain the feelings of attrition mentioned in other studies. The second explanation had to do with skills tested. It is a well known finding in psycholinguistic research that generally, language perception is easier than language production. Accordingly it is conceivable that productive skills will be more vulnerable to attrition than receptive skills. In a second investigation, Grendel tested some 250 Dutch informants representing a range of levels of proficiency as measured by years of education in French and a range of years of non use. Rather surprisingly, she found that even over a period of 20 years after course completion, no attrition was found, for receptive, or for productive language skills (Grendel et al., 1996). Oral proficiency scores even increased rather than decreased over time. It was concluded that in the Netherlands, foreign language attrition is unlikely to occur because of the relatively rich linguistic environment: there is virtually continuous foreign language input from the media and close to half of the population spends its holidays abroad. The findings of this study support the Bahrick (1984) data in that linguistic skills have remained stable over a very long period of time.

One of the few studies on foreign language attrition in the US was conducted by Hedgcock (1991). He looked at the loss of Spanish among college undergraduates. The study aimed at providing evidence for two versions of the regression hypothesis: 'last-learned = first forgotten' vs. 'best learned = last forgotten'. The students were tested at the end of their second semester of Spanish and four months later. Rather surprisingly, "subjects improved their accuracy on 9 of the 14 items on the test: likewise, 16 of the 22 subjects also improved their overall performance from test 1 to test 2" (50).

Harley (1993) tested English Canadians who had learned French either through immersion or in core language courses in various parts of Canada. She found (as did Bahrick and Weltens) that a higher level of original proficiency is predictive of a higher level of retained knowledge. Using Can-do type of self-evaluations, she also compared estimated level of proficiency now and at the end of formal training. The immersion group showed no real differences between points in time, but interestingly, the core French graduates felt that their proficiency had actually improved. There was a moderate correlation between recency of contact with French and level of proficiency.

WORK IN PROGRESS

On the basis of the earlier study on attrition of productive and receptive skills in French, which showed no decline of skills in the Netherlands, Grendel et al. (1996) replicated this study in the US. Sixty-six informants participated in this study in which the same tests were used as in the original study. The results showed that there was no attrition for the cloze test and the grammar test, but there was significant attrition of oral proficiency. This outcome seems to support the suggestion made earlier that characteristics of the linguistic environment have an impact on the retention of linguistic skills, but what characteristics actually explain the difference between the Netherlands and the US is still unclear.

In a recent study by Driessen et al. (1996) the factors 'time pressure' and 'productive vs. receptive skills' were combined in an experiment in which Dutch informants had to perform two tasks: a translation task (Dutch-French and vice versa) and a translation-verification task. In the first task subjects saw a Dutch word on a screen and they had to translate it as quickly as possible. Latencies were measured with the aid of a voice key. The words to be translated were taken from a widely used word list, which is also used as a basis for final examinations at the end of secondary education. One of the groups tested was first year students who had done French in secondary education, and who were expected to know all the words in the word list. The data showed that this group had a 66% correct score for translation of French into Dutch, but only a 34% correct score for translation of Dutch into French. This reflects the perception bias discussed earlier. More interestingly, the same informants showed a 87% correct score in a translation verification task in which they were presented with a word in French and a word in Dutch and they had to indicate whether these two were translation equivalents. This seems to suggest that there may be attrition in the productive skills of these subjects, while their receptive skills are still intact, which is in line with earlier findings (Cohen, 1989, Hakuta & D'andrea, 1992).

Although his study is on first rather than foreign language attrition, Ammerlaan's (1996) study is relevant here. He looked at the attrition of Dutch in a group of what he called 'dormant' speakers of Dutch in Australia who had not used their language at all in the years preceding the testing. The informants had to name pictures of common objects in Dutch, and for those objects they could not name they were given a multiple choice recognition task. The outcomes supported the earlier findings that it is easier to recognize a word than to find it in a naming task. More interestingly the transcriptions revealed aspects of the process of retrieval that are very relevant for our understanding of the attrition process. The verbal reports and introspective data on word finding problems are a major source of information on ongoing processes in language production: when presented with a picture of a broom, one subject called that 'Een zwepertje' and he explained that he had used a Dutch nominalization procedure on an English lexical item ('sweep') which accordingly was combined with a Dutch diminutive morpheme ('tje') and pronounced with Dutch sounds. The combination of on-line processing measurements and qualitative data in Ammerlaan's study is a promising one that can be applied in other studies on language attrition.

There are signs of an increased interest in long term retention testing in acquisition studies. A recent example of this is a study by Mondria (1996) who looked at the effect of different methods of presentation on the retention of lexical skills. In addition to the 'normal' post-treatment assessment, he used parallel tests four weeks later in order to find out whether the different treatments ('guessing' vs. 'presentation') had differential effects on longer term retention. His data showed no clear relation between method of presentation and retention.

PROBLEMS AND DIFFICULTIES

In research on attrition a number of very specific problems have to be solved. The first problem has to do with research designs. Ideally data should be gathered using longitudinal designs. Only longitudinal designs can provide us with data on intra-individual development over time. As has been shown, attrition is likely to be a very slow process that may take many years. Apart from the fact that it is virtually impossible in any country to get research money for such lengths of time, there are the problems of test-effects, and assessing language intake between measurements. Test-effects have to do with the effect of recurrent testing on the attrition process itself: In a number of studies, informants indicate that their participation in the study itself led them to pay more attention to that language. That will no doubt have an effect on the next measurement. Also the length of the intervals between measurements is a problem: testing too often will lead to relearning, while testing with very large intervals may mean that important changes are missed (cf. Jaspaert, Kroon & van Hout, 1986).

Language contact is an even more problematic point: It is very difficult, if not impossible to get an accurate picture of the contacts subjects may have had with the language during what Gardner, Lalonde and MacPherson (1985) have labeled the 'incubation period' and what the impact of these contacts has been. It is unclear whether global measures of language contact provide us with the kind of information needed. The main problem is that there is probably no direct relation between amount of contact and loss. The same amount of input may have totally different effects on different individuals and accordingly on their learning or retention of the language.

FUTURE DIRECTIONS

Study abroad effects

There are some areas or topics that cry out to be looked at from a language attrition perspective. In recent years the interest of student exchange programs has grown dramatically in many parts of the world. One of the aims of those exchange programs is the enhancement of the proficiency of the students in the language of the host country. Recently a number of studies have been carried out to establish the effects of study abroad on language proficiency. What happens with the acquired skills once the students return home is a question worth studying. As Freed (1995) indicates in her introduction to a volume on 'Second Language Acquisition in a Study Abroad Context', one of the topics for future work is: 'What should students be encouraged to do upon their return to maintain and improve these skills'. (18).

In some of the study abroad reports, a wealth of data have been gathered on language use, sociolinguistic background and language proficiency before departure and after arrival (e.g. Brecht, Davidson & Ginsberg 1995). We could learn a lot about language attrition if the students in those programs were retested (preferably more than once, e.g. after one and after five years) after their return.

A language processing perspective on attrition

More attention is needed to the processing side of language attrition. In recent years comprehensive psycholinguistic models of language production and perception have been developed that can also serve as developmental models (e.g. Levelt, 1989, 1993). In those models the various components of the processing system are laid out, and experimental data have been gathered to elucidate the mechanics of those components and their interaction. If language attrition does take place, we have to find out in what part of the system it is likely to occur. As yet the attrition process has been looked at as a black box rather than a decomposable complex of subprocesses.

Individual differences and learner characteristics

Very little is known about the role of learner characteristics such as age, aptitude, cognitive style and earlier learning experiences. A study on the attrition of English in Hebrew speaking children revealed an effect of age on attrition with younger children showing more attrition than older ones (Olshtain, 1989). No data on the relation between any of the other characteristics and language attrition have been published so far. One characteristic that could also be tested in the study-abroad programs discussed earlier is the extent to which learning a foreign language has a positive effect on the learning and retention of the next one(s).

Cross-linguistic comparisons

Finally, comparisons of different language pairs are called for. While the role of cross-linguistic influence in second language acquisition is well attested, we know basically nothing about its role in attrition or retention. In the Dutch research on the retention of skills in French, there is at least a suggestion that frequent contact with cognate languages (English/French) may have a positive effect on retention of skills. There are hardly any data on less cognate languages. In that respect, some of the languages in the study abroad reports, like Russian, seem to offer interesting possibilities. See the review by Sandra in Volume 6.

University of Nijmegen, the Netherlands

REFERENCES

Ammerlaan, T.: 1996, '"You get a bit wobbly . . . " Exploring Bilingual Retrieval Processes in the Context of First Language Attrition'. Unpublished doctoral dissertation, University of Nijmegen, Nijmegen.

Andersen, R.: 1982, 'Determining the linguistic attributes of language attrition', in: R. Lambert, & B. Freed (eds.), The Loss of Language Skills, Newbury House, Rowley, Mass, 83–118.

Bahrick, H.: 1984, 'Fifty years of second language attrition: Implications for programmatic research', Modern Language Journal 68, 105–118.

Brecht, R., Davidson, D., & R. Ginsberg: 1995, 'Predictors of foreign language gain during study abroad', in B.J. Freed (ed.), Second Language Acquisition in a Study Abroad Context, John Benjamins, Amsterdam/Philadelphia, 37–66.

Cohen, A.: 1989, 'Attrition in the productive lexicon of two Portuguese third language speakers', Studies in Second Language Acquisition, 11, 135–149.

De Bot, K. & Weltens, B.: 1991, 'Recapitulation, regression and language loss', in: H. Seliger & R. Vago (eds.), First Language Attrition: Structural and Theoretical Perspectives, Cambridge University Press, Cambridge, 87–98.

Driessen, C. de Bot, K. & Schreuder, R.: 1996, 'The language asymmetry in translation', Internal Report, University of Nijmegen.

Ebbinghaus, H.: 1885, Ueber das Gedächtnis. Untersuchungen zur experimentellen Psychologie, Duncker & Humblot, Leipzig.

Freed, B.: 1995. 'Language Learning and Study Abroad', B. Freed (ed.), Second Language Acquisition in a Study Abroad Context, John Benjamins, Amsterdam/Philadelphia, 3–33.

Gardner, R., Lalonde, R., & MacPherson, J.: 1985, 'Social factors in second-language attrition', Journal of Language and Social Psychology 35, 519–540.

Grendel, M., Weltens, B., & de Bot, K.: 1993, 'Language attrition: Rise and fall of a research topic?', Toegepaste Taalwetenschap in Artikelen 46/47, 59–68.

Grendel, M.: 1993, 'Verlies en herstel van lexicale kennis', unpublished doctoral dissertation, University of Nijmegen, Nijmegen.

Grendel, M., Freed, B., Weltens, B. & de Bot, K.: 1996, 'Attrition of French in The

Netherlands and the US: A comparative study', paper presented at the 1996 Annual AAAL conference, Chicago.

Hakuta, K. & D'Andrea, D.: 1992, 'Some properties of bilingual maintenance and loss in Mexican background high-school students', *Applied Linguistics* 13(1), 72–99.

Harley, B.: 1993, 'Maintaining French as a second language in adulthood', paper presented at the 10th AILA world congress, Amsterdam.

Hedgcock, J.: 1991, 'Foreign language retention and attrition: A study of regression models', *Foreign Language Annals* 24, 43–55.

Jaspaert, K., Kroon, S., & van Hout, R.: 1986, 'Points of reference in first-language attrition research', in B. Weltens, K. de Bot, & T. van Els (eds.), *Language Attrition in Progress*, Foris Publications, Dordrecht/Providence, 37–49.

Kennedy, L.: 1932, 'The retention of certain Latin syntactical principles by first and second year Latin students after various time intervals', *Journal of Educational Psychology* 23, 132–146.

Lambert, R., & Freed, B. (eds.): 1982, *The loss of Language Skills*, Newbury House, Rowley, Mass.

Levelt, W.J.M.: 1989, *Speaking. From Intention to Articulation*, The MIT Press Cambridge, Mass.

Levelt, W.J.M.: 1993, 'Language use in normal speakers and its disorders', in G. Blanken, E. Dittman, H. Grimm, J. Marshall, & C. Wallesch (eds.), *Linguistic Disorders and Pathologies. An International Handbook*, Walther de Gruyter, Berlin, 1–15.

Mondria, J.-A.: 1996, *Vocabulaireverwerving in the vreemde-talenonderwijs* (Vocabulary acquisition in foreign language teaching), unpublished dissertation University of Groningen.

Moorcroft, R., & Gardner, R.: 1987, 'Linguistic factors in second language loss', *Language Learning* 37, 327–340.

Neisser, U.: 1984, 'Interpreting Harry Bahrick's discovery: What confers immunity against forgetting?', *Journal of Experimental Psychology: General* 113, 32–35.

Olshtain, E.: 1986, 'The attrition of English as a second language', in B. Weltens, K. de Bot, & T. van Els (eds.), 185–202.

Scherer, G.: 1957, 'The forgetting rate in learning German', *German Quarterly* 30, 275–277.

Seliger, H., & Vago, R. (Eds.): 1991, *First Language Attrition: Structural and Theoretical Perspectives*, Cambridge University Press, Cambridge.

Weltens, B.: 1989, *The attrition of French as a Foreign Language*, Foris Publications, Dordrecht/Providence.

Weltens, B., de Bot, K., & van Els, T. (eds.): 1986, *Language Attrition in Progress*, Foris, Dordrecht/Providence.

Section 3

Focus on the Delivery of Instruction

DICK ALLWRIGHT

CLASSROOM-ORIENTED RESEARCH IN SECOND LANGUAGE LEARNING

Classroom-oriented research is an odd category in at least two important ways. Firstly, it may seem very odd to any reader who is a newcomer to the field to discover that research on language education apparently needs to mark out a special area that is self-consciously 'oriented' to the classroom. It would surely not be unreasonable to assume that a thoroughgoing *classroom* orientation could be taken for granted, leaving *non*-classroom-oriented research to be the special case needing separate treatment. However, after several decades of work attempting to establish the classroom as the obvious focus for research attention, it is salutary to note that Nunan's 1991 review revealed that of the fifty carefully selected 'classroom-oriented' research studies he surveyed ('carefully selected' for their overall representativity of the field over twenty-five years) only fifteen drew their data 'directly from the language classroom' (p. 255). If we accept Nunan's analysis, and if we believe that there is a compelling prima facie case for research in this area to focus on what happens in classrooms, then we are forced to conclude that, for all practical purposes, the argument is not yet won.

Secondly, it is an odd category because it lacks substantive content. Other subtopics in this section clearly have substantive content (in terms of learner differences, for example). This subtopic, however, is a category of research itself, aligned to no particular content except via the very general notion of a focus on the 'delivery of instruction', which is itself spelled out in the headings for the other subtopics. It is thus in a sense an empty category (or at the very least a wide-open one), unless treated more as a philosophy of science matter. What follows will therefore attempt to deal with 'classroom-oriented' research both as a choice of research approach and as an approach that has dealt with a variety of substantive issues over the decades. I will necessarily run the risk of straying into the territory of other subsections, but some such overlap is perhaps inevitable and not altogether regrettable.

EARLY DEVELOPMENTS

Classroom-oriented research on second language acquisition can be traced back to three distinct sources in the 1960s. By the end of the 1960s one of

G.R. Tucker and D. Corson (eds), Encyclopedia of Language and Education,
Volume 4: Second Language Education, 63–74.
© *1997 Kluwer Academic Publishers. Printed in the Netherlands.*

these sources – large-scale research comparing competing language teaching methods – was in decline, while the other two – the development of an analytical approach to teacher effectiveness research and the simultaneous but independent development of a descriptive approach to language teacher training – were in the ascendant.

The source of classroom-oriented research in comparisons of competing language teaching methods is best exemplified by the Pennsylvania Project (Smith, 1970), or rather in the criticism that it gave rise to, which pointed out (Clark, 1969) that the results, however disappointing to the Project Staff because they apparently failed to establish clear superiority for any one language teaching method, were actually better treated as uninterpretable because of the lack of systematic observational evidence that the teachers involved in the project had been able to keep strictly to the designated methods. There was also some anecdotal but highly damaging evidence that teachers had deviated significantly from them. It thus became clear that progress was only going to be possible if a more systematic approach was adopted to the problem of knowing exactly what teachers did in their own classrooms.

Jarvis had already got this far in his own work (1968) on language teacher effectiveness, developing his own 'behavioral observation system for classroom foreign language skill acquisition activities'. And for this he had moved well away from the notion of method because he had already seen the possibility of analysing and then defining effective language teaching in terms of observed individual behaviours.

This new concern among educational researchers in the language area (some, especially those in the field of English as a second or foreign language, soon to prefer calling themselves 'applied linguists') for the development of systematic techniques to analyse and describe language teacher classroom behaviour found an echo in our third source: the area of language teacher training. In the USA Moskowitz (1968), for example, was already using and adapting the general educational work of Flanders (1960) to develop observation schemes (essentially lists of categories of what to look for) for the description and analysis of teacher behaviour in the language classroom. But where the underlying purpose of the methodological comparisons research, and of Jarvis's teacher effectiveness research, had been to put the profession in a position to *pre*scribe to teachers how to teach a language most effectively, the purpose of the work in language teacher training was to provide *de*scriptive feedback to trainees about their classroom performance, so that they could attempt to change their behaviour in whatever way or ways seemed likely to be helpful, and could then systematically observe their classroom performance again to see if they had successfully changed their behaviour in the intended direction.

This difference of purpose proved historically important to later developments, as did teacher training's probably inevitable focus on teacher behaviour (sometimes almost to the extent that learner behaviour became excluded from serious consideration) and teacher training's inevitable need for observation schemes that would be simple enough to be used by novices after a minimum of special training.

MAJOR CONTRIBUTIONS

The search for an observation scheme that would be comprehensive enough to be used for research purposes but also simple enough to be used, selectively, by novice teachers, found its culmination in the work of Fanselow in New York (1977a). Fanselow devised FOCUS, a system of observational categories that was derived from Bellack's general educational work (later to be also a major source for Sinclair and Coulthard's (1975) pioneering 'discourse analysis' work in the UK). The full version of the acronym FOCUS – Foci for Observing Communications Used in Settings – reveals Fanselow's ambitious intent to offer the world a universally applicable system of categories, not one restricted to educational settings.

Despite its universalistic intent, Fanselow's system, later set down as the centrepiece of a whole book on language teaching (Breaking Rules, 1987), has not proved universally attractive for teacher training purposes, and has not fed into a major research programme. It can be said to represent a major intellectual enterprise for the field, but one that has, sadly, served mainly to demonstrate the limitations of the approach it embodies.

In the early 1980s a team of researchers in Canada (see Allen et al., 1984; Fröhlich et al., 1985) later developed another complex analytical system of observational categories, but this time with the more limited intent of enabling assessments to be made, for research rather than teacher training purposes, of the extent to which lessons could be said to be 'communicative', as indicated by the acronym COLT – the Communicative Orientation of Language Teaching. This was a direct reflection of the contemporary development and widespread influence of the so-called 'communicative approach' to language teaching (see Littlewood, 1981) that had filled the gap left by the failure of the 1960s methodological experiments to identify the 'best' method for language teaching. Although, as with FOCUS, it is not easy to see widespread adoption of COLT for research projects worldwide, given how difficult it seems to be to enable readers of such complex category systems to feel confident in using them satisfactorily without training from the systems' inventors, COLT has been used by its originators for a major project in Canada (Harley et al, 1987), and the recent publication of the system in book form reinforces its claims to continued consideration as a research tool.

A parallel development begun in the 1970s saw classroom-oriented research taken up by academics less concerned with contributing to teacher education or to large-scale notions of language teaching method and much more concerned with contributing to our understanding of classroom events regardless of the 'method' in use, and thus potentially contributing to theoretical developments in second language acquisition (soon known as SLA – a new field that owed more to work in general linguistics and in psycholinguistics than to education). SLA's earlier focus was on learner error as a source of information about second language development, and it is thus not surprising to find classroom-oriented research on the same topic. Fanselow did pioneering work in the area in the early 1970s (not published until 1977), but without making the connection with SLA. This came later, in British applied linguistics work, with publications by Allwright (1975), and Long (1977) that set out conceptual analyses of the possible components of the classroom treatment of learner error, rather than sets of observational categories of teaching behaviour in the Fanselow manner. Such analyses, further developed by Chaudron (1977), eventually served, like Fanselow's category system, more to draw attention to the limitations of observation as a research tool than to start off a fruitful line of observational research.

Another line of enquiry pursued from the mid 1970s onwards by academic researchers doing classroom research was that of the nature of interaction in the language classroom. This was less directly connected historically with work in SLA, taking its original impetus from more general work in discourse analysis (as in Larsen-Freeman, 1980), but it soon proved relevant to SLA as work in that area (see Long, 1981), under the influence of Krashen's Input Hypothesis (1985) began to look at interaction as the potential driving force for linguistic development (technically termed 'acquisition' in Krashen's conception) via the process of interactive negotiation that was expected, again following on from Krashen's conception, to make input comprehensible, thus triggering the non-conscious acquisition process. Such issues formed the topic for a major conference on input in second language acquisition in 1983 (see Gass & Madden, 1985).

The work on classroom interaction marked a shift in focus well away from the teacher towards the learner, with the major effort now being concentrated on using observational techniques to study learner behaviour. Throughout this time, however, other researchers had become aware, as noted above, of the potentially severe limitations of observation as a research technique, and had begun to adopt what was called a 'mentalistic' approach to research on classroom language learning. This 'mentalistic' approach involved direct canvassing of learners' own reports of their mental activity. Cohen, for example, pioneered such techniques as stopping a lesson in mid-flow to ask learners to note down what was in their heads, what they were thinking, at the moment they had been asked to stop (see Cohen & Hosenfeld, 1981). At about the same time Schumann and Schumann (1977) pioneered the use of learner diaries of classroom language learning experiences (offering their own double diary study as an example of what might be learned from such data).

WORK IN PROGRESS

Towards the end of the 1980s three books appeared, all in the same year, that simultaneously signalled both how well established classroom-oriented research apparently was (pace Nunan, 1991), and, at the same time, for some at least, how little it had achieved in traditional research finding terms. In my own backwards-looking1988 book on the first decade or so of language classroom observation studies, for example, I found it necessary to conclude with warning words about the future of classroom-oriented studies based primarily on observational data. In his authoritative survey of the field Chaudron showed, intentionally or not, how generally inconclusive classroom-oriented research was and seemed doomed to be both as a source of theory development and as a source of firm and unequivocal advice to classroom practitioners, while van Lier, in his more forward-looking volume, showed how a new approach was perhaps needed, via a move away from the SLA tradition of relatively positivistic research towards a rapprochement with more sociological perspectives on language education, making use of such notions as classroom ethnography, and taking up the challenge implied in Breen's 1985 paper entitled: 'The Social Context for Language Learning – A Neglected Situation', where the 'neglected situation' he had in mind was precisely the classroom itself (see the reviews by Watson-Gegeo, Garcez, May and Peirce in Volume 8).

Since the late 1980s, however, not a great deal has happened to change the picture significantly. Some potential reasons for this state of affairs are set out in the following section, dealing with 'problems and difficulties'. As will be seen, they are fundamental issues, rather than small issues of detail and refinement. They add up to a major shift in focus, with a return to a central concern for the teacher, but no longer simply for the sake of studying the effectiveness, or otherwise, of a teacher's observable behaviour in class. The interest now is in the teacher as a thinking person, developing his or her own theories of language learning and language teaching, through reflection, if not through his or her own active research programme. This takes us squarely into the realm of teacher development, and thus beyond the immediate scope of this section.

From the foregoing it would appear that perhaps classroom-oriented research has outlived its usefulness. This is probably an overstatement, but it is at least arguable that classroom-oriented research, narrowly conceived as research relying exclusively (or even primarily) on observational data from classroom lessons, can no longer be seen as adequate if we are seeking a rich understanding of what goes on in language classrooms. The initial concern for observational data was in its day an important advance on previous approaches which seemed to take for granted that we already knew what actually happened in classrooms, but the focus on observable behaviour ultimately drew attention to the enormous complexity of that behaviour, and thus to the impossibility of reaching an adequate understanding of it through the study of observable data alone. As soon as we went beyond observable behaviour, however, we came up against the enormous complexity of teachers' mental behaviour.

This realisation, coupled with serious disquiet about the relationship between academic research and the world of language teaching practitioners, has led to the substantial problems that are discussed at some length in the following section.

PROBLEMS AND DIFFICULTIES

Three sets of fundamentally practical problems have emerged over recent years. Firstly, who should conduct classroom-oriented research – academics or practitioners? Secondly, what model of research should be followed, and should it depend upon who is conducting the research? And, thirdly, if practitioners are to conduct research in their own classrooms, how is this to be made sustainable within the practitioners' normal working life? A fourth set of practical problems arises as a by-product in connection with the inclusion of a research element in teacher training and development work. I shall deal with this by asking the question: why should practitioner research be sustainable?

These sets are complexly related to one huge underlying question of principle for the entire field: what is research for? This question can be usefully subdivided into two less cosmic formulations. Firstly, what is the nature of the optimal relationship between classroom-oriented research and the development of theory? And, secondly, what is the nature of the optimal relationship between research and classroom practice? These major issues will be left for the last section, where we will consider future directions for the field of classroom-oriented research.

Who should conduct classroom-oriented research?

From the academic point of view, research, if it is to be done at all, must be done in such a way that its results are valid, by the standards of academic research. In practice this means that research should be conducted by people who are well enough trained, and well enough supported in terms of the required supporting resources (including research time of course). In practice this leads inevitably to the conclusion that it is academics themselves, with their professional commitment to research as a proper part of their working lives, who should conduct whatever research is to be done.

From the practitioners' point of view, however, research can be seen as something that is far too good to be left to the 'experts' – the academics. Academics may have their own high standards, but they also have their own research agendas, and these may well not coincide with what practitioners find relevant or important to their work. In order for research to meet the professional requirement of relevance, then, it may have to be conducted by the practitioners themselves.

There is also the major problem in the field of education that research conducted by academics, even when it is conducted in the classroom itself, is commonly seen by practitioners as a parasitic enterprise. This perception may have a number of causes, but it is exacerbated by the additional perception that academics generating theory seem typically to see no reason to want to hear what teachers have to say about the phenomena that the academics are investigating. They therefore reach their conclusions without giving teachers a chance to contribute their understandings, and then the academic researchers publish their findings for each other to read, rather than for practitioners. We therefore have a situation in which there is a mutual and debilitating distrust between academics and classroom practitioners, with neither side typically finding it profitable to try to talk to the other. From the point of view of practitioners academics are pursuing irrelevant topics, treating practitioners' own understandings as irrelevant, and publishing only for each other. They therefore are not worth talking to. From the academics' point of view practitioners are hopelessly impatient for usable findings, and lack the research expertise either to contribute usefully to the research enterprise in the first place, or to benefit from reading about it afterwards.

To oversimplify, the question of who should conduct classroom-oriented research has thus become a battle, from the points of view of both academics and practitioners, between 'quality' and 'relevance'. The practitioners' concern for relevance (in their terms, of course) seems to the academics to prejudice research quality, and the academics' concern for quality (in their terms, again) seems to the practitioners to prejudice research relevance. In such circumstances it is hardly surprising that there is also controversy over what might be the most appropriate model for classroom-oriented research to follow, and that this controversy is directly related to the issue of who should actually conduct the research. See McCarty's review on teacher research methods in Volume 8.

What model of research should be followed?

Within academic classroom-oriented research there is still some evidence of futile dichotomising between 'quantitative' and 'qualitative' research, although there is probably an increasing consensus that the dichotomy is indeed futile and unhelpful, since in practice research projects typically make demands on both 'quantitative' and 'qualitative' approaches. When we move to consider what model of research would be appropriate for practitioners to adopt in their own classrooms, however, we then have to face a different dichotomy. This new dichotomy is between, on the one hand, from the academic tradition, research that sees a major distinction between research findings and their application to real-world settings, aiming first and foremost to develop our understanding, and on the other hand, from the profession's practitioners, research that is concerned to bring about, as quickly as possible, desired changes in practice. The academic tradition is itself divided into research that involves the conduct of controlled experiments (an approach borrowed in our field largely from individualistic psychology), and research which is essentially descriptive of the status quo (borrowing more from the social sciences), on the understanding that a descriptive base is essential before any sensible decisions can be taken about what sorts of changes, if any, might be appropriate. Practitioners concerned to change the status quo as quickly as possible point out both that the descriptive approach simply delays much-needed reform, and that the controls essential to the experimental model are extremely difficult to provide within real school settings. In any case, they argue, the notion of experimental control means that a teacher involved in an experiment is expected to pursue an experimental way of teaching 'to the bitter end' even if it is demonstrably failing the learners involved, because otherwise the research design itself will be compromised and the project rendered inconclusive. The term 'action research' was originally coined to capture the notion that practitioner research could legitimately dispense with both the descriptive work and with the controls insisted upon by the psychological model, and could therefore continuously change (act upon) the situation being studied, in the hope of continuously improving the situation for the learners (see Volume 8).

The problem of sustainability?

'Action research' may dispense with the control element of academic experimental research, but otherwise it depends upon the research techniques and procedures (e.g. questionnaires, observation schemes, interview schedules) developed in the academic world. These techniques are not easy to use well and require both special training and a considerable investment of time. Both the training and the time-investment may well be available when practitioners are engaged in teacher education courses, but when they are 'back in the classroom', trying to cope with all the other demands made upon them, there is a strong risk that they will not feel able to undertake further research, or, if they do try to do so, they will 'burn-out' on classroom research and drop it quite quickly in any case. So, practitioner research is likely to happen principally when practitioners are on courses. It will therefore be novice research, in the main, and, perhaps more crucially, not part of a continuous enterprise for the practitioners concerned, simply because it is not seen as a sustainable addition to an already busy professional life.

But why should practitioner research be sustainable?

The obvious reason to give first is that if practitioners are to become proficient researchers then they will need to go well beyond their first novice efforts. Only in this way will the quality of the research produced be high enough to justify taking it seriously as a contribution to our developing knowledge of the field of classroom second language teaching and learning. There is currently a considerable risk that moves made to introduce a research project into pre-service or in-service teacher training and development work will engage trainees very effectively, so effectively that they will be willing to make a major intensive effort, while they are on the training course, but that this will be a level of intensity they will be quite unable to sustain thereafter, in their normal working lives as teachers, and so the whole idea of carrying on with research will be dropped. (There is also a strong argument, related to the above discussion of the most appropriate research model, that a training course research project is most likely to be conducted in accordance with an academic model of research, because it is likely to be associated with a professional academic qualification, and that this model will not itself be sustainable thereafter, because of the time-consuming and intellectually demanding burdens it places upon teachers.)

Quite independently of this 'quality' argument, however, is the very different suggestion that practitioner research is capable of making a major contribution to the professional development of the individual practitioner. And, if we see professional development itself as a continuous matter, then practitioner research must also be seen in such terms. For it to make its full contribution, then, practitioner research must take a form that is indefinitely sustainable, a form that does not depend on an unsustainable level of personal commitment from the individual practitioner (or an unsustainable level of institutional support), that does not lead to early 'burn-out'. Going one stage further in the argument, we might now even propose that, at least in terms of its relationship to the 'standards' of academic research, the 'quality' of the research produced by practitioners is less important than its role in practitioners' professional development.

FUTURE DIRECTIONS

So, what is classroom-oriented research for?

Two distinct but related aims can now be delineated, corresponding to the distinction made at the beginning of the previous section between a concern for finding the optimal relationship between research and *theory* on the one hand, and between research and *practice* on the other. In classical thinking in this area, however, these are not two separate, parallel issues, but rather three terms best seen in a linear relationship in which research generates theory which in turn informs practice. This is a product-oriented view of research, however, which is based on the claim that the sole value of research *for practice* is to be found in its products: theories which can then inform, perhaps even transform, practice. This claim, however, fails to take into account two factors. The first of these is the practical, and severe, problem of communication between research and practitioners, as we have seen above. The second is the more encouraging possibility that research, when conducted by practitioners in their own classrooms, may be able to have a more direct relationship with practice, via the contribution that being involved in classroom research might make to the professional development of the individual practitioner. And this contribution may conceivably depend more upon the *process* than the product. It may not be from the findings of their research projects that practitioners draw the most benefit, but from the process of conducting the research themselves, a process that may generate understandings that cannot be reduced to sets of identifiable findings.

To return to our two aims, however: firstly, then, there is the 'academic' aim of furthering the development of our theoretical understanding of the phenomena of classroom language learning and teaching. And secondly there is the 'professional' aim of furthering the professional development of individual practitioners. These two aims could of course, and might, go their separate ways and develop independently of each other. In principle, academic research could carry on developing academic theory, and could carry on having a chronic problem of reaching the practitioners in the field. And, simultaneously, practitioner research could carry on conducting its own local investigations, largely for personal professional development purposes. There are alternative possibilities, however.

Firstly, thoughtful practitioners conducting their own investigations could find themselves dissatisfied with the 'amateurishness' of their work, and that reaction could generate a demand for input from professional academic researchers. This could help significantly with the dissemination problem noted above, if academic researchers are willing to respond sensitively to the demand.

Secondly, other thoughtful practitioners, faced with the same feeling of dissatisfaction at their ability to copy the academic research model adequately, could develop their own independent conception of what constitutes viable research, and their own independent notion of relevant theory. This is the approach adopted by the largest professional organisation for teachers of English as a second language – TESOL (Teachers of English to Speakers of Other Languages), who, partly prompted by decreasing satisfaction with relationships with the academic research tradition in the field, set out in the mid-1990s to rethink the role of research for the profession, and for a professional association.

Lancaster University, England

REFERENCES

Allen, J.P.B., Frölich, M. & Spada, N.: 1984, 'The communicative orientation of language teaching: An observation scheme', in J. Handscombe, R. Orem,& B. Taylor (eds.), *ON TESOL '83: The Question of Contro* TESOL, Washington, DC, 231–252.

Allwright, R.L.: 1975, 'Problems in the study of the teacher's treatment of learner error', in M.K. Burt & H.C. Dulay (eds.), *ON TESOL '75: New Directions in Second Language Learning, Teaching and Bilingual Education*, TESOL, Washington, DC, 96–109.

Allwright, R.L.: 1988, *Observation in the Language Classroom*, Longman, London.

Bellack, A.A., Kliebard, H.M., Hyman, R.J. & Smith, F.L.: 1966, *The Language of the Classroom*, Teachers College Press, New York.

Breen, M.P.: 1985, 'The social context for language learning – a neglected situation', *Studies in Second Language Acquisition* 7(2), 136–158.

Chaudron, C.: 1977, 'A descriptive model of discourse in the corrective treatment of learners' errors', *Language Learning* 17, 29–46.

Chaudron, C.: 1988, *Second Language Classrooms*, Cambridge University Press, Cambridge.

Clark, J.L.D.: 1969, 'The pennsylvania project and the "audio-lingual vs traditional" question', *Modern Language Journal* 53, 388–396.

Cohen, A.D. & Hosenfeld, C.: 1981, 'Some uses of mentalistic data in second language research', *Language Learning* 31, 285–313.

Fanselow, J.F.: 1977, 'The treatment of error in oral work', *Foreign Language Annals* 10(4), 17–39.

Fanselow, J.F.: 1977a, 'Beyond rashomon: conceptualising and describing the teaching act', *TESOL Quarterly* 11(1), 17–40.

Fanselow, J.F.: 1987, *Breaking Rules*, Longman, New York.

Flanders, N.A.: 1960, *Interaction Analysis in the Classroom: A Manual for Observers*, University of Michigan Press, Ann Arbor.

Frölich, M., Spada, N. & Allen, J.P.B.: 1985, 'Differences in the communicative orientation of L2 classrooms', *TESOL Quarterly* 19(1), 27–57.

Gass, S.M. & Madden, C.G. (eds.): 1985, *Input in Second Language Acquisition*, Newbury House, Cambridge, Mass.

Harley, B., Allen, P.J.B., Cummins, J. & Swain, M.: 1987, *Development of Bilingual Proficiency: Final Report*, Ontario Institute for Studies in Education, Toronto (mimeo).

Jarvis, G.A.: 1968, 'A behavioral observation system for classroom foreign language skill acquisition activities', *Modern Language Journal* 52, 335–341.

Krashen, S.D.: 1985, *The Input Hypothesis: Issues and Implications*, Longman, London.

Larsen-Freeman, D.E. (ed.): 1980, *Discourse Analysis in Second Language Research*, Newbury House, Rowley, Mass.

van Lier, L.: 1988, *The Classroom and the Language Learner*, Longman, London.

Littlewood, W.T.: 1981, *Communicative Language Teaching*, Cambridge University Press, Cambridge.

Long, M.H.: 1977, 'Teacher feedback on learner error: Mapping cognitions', in H.D. Brown, C.A. Yorio, & R.H. Crymes (eds.), *ON TESOL '77: Teaching and Learning English as a Second Language: Trends in Research and Practice*, TESOL Washington, DC, 278–293.

Long, M.H.: 1981, 'Input, interaction and second language acquisition', in H. Winitz (ed.), *Native Language and Foreign Language Acquisition*, New York Academy of Sciences, New York, 259–278.

Moskowitz, T.: 1968, 'The effects of training foreign language teachers in interaction analysis', *Foreign Language Annals* 1(3), 218–235.

Nunan, D.: 1991, 'Methods in second language classroom-oriented research: A critical review', *Studies in Second Language Acquisition* 13(2), 249–274.

Schumann, F.M. & Schumann, J.H.: 1977, 'Diary of a language learner: An introspective study of second language learning', in H.D. Brown, C.A. Yorio & R.H. Crymes (eds.), *ON TESOL '77: Teaching and Learning English as a Second Language: Trends in Research and Practice*, TESOL, Washington, DC, 241–249.

Sinclair, J. McH & Coulthard, R.M.: 1975, *Towards an Analysis of Discourse*, Oxford University Press, Oxford.

Smith, P.D.: 1970, *A Comparison of the Cognitive and Audiolingual Approaches to Foreign Language Instruction: The Pennsylvania Project*, Center for Curriculum Development, Philadelphia.

JOANN CRANDALL

LANGUAGE TEACHING APPROACHES FOR SCHOOL-AGED LEARNERS IN SECOND LANGUAGE CONTEXTS

The growing movement of peoples across national borders (refugee resettlement, immigration, or temporary migration for employment or education) and the legacy of colonialism have led to the development of educational programs which require students to receive at least part of their education through the medium of a second language, usually one with national, official, or international status.

For example, English is used as a medium of instruction for at least a portion of schooling in "inner circle" countries (Kachru, 1988) such as Australia, Canada, New Zealand, the United Kingdom, and the United States, where English is the primary language of a majority of students and a national or official language; in "outer circle" countries such as Botswana, India, Jamaica, Kenya, Namibia, Nigeria, the Philippines, Singapore, South Africa, Sri Lanka, or Zambia, where English is the primary language of few students; and beyond these circles to Asian or Central or South American countries, where English is a medium of instruction at progressively earlier grades in elite bilingual schools (see the review by Phillipson in Volume 1).

Other former colonial languages also serve as media of instruction (French in Francophone Africa and the Mahgreb; Spanish in Central and South America), and many other national languages are taught as second languages and later used as media of instruction as well (cf. Hebrew in Israel; Swedish in Sweden; and Dutch in the Netherlands). See Part Five of this volume.

The discussion which follows reviews both program models and instructional approaches to help school-aged children learn second languages and make the transition to academic instruction through those languages. While many of the approaches and some of the program models are also used in foreign language education (i.e., the study of additional languages such as Russian in the United States or English in Finland where the language is not used substantially as a medium of education), the focus throughout this chapter is on second language education for school-aged learners, i.e., the formal instruction which is provided for children during at least the compulsory years of primary and secondary education. Throughout the chapter, the term "primary" language is used, rather than the more familiar "home language" or "mother tongue," since many languages may be

G.R. Tucker and D. Corson (eds), Encyclopedia of Language and Education,
Volume 4: Second Language Education, 75–84.
© *1997 Kluwer Academic Publishers. Printed in the Netherlands.*

spoken at home and the primary language may be that of the father. In this chapter, as well, "approach" and "method" are used interchangeably, though "approach" has traditionally referred to the theoretical underpinnings (the theories of language and learning) which guide instruction, while "method" is the stipulation of the actual classroom procedures and instructional activities involved (cf. Anthony, 1963; Richards & Rodgers, 1986).

EARLY DEVELOPMENTS

School-aged learners can participate in a number of models of second language instruction. What differentiates them are: (1) the degree of planned support for the primary language; (2) the instructional approach to develop second language competence; and (3) the type of program to transition learners from second language classes to instruction through that language in courses across the curriculum (e.g., sciences, mathematics, and social sciences).

In one of the earliest approaches to teaching second languages, tutors were brought into the homes of nobility to instruct the children in other languages, teaching directly through the language. What has subsequently been termed the "direct method" continues to be used in formal instruction, but more commonly in private or adult language classes. Another early approach, grammar-translation, was for centuries the dominant approach to teaching second languages such as Latin or French, and today it is still widely used, but more for the teaching of foreign languages. With grammar-translation, the focus of instruction is the written language, and classroom activities include translation of literary texts, vocabulary study, and grammar analysis, with much of the instruction conducted in the student's primary language. It is especially amenable to classical languages or languages in which oral proficiency is not expected. (Richards & Rodgers, 1986 and Larsen-Freeman, 1986 provide a more thorough discussion of these and other approaches.)

During the last half of the twentieth century, the aural-oral or audiolingual approach was developed (Lado, 1964) based on behaviorist psychology (Skinner, 1957) and structural or descriptive linguistics (Hockett, 1958). In contrast to grammar-translation, audiolingual instruction focuses on oral language development with limited use of the student's primary language. In audiolingual classes, a limited set of patterns are practiced through repetitive drills and memorized dialogs, until the pattern becomes habitual and unconscious. A grammatical or structural syllabus specifies the elements to be learned, and teachers restrict the number of grammatical and lexical units to encourage error-free responses from the learners and to prevent interference from the first language if students try to go beyond their proficiency in the second language.

MAJOR CONTRIBUTIONS

The audiolingual approach is still widely used, especially where teachers have limited proficiency in the second language, but it is being gradually replaced by more communicative and cognitive approaches which have been influenced in their development by generative-transformational linguistic theories (Chomsky, 1965), speech act theory (Austin, 1962; Searle, 1969), ethnography of communication (Hymes, 1972), and more learner-centered educational approaches.

In communicative language teaching (Widdowson, 1978; Van Ek, 1975; Wilkins, 1976), discourse (particularly oral discourse) replaces the sentence as the major focus of instruction and the structural syllabus is either replaced or subsumed in a syllabus which specifies language functions (e.g., requesting, apologizing, describing), notions (e.g., quantity, quality, space, time), or contexts of language use (e.g., social, academic, professional). Some attention to pattern practice and memorization still occur, but the major instructional focus is on activities which simulate and stimulate authentic language use and require students to negotiate meaning, for example, through information-gap activities in which learners who each know only a portion of the required information must interact and exchange that information to complete a task.

The goal of communicative language teaching is communicative competence, a complex measure of ability to function in a language which, according to Canale and Swain (1980), includes grammatical and sociolinguistic competence, (knowledge of the rules of the language and appropriate language use) and discourse and strategic competence (strategies to develop and maintain conversation or write texts beyond a sentence).

Humanistic and cognitive psychological theories also fostered the development in the 1960s and 1970s of a number of language teaching approaches such as Curran's Counseling-Learning, Lozanov's Suggestopedia, and Gattegno's Silent Way. (See Richards & Rodgers, 1986 and Larsen-Freeman, 1986 for discussion). They have been more frequently used in teaching foreign languages and adult language instruction, but activities from these approaches are often incorporated by second language teachers as well.

Drawing upon Chomsky's concept of a Language Acquisition Device (LAD), Krashen (1982) has developed the Monitor Theory, which distinguishes between natural language acquisition and formal language learning and hypothesizes that individuals can acquire (not learn) second languages in a manner similar to the way in which they acquire their first, if certain conditions are met: that is, if learners receive comprehensible input (input which is understandable but just beyond the learner's current level of development), in a context where the focus is on meaning (rather than form), and where the learner's anxiety level (or affective filter) is low.

While comprehensible input is necessary for language acquisition, Swain (1985) has pointed out that it is not sufficient. Also needed is comprehensible output: an opportunity to use the language to negotiate meaning with peers and to receive feedback from more proficient language users.

Based on this theory, Krashen and Terrell (1983) have developed the Natural Approach, a communicative approach that simulates the stages of natural first language acquisition, focusing first on concrete and relevant listening and reading activities to build comprehension, allowing learners a silent period before they are expected to speak. Included are activities from Total Physical Response (Asher, 1969), in which students respond initially only through actions to increasingly more complex teacher commands.

Another approach which draws upon first language instruction and natural language acquisition is Whole Language (Goodman, 1982), which emphasizes the interdependence of language skills (listening, speaking, reading, and writing), the importance of developing fluency in oral and written communication through process-oriented activities, and the need for meaningful and relevant learner activities (including reading appropriate literature and engaging in authentic writing to share with peers).

WORK IN PROGRESS

School-aged learners may receive instruction through any of these approaches in a separate second language class (for example, English or French as a Second Language), in second language instruction in a bilingual educational program, or in a mainstream class where specially trained content teachers adapt instruction to enable second language learners to participate with primary language speakers in the same class through sheltered instruction (discussed below).

In bilingual programs, second language students are introduced to literacy and receive at least a part of their initial academic instruction in their primary language, while also receiving second language instruction. In the most promising bilingual program model, two-way immersion or developmental bilingual education, students from two linguistic groups are brought together in a structured program where each group is exposed to and learns the other's language for use across the curriculum, while also receiving primary language literacy and language arts instruction. Students in these programs have been found to function at or above grade level in both languages at the end of primary education, when the program usually ends (Genesee, 1987; Lindholm, 1990).

Students in maintenance or late-exit bilingual education ("gradual transfer"), may receive instruction through both languages for five or six years (as in the United States) or throughout their education (as in the Philippines and Brunei); the goal is primary language development and continuity of cognitive development across both languages. (Tucker, 1997, reviews a number of these programs around the world.)

In transitional or early-exit bilingual education ("sudden-transfer"), students receive two or three years of education through both languages for initial literacy and academic support in the primary language and second language development before transitioning entirely to that second language as the medium of instruction.

Some support for the primary language may be provided after transition from these programs through continued primary language study (e.g., courses in Spanish for Spanish Speakers in the United States; in heritage languages in Canada and Australia; and national languages in Namibia).

There is substantial evidence that students who participate in effective bilingual education programs develop linguistic competence in the second language equivalent to those who participate only in second language instruction, and they are able to do so while continuing cognitive and academic development in their first language. (See the Winter/Spring 1992 Special Issue of the *Bilingual Research Journal*.) Those transitioned too early or placed in submersion ("sink or swim" or "straight for English") programs, face substantial academic difficulty and may fall progressively behind in school. According to Lambert (1980), students from minority linguistic and cultural backgrounds who are schooled through a second language by teachers who neither understand their language nor make sufficient accommodations for their degree of second language proficiency, experience a kind of subtractive bilingualism in which the second language is developed at the expense of the first, with negative social and cognitive consequences. This contrasts with the situation of middle or upper middle class children schooled through a second language (English-speaking Canadian children learning through French or Spanish-speaking Uruguayan children learning through English), in which the second language offers cognitive and social enrichment (additive bilingualism) and where the teacher is likely to both understand the students' language and make accommodations to their language learning needs through structured immersion.

Cummins (1980), Collier (1992), and MacDonald (1990) have documented the difficulties of second language learners who are transitioned to instruction in a second language when they are seemingly fluent in informal, social uses of the language but lack the academic language proficiency required for reading academic texts and performing academic tasks such as answering mathematical word problems or writing science lab reports in the second language. Cummins identifies two factors which affect the difficulty of second language acquisition: (1) the degree of context-embeddedness (access to sources of meaning outside of the language), and (2) the degree of cognitive complexity of the content (the level of abstractness or difficulty of the ideas in the text). Learners are able to function

in second language (social) contexts within one or two years if sources
for meaning clarification (such as gestures, concrete referents, or shared
information) are available and the content is relatively simple. However,
they may take five to seven years to function in (academic) contexts with
cognitively demanding content where meaning is increasingly conveyed
through language and text.

Based on Cummins' theory of social and academic language proficiency,
a number of integrated approaches to the teaching of language and content
have been developed which are useful for all second language learners
making the transition to learning through that language, but they are especially important for contexts in which learners speak a number of primary
languages and there is limited instructional use of these languages. Referred to as "language across the curriculum," "integrated language and
content instruction," "content-based language teaching," and "sheltered instruction," all involve some combination of attention to academic language
and academic content, with the focus and degree of attention determined
by who is doing the teaching and the purpose of instruction (Crandall,
1993; Crandall & Tucker, 1990).

In content-based second language classes, language teachers draw from
the vocabulary, texts, tasks, and tests from other content areas to help
students develop academic language and skills, referred to variously as
thinking and study skills or more recently, as cognitive and metacognitive
strategies (Oxford, 1990).

In sheltered content classrooms, the science, mathematics, or social
studies teacher uses techniques familiar to language teachers to increase
the embeddedness and decrease the cognitive complexity of the material.
Originally defined as classrooms where all students were second language
learners and intended for those students who had achieved intermediate
proficiency in the second language (Krashen, 1991; Chamot & O'Malley,
1987), the term has been extended to describe any content area teaching
where adaptations and accommodations are made for second language
learners to increase the comprehensibility of the instruction and foster
continued cognitive-academic development. These include: simplifying
or modifying the input; increasing the sources of contextual clues through
demonstrations, multiple media and graphic organizers; engaging students
in small group and cooperative tasks; integrating language and academic
skill objectives with the academic concepts; and checking frequently for
understanding (Crandall & Tucker, 1990; Chamot & O'Malley, 1987;
Mohan, 1986). Increasingly important is attention to learner training, i.e.
to helping learners become more aware of the cognitive and metacognitive
strategies they (could) use in developing academic language proficiency.

Where teachers work together in teams, or when one teacher provides
most of the instruction for a child, as is likely to be the case in elementary and middle schools, it is possible to integrate language, cognitive

and metacognitive strategy instruction, and academic concepts from multiple areas of the curriculum through the development of thematic units which form the basis of instruction for days or weeks, consistent with the Whole Language Approach. Thus, a unit on water pollution could involve stream monitoring (requiring both scientific and mathematical constructs), environmental awareness and outreach activities (involving social studies constructs), and a variety of oral and written reports of results. These could be organized by a number of teachers who are assigned the same students or by one teacher who is responsible for multiple areas of the curriculum.

PROBLEMS AND DIFFICULTIES

As the above discussion demonstrates, the development of second language teaching has moved from a focus on teacher-centered to more learner-centered or learning-centered classrooms; from the use of carefully prepared materials with limited linguistic and conceptual range to more authentic and meaningful texts; from separation of language and content instruction to more integrated approaches in both language and content area classrooms; and from teacher-whole class instruction to more small group and cooperative activities where learners need to use the language to negotiate meaning.

In practice, second language learners need both communicative and content-based instruction, with focus on form, as well as meaning, both in terms of attention to linguistic features and rhetorical genres. Teachers need to be able to balance holistic, process-based approaches focused on learner-centered development of fluency and creative language use, with more academically-oriented, product-oriented approaches, focused on helping learners to become more aware of linguistic forms and texts and better able to produce appropriate academic texts.

To do so requires changes in (language) teacher education to enable teachers to create classroom contexts which foster both social and academic language and cognitive development. Teachers need a range of strategies and techniques (or methodology, drawn from the approaches discussed in this chapter) as well as a principled approach to making instructional decisions. The increasing numbers of second language speakers in education requires all teachers to learn how to shelter instruction and enable learners to develop second language proficiency as they are also learning academic concepts. The roles of language and content teachers are also changing, with more language teachers team-teaching with content teachers for part of the school day in Australia, Canada, and parts of the United States, necessitating changes in instructional planning as well. It will be important to monitor team-teaching (inclusion) closely to ensure that language needs are being properly addressed and that learners do not find themselves once again in submersion programs (see the reviews by Brumfit in Volume 6 and by Widdowson in this volume).

FUTURE DIRECTIONS

The construct of academic language is still vague. A large part of it is vocabulary (Saville-Troike, 1984; Crandall, 1993), but studies of mathematics English, for example, demonstrate that comparatives (e.g. *greater than* or *as much as*), prepositions (*divided by* or *into*), or specialized meanings (*square* or *root*), may be as difficult as technical vocabulary such as *additive inverse* or *hypotenuse*, which are terms that primary language speakers learn in school as well. Additional study of second language learners engaged in content area tasks is needed to provide illumination on what constitutes academic language and how best to help students to acquire it and also to assess student competence in using it, separating linguistic from academic content knowledge. See the review by Olson in Volume 3.

Currently, the following represents the author's evaluation of the various approaches, from those which offer the most support for the primary language and the most effective bridge to instruction through a second language, to those which provide the least support and the least effective bridge:

> *Most*
>
> Two-way bilingual education + sheltered instruction + second language instruction
>
> Late-exit bilingual education + sheltered instruction + second language instruction
>
> Early exit bilingual education + sheltered instruction + second language instruction
>
> Second language instruction + content-based language instruction + sheltered instruction
>
> Second language instruction + content-based language instruction
>
> Structured immersion (sheltered instruction)
>
> Second language instruction
>
> Submersion (no accommodation)
>
> *Least*

Close observation and evaluation of students from differing linguistic and cultural backgrounds enrolled in various program models and learning through various instructional approaches is needed to document the costs and benefits of participation in each of the contexts listed above. This research needs to be undertaken in diverse settings around the world (e.g. Singapore, South Africa, Australia, the United States) to inform language education policy and practice not only in those countries, but in all countries in which a decision is made to provide academic instruction through the medium of a second language.

University of Maryland Baltimore County, USA

REFERENCES

Anthony, E.M.: 1963, 'Approach, method and technique', *English Language Teaching* 17, 63–67.
Austin, J.L.: 1962, *How to Do Things with Words*, Oxford University Press, Oxford.
Canale, M. & Swain, M.: 1980, 'Theoretical bases of communicative approaches to second language teaching and testing', *Applied Linguistics* 1, 1–47.
Chamot, A.U. & O'Malley, J.M.: 1987. 'The cognitive academic language learning approach: A bridge to the mainstream', *TESOL Quarterly* 21, 227–249.
Chomsky, N.: 1965, *Aspects of the Theory of Syntax*, M.I.T. Press, Cambridge, MA.
Collier, V.P.: 1992, 'A synthesis of studies examining long-term language minority student data on academic achievement', *Bilingual Research Journal*, 16, 187–212.
Crandall, J.A.: 1993: 'Content-centered learning in the United States', *Annual Review of Applied Linguistics* 13, 111–126.
Crandall, J.A, & Tucker, G.R.: 1990, 'Content-based language instruction in second and foreign languages', in A. Sanivan (ed.), *Language Teaching Methodology for the Nineties*, SEAMEO Regional Language Centre, Singapore, 83–96.
Cummins, J.: 1980, 'The cross-lingual dimensions of language proficiency: implications for bilingual education and the optimal age issue', *TESOL Quarterly* 14, 175–187.
Genesee, F.: 1987, *Learning Through Two Languages: Studies of Immersion and Bilingual Education*, Newbury House, Cambridge, MA.
Goodman, K.: 1982, *Language and Literacy*, Routledge and Kegan, London.
Hockett, C.F.: 1958, *A Course in Modern Linguistics*, Macmillan, New York.
Hymes, D.: 1972, 'Introduction', *Language in Society* 1, 1–14.
Kachru, B.B.: 1988, 'Teaching world Englishes', *ERIC/CLL News Bulletin* 12, 1,3–4,8.
Krashen, S.: 1982, *Principles and Practices in Second Language Acquisition*, Pergamon, Oxford.
Krashen, S.: 1991, 'Sheltered subject matter teaching', *Cross Currents* 18, 183–189.
Krashen, S. & Terrell, T.D.: 1983, *The Natural Approach*, Prentice-Hall Regents, Englewood Cliffs, NJ.
Lado, R.: 1964, *Language Teaching: A Scientific Approach*, McGraw Hill, New York.
Lambert, W.E.: 1980, *The Two Faces of Bilingual Education*, Forum, No.3, National Clearinghouse on Bilingual Education, Washington, DC.
Larsen-Freeman, D.: 1986, *Techniques and Principles in Language Teaching*, Oxford University Press, NY.
Lindholm, K.J.: 1990, 'Bilingual immersion education: Criteria for program development', in A.M. Padilla, H.H. Fairchild, & C.M. Valadez (eds.) *Bilingual Education: Issues and Strategies*, Sage, Newbury Park, CA, 91–105.
MacDonald, C.A.: 1990, *Crossing the Threshold into Standard Three to Black Education. The Consolidated Main Report of the Threshold Project*, Human Sciences Resource Council, Pretoria.
Mohan, B.: 1986, *Language and Content*, Newbury House, Reading, MA.

Oxford, R.L.: 1990, *Language Learning Strategies: What Every Teacher Should Know*, Newbury House, New York.

Richards, J.C. & Rodgers, T.S.: 1986, *Approaches and Methods in Language Teaching*, Cambridge University Press, Cambridge.

Saville-Troike, M.: 1984, 'What *really* matters in second language learning for academic achievement', *TESOL Quarterly* 18, 199–219.

Searle, J.B.: 1969, *Speech Acts*, Cambridge University Press, Cambridge.

Skinner, B.F.: 1957, *Verbal Behavior*, Appleton-Century Crofts, New York.

Swain, M.: 1985, 'Communicative competence: Some roles of comprehensible input and comprehensible output in its development', in S. Gass & C. Madden (eds.) *Input in Second Language Acquisition*, Newbury House, Rowley, MA, 235–253.

Tucker, G.R.: 1997, 'A global perspective on multilingualism and multilingual education', in J. Cenoz & F. Genesee (eds.) *Beyond Bilingualism: Multilingualism and Multilingual Education*, Multilingual Matters, Clevedon.

Van Ek, J.A.: 1975, *The Threshold Level*, Council of Europe, Strasbourg.

Wilkins, D.A.: 1976, *Notional Syllabuses*, Oxford University Press, Oxford.

Widdowson, H.G.: 1978, *Teaching Language as Communication*, Oxford University Press, Oxford.

ELSE V. HAMAYAN

TEACHING EXCEPTIONAL SECOND LANGUAGE LEARNERS

In this chapter, I will address two kinds of exceptionality: (1) cognitive, perceptual, neurological, sensorial, or behavioral disabilities and (2) normal difficulties that result from lack of prior schooling. For both types of exceptionalities, the focus will be on school age learners from minority backgrounds who are typically forced to learn the language of the majority. Much of the literature on second language learners with special needs has focused on assessment, instructional strategies and programmatic designs. One of the most pressing issues facing educators in several countries with large numbers of minorities, immigrants and refugees is the likelihood of students who are simply having difficulties in the second language being misidentified as having a disability. For this reason, it is important to include a discussion about this large group of students who do not necessarily have disabilities but are likely to be identified as having disabilities as they progress through school (Baca & Almanza, 1991; Naicker, 1995).

EARLY DEVELOPMENTS

The study of exceptional second language learners is a rather new field as a result of large influxes of immigrants whose children are receiving instruction in languages in which they are not proficient. Many of those immigrants or their children live in poverty, and they clearly represent a disempowered political and social minority. A number of learners are entering school with little or no proficiency in the language of instruction, some with atypical educational experiences (Gersten & Woodward, 1994). In the past, these students' limited success in school was often attributed to cognitive confusion and language handicaps (Mercer, 1974; Ortiz & Yates, 1989; Cloud, 1994). As a result, much of the early North American research focused on the distinction between normal second language difficulties and longer-term disorders. Some authors (Cummins, 1986) suggested that the identification of minority students as having disabilities and their placement into special education programs was a result of discriminatory treatment in society and in the public schools. But much of the blame was placed on traditional testing procedures which generally do not allow for adaptations to accommodate the fact that the learner may not be fully proficient in the language of testing and may not be familiar with

G.R. Tucker and D. Corson (eds), Encyclopedia of Language and Education,
Volume 4: Second Language Education, 85–93.
© *1997 Kluwer Academic Publishers. Printed in the Netherlands.*

the cultural context of the test. Thus, investigations began on the use of alternatives to traditional testing.

Another body of research in the eighties addressed the issue of whether students with identified language or learning difficulties could master a second language in addition to their mother tongue. Most of the research came from Canada and asserted that immersion into a second language was suitable for children with language or learning difficulties (Naiman, Frohlich & Todesco, 1975; Bruck, 1978; Galloway, 1983). This research indicated that there is no justification for excluding students who are not excelling academically from second language learning. It was suggested that in order to succeed in learning a second language, one does not need to be a high academic achiever. There is no need, then, to exempt students with disabilities from foreign or second language study, as is typically done in the US, for example.

EXTENSION TO THE PRESENT

The difficulty of distinguishing short-term second language learning problems from longer-term disorders has continued to dominate much of the literature on exceptional second language learners. Perhaps as a reaction to the misidentification of normal second language learning difficulties as disorders, psychologists and teachers became reluctant to refer second language learners to any formal assessment or to special education services. In the case of some indigenous populations in Canada, special education services are still not readily available (Hull, 1995). Thus, in addition to the well known overrepresentation of language minority students in special education, many writers pointed out the existence of underrepresentation as well (Ovando & Collier, 1985; Baca & Cervantes, 1989).

This dilemma led to the development of sophisticated prereferral procedures and the adoption in many schools of prereferral as a routine part of the assessment process. Prereferral is the time period following an indication that the student has some kind of problem, but before a formal referral for special education occurs (Baca & Almanza, 1991). It provided a way to avoid unnecessary placement into special education. The wide use of prereferral procedures led to a perceived need for more extensive information gathering and a search for better ways of assessing second language learners with possible disabilities. Pluralistic models of assessment were recommended that would include sociocultural and linguistic information when interpreting IQ test scores (Baca & Cervantes, 1989). Variations on testing procedures such as additional time allowance and the use of two languages in testing were also considered (Fradd & McGee, 1994).

In the assessment of cognitive ability, many (Rueda, 1989; Holtzman & Wilkinson, 1991) suggested that the accurate identification of exceptionalities in second language learners requires a shift of focus from standardized psychometrics to modifications of learning environments such as the approach used by Feuerstein (1979) in the Learning Potential Assessment Device (LPAD). In this model, the growth from unassisted performance to mediated or assisted performance is measured rather than performance on a static task. The examiner teaches by mediation a strategy that will correct a specific deficit and then ascertains how well the learner can apply the strategy to new material, thus getting an indicator of their learning potential. Dynamic assessment approaches, also referred to as "reciprocal teaching" establish a strong link between testing and teaching. Although the application of these non-traditional approaches are fraught with difficulty, they are seen as more appropriate for minority students because they provide a more contextualized way of assessing students' abilities (Cummins, 1984.)

For assessing language proficiency and communicative ability, it was suggested that pragmatic rather than structural aspects of language be tested (Damico, 1991). By putting the emphasis on pragmatics, language is tested as an integrated process rather than a disconnected system of symbols, words, and rules of grammar and phonetics. When language proficiency and communicative ability were assessed in authentic contexts and for authentic purposes, learners were referred for special education services with greater accuracy than if they were tested using more traditional structural-oriented criteria (Damico, 1991; Fradd & McGee, 1994).

Along with the attempts to introduce and validate alternative procedures to traditional testing, some research efforts went into characterizing behaviors of the most common disorder, learning disability, for second language learners. Comparisons between characteristics of students with learning disabilities and those who were simply having difficulties in the second language yielded widely overlapping pictures (Mercer, 1974). Discrepancy between verbal and non-verbal performance on IQ tests, academic learning difficulties, language difficulties, perceptual difficulties, social/emotional problems, and attention and memory problems were all indicators of either a learning disability or a second language learning difficulty, making it very hard to distinguish between the two (Ortiz & Maldonado-Colon, 1986).

Despite the call for multi-referenced assessment, the inclusion of the native language and culture in the assessment process, and for ecologically sound and contextualized testing (Damico & Hamayan, 1991), many second language learners continue to be tested inappropriately. Figueroa (1989) conducted an extensive review of psychological testing and found that the impact of bilingualism on test scores was consistently ignored and the existing practices in school psychology related to intelligence testing have not changed much over the past 70 years. The fact still remains that second language learners with disabilities from minority backgrounds are often at risk because schools are not sufficiently prepared to meet their

needs (Baca & Almanza, 1991). And it is still the case that little attention has been given to ensuring effective instruction of second language
learners who may be handicapped.

WORK IN PROGRESS

Much of the current work on second language learners who encounter special difficulties in school revolves around the socio-political factors that
determine academic success for students who come from disadvantaged
or minority backgrounds. It has been suggested that social disadvantages
may lead to perceptions of disabilities that eventually lead students to be
placed in special education programs (Ogbu, 1992). The following factors have been highlighted as major social contributors to second language
learners' academic difficulties: degree of similarity or difference between
the cultural and linguistic context of the child's home environment and
that of the educational setting, and the degree of acceptance or nonaccep-
tance within the school environment of particular home culture values and
behaviors (Ogbu, 1992). Thus, it is argued that it is not so much ability
as it is dissonance between cultural and linguistic contexts that interferes
with many learners' performance and leads to the arrested development of
bilingual minority students, language loss and subtractive bilingualism.

   Cloud (1994) suggests that the interplay between external conditions
of the learning context and the learner's internal conditions can be used
to understand the effect that potential disabilities can have on a learner's
performance. In this model, four areas influence learning outcomes: (1) the
present knowledge that the learner has; (2) the constitutional characteristics
of the learner that are involved in receiving, processing, storing, retrieving
and expressing information and concepts; (3) the motivation that the learner
has in the learning process; and (4) opportunities that the learner has for
learning.

   More generally, some writers have turned their attention to the characteristics that place students at risk (Schwenn, 1994). Many second language
learners come from backgrounds of poverty and trauma, but the effects of
trauma on cognitive development and academic behavior and achievement
have begun to be investigated only recently. This research is particularly
germane to a growing population of learners: students who come from
low-literacy or underschooled backgrounds. Many of those students also
come with a history of trauma and face a particularly difficult struggle
in academic settings, where success rests on the ability to read (Barton,
1988).

   Little is known about adolescent students who enter school without any
literacy in their native language. For the most part, these are students who
come with interrupted prior schooling from war-torn countries, or students
who come from extremely impoverished rural environments, whose lives

prior to emigration have not been literacy rich. Besides the fact that these students are entering school with a tremendous disadvantage, their approach and understanding of literacy differs drastically from those of literate students (Hamayan, 1994). These students' lack of familiarity with the different forms and functions of literacy have a significant effect on their schooling.

Students from low-literacy backgrounds are typically three or more years below their age appropriate grade level in school and their climb to literacy is typically slow and arduous (Cloud, 1994). Partly at fault is the fact that most literacy programs in English are based on phonetic approaches that assume mastery of the sound system that recent non-literate learners do not have. Rather than teaching students the abstract phonetic codes of the language, it may be more helpful to provide students with meaning-based literacy experiences that correspond closely to their oral language (Hamayan, 1994).

Regardless of whether students come in with insufficient exposure to literacy or whether they have a disability, a long-term language use plan must be formally established that would specify who teaches what content area through which language (Ortiz & Yates, 1989). For students who have been formally identified as having a disability, this plan is a formal contract that also specifies the appropriate teaching, mediation or remediation strategies to be used. Appropriate teaching strategies that allow for instruction to take place without watering down the curriculum include: meaning-based instruction (Gersten & Woodward, 1994), instruction in the students' stronger language, which is often the native language (Baca & Almanza, 1991), allowing literacy to emerge holistically and developmentally (Hamayan, 1994), connecting the curriculum to the students' homes and their personal experiences (Ruiz, 1989), structuring lessons in a way that particularly helps students with learning disabilities focus on the task, clustering and categorizing new concepts that are being introduced, making use of learning strategies, allowing students to learn collaboratively and through the use of technology (Cloud, 1994), and to learn by doing (Galloway, 1983).

Although the types of programs that are available to second language learners with exceptional needs vary, they are typically highly specialized. Programs for these students can be formed by integrating special education services with bilingual or second language support services (Cloud, 1994). Four instructional models have been described (Ambert & Dew, 1982): (1) the bilingual support model where monolingual English special education teachers are teamed with native language tutors or paraprofessionals to provide special education services; (2) the coordinated service model in which second language learners are served by a monolingual English-speaking special education teacher and a bilingual teacher; (3) the integrated bilingual special education model where teachers who are trained to serve students with disabilities can also provide instruction in both the native language and ESL; (4) the consultant teacher model where a specialist in ESL and crosscultural education might help the special education teacher as a consultant.

Although the research does not provide unqualified support for it, there has recently been a trend in several countries (for example, Australia, Canada, England, Scotland, and the US) to serve students with special needs as much as possible within the mainstream classroom (Klassen, 1994). The challenge of mainstreaming, or inclusion as it is also known, for special needs students who are learning through their second language is to ensure that quality support is given not only for their disability but also for their bilingual development.

Regardless of the type of program, two factors are key to providing quality education to second language learners with special needs. First, it is essential that special education services for these students be framed in the cultural and linguistic context that is optimal for each student's maximum cognitive and affective development (Baca & Almanza, 1991). Second, the instructional delivery system must have the flexibility to incorporate a continuum of bilingual and/or ESL services over the duration of schooling and for those services to be tailored to individual students' needs (Baca & Almanza, 1991).

PROBLEMS AND DIFFICULTIES

Distinguishing between normal second language learning difficulties and more permanent disorders continues to be one of the biggest challenges for educators working with second language learners with special needs (Cloud, 1994). Although assessment of second language learners has improved significantly over the last decade, the fact still remains that even with the most extensive and most contextualized assessment, the conclusion that is drawn as to whether a student is experiencing normal second language difficulties or whether that student has a long-term disorder is, at best, an educated guess that a professional or a group of professionals make. School systems often cannot cope with ambiguities such as that, both for programmatic as well as legal reasons.

Programmatically, special education in several English-speaking countries (for example, Canada, England, and the US) is set up in such a way that a formal referral and a formal label are necessary before a student is given specialized support. Once a student is placed in a special education classification, it is highly unlikely that he or she will leave that category. This poses some problems for second language learners with special needs. First, because of the likelihood of a student being misidentified as having a disability, more flexibility is needed to be able to reclassify second language learners with special needs, or better still, to provide them with

the support they need without having to classify them as "special education students." Second, many of these students' needs stem from their
linguistic, cultural and educational diversity in addition to a disability.
Oftentimes, due to rigid scheduling constraints, placement into special education results in the reduction or elimination of native language, second
language or culture learning support services. Third, as students adjust to
their new environment and become more proficient in ESL, in the mainstream culture and in school skills, their seeming disabilities may change
as well. The system needs to be flexible in order to support those changing
needs. Models such as the one used in Scotland, where individual needs
are seen as a continuum and are interpreted strictly in the context of the
child's environment, provide a much larger degree of flexibility and must
be studied carefully over the years (Morris, 1995).

Second language learners who are coming ill prepared to enter school
also continue to challenge the educational system. These students tend to
be so different from the norm of the mainstream that their 'at risk' status
for particular disabling conditions is increased (Cloud, 1991). With the
growing interest in setting standards for academic achievement in the US
and with the national academic standards that several English-speaking
countries already have, it is not clear how these students fit into the school
mold. Cloud (1991) has suggested extensive information gathering and a
thorough assessment of these students' educational and home background
in order to plan responsive programs.

FUTURE DIRECTIONS IN RESEARCH AND PRACTICE

First, the validity of alternatives to traditional academic, cognitive, and
language testing must continue to be investigated, as well as the best way
to put them to use in the assessment of second language learners with
special needs. As the traditional assessment paradigm has come into question for all students, concerns for this particular group of students have
not abated. Psychologists and other personnel who administer tests need
to expand their knowledge of second language learning and the effects
of diversity on performance. Second, research must go beyond establishing valid assessment and placement procedures to the development of
effective instructional strategies that integrate special education, bilingual
and ESL teaching approaches. Third, the slackening of the rigid program
design that currently exists must be advocated to allow flexibility in the
provision of services. The purpose of this flexibility would be to give
students the specific support they need without the binding regulations
that often result from categorical programming. Fourth, as an increasing
number of second language learners with special needs enter the mainstream classroom, teachers need to be given the necessary support to deal

with diverse students with atypical educational backgrounds. This staff development becomes more essential as special education personnel continue to move into collaborative and inclusion-oriented delivery models. Finally, extensive and long-term research is much needed on the academic performance of second language learners with various atypical educational backgrounds. Guidelines need to be developed as to what can be expected from students with low-literacy backgrounds so that they are given the opportunity to achieve the highest standards possible.

Illinois Resource Center
USA

REFERENCES

Ambert, A. & Dew, N.: 1982, *Special Education for Exceptional Bilingual Students: A Handbook for Educators*, Midwest National Origin Desegregation Assistance Center, University of Wisconsin, Milwaukee WI.

Baca, L. & Almanza, E.: 1991, *Language Minority Students with Disabilities*, The Council for Exceptional Children, Reston VA.

Baca, L. & Cervantes, H.: 1989, *The Bilingual Special Education Interface*, Merrill, Columbus OH.

Barton, L.: 1988, *The Politics of Special Educational Needs*, Taylor & Francis, Washington, DC.

Bruck, M.: 1978, 'The suitability of early french immersion programs for the language disabled child', *Canadian Modern Language Review* 34, 884–887.

Cloud, N.: 1991, 'Educational assessment', in E.V. Hamayan & J. Damico (eds.), *Limiting Bias in the Assessment on Bilingual Students*, Pro-Ed, Austin TX, 220–245.

Cloud, N.: 1994, 'Special education needs of second language students', in F. Genesee (ed.), *Educating Second Language Children*, Cambridge University Press, New York, 243–275.

Cummins, J.: 1984, *Bilingualism and Special Education: Issues in Assessment and Pedagogy*, College-Hill Press, San Diego.

Cummins, J.: 1986, 'Empowering minority students: A framework for intervention', *Harvard Educational Review* 56, 18–36.

Damico, J.S.: 1991, 'Descriptive assessment of communicative ability in limited English proficient students', in E.V. Hamayan & J. Damico (eds.), *Limiting Bias in the Assessment on Bilingual Students*, Pro-Ed, Austin TX, 157–217.

Damico, J.S. & Hamayan, E.V.: 1991, 'Implementing assessment in the real world', in E.V. Hamayan & J.S. Damico (eds.), *Limiting Bias in the Assessment of Bilingual Students*, Pro-Ed, Austin TX, 303–316.

Feuerstein, R.: 1979, *The Dynamic Assessment of Retarded Performers: The Learning Potential Assessment Device*, University Park Press, Baltimore MD.

Figueroa, R.: 1989, 'Psychological testing of linguistic-minority students: Knowledge gaps and regulations', *Exceptional Children* 56, 145–153.

Fradd, S.H. & McGee, P.L.: 1994, *Instructional Assessment: An Integrative Approach to Evaluating Student Performance*, Addison-Wesley, Reading MA.

Galloway, V.: 1983, 'Foreign language and the "Other" student', in R.G. Mead, Jr. (ed.), *Foreign Languages: Key Links in the Chain of Learning*, Northeast Conference on the Teaching of Foreign Languages, Middlebury VT, 96–119.

Gersten, R. & Woodward, J.: 1994, 'The language-minority student and special education: Issues, trends, and paradoxes', *Exceptional Children* 60, 310–322.

Hamayan, E.V.: 1994, 'Language development of low-literacy students', in F. Genesee (ed.), *Educating Second Language Children*, Cambridge University Press, New York, 278–300.

Holtzman, W.H. & Wilkinson, C.Y.: 1991, 'Assessment of cognitive ability' in E.V. Hamayan & J. Damico (eds.), *Limiting Bias in the Assessment of Bilingual Students*, Pro-Ed, Austin TX, 247–280.

Hull, J.: 1995, 'Indian control and the delivery of special education services to students in band-operated schools in Manitoba', *Alberta Journal of Educational Research* 41, 36–62.

Klassen, R.: 1994, 'Research: What does it say about mainstreaming', *Education Canada* 34, 27–35.

Mercer, J.R.: 1974, 'A policy statement on assessment procedures and the rights of children', *Harvard Educational Review* 44, 125–141.

Morris, L.: 1995, 'Pupils with special needs: A scottish perspective', *Journal of Learning Disabilities* 28, 386–390.

Naicker, S.: 1995, 'The need for a radical restructuring of specialized education in the new South Africa', *British Journal of Special Education* 22, 152–154.

Naiman, N., Frohlich, M. & Todesco, A.: 1975, 'The good language learner', *TESL Talk* 6, 58–70.

Ogbu, J.U.: 1992, 'Understanding cultural diversity and learning', *Educational Researcher* 21, 5–14, 24.

Ortiz, A. & Maldonado-Colon, E.: 1986, 'Reducing inappropriate referrals of language minority students to special education', in A.C. Willig & H.F. Greenberg (eds.), *Bilingualism and Learning Disabilities: Policy and Practice for Teachers and Administrators*, American Library Publishing, New York, 37–50.

Ortiz, A. & Yates, J.R.: 1989, 'Staffing and the development of individualized educational programs for the bilingual exceptional student', in L. Baca & H.T. Cervantes (eds.), *The Bilingual Special Education Interface*, Merrill Publishing Company, Columbus OH, 183–204.

Ovando, C. & Collier, V.: 1985, *Bilingual and ESL Classrooms: Teaching in Multicultural Contexts*, McGraw-Hill, New York.

Rueda, R.: 1989, 'Defining mild disabilities with language-minority students', *Exceptional Children* 56, 121–129.

Ruiz, N.: 1989, 'An optimal learning environment for rosemary', *Exceptional Children* 56, 130–144.

Schwenn, J.O.: 1994, 'Serving culturally and linguistically diverse exceptional students in the REI', in A.F. Rotatori, J.O. Schwenn & F.W. Litton (eds.), *Advances in Special Education: Perspectives on the Regular Education Initiative and Transitional Programs*, Jai Press, Greenwich, CT, 53–74.

BARBARA BURNABY

SECOND LANGUAGE TEACHING APPROACHES FOR ADULTS

Every day, thousands of adults gather in classrooms, union halls, church basements, and the like to learn a second language. In addition to the characteristics of the learners and the purposes they have set for their learning, an understanding of how language should be taught colours the way they work. Such understandings or 'approaches', reflecting the culture and climate of the time and place, are the main topic of this discussion. Specifying 'teaching' in the topic narrows the scope to learning opportunities deliberately provided in formal settings, although many L2 learners do all or most of their learning on their own. This factor implies the influence of educational institutions, governments, or non-governmental organizations and relationships in which certain people are designated as teachers. The importance of specifying second language (L2), as opposed to minority or foreign languages, and adults, as opposed to children, will be discussed below.

The elusive concept of 'approach' in L2 teaching has overlapped that of several other terms. Anthony (1963) distinguished between 'approach' (assumptions and beliefs about language and language learning), 'method' (putting theory into practice and making decisions about skills, content, and order), and 'technique' (classroom procedures) (see Richards & Rogers, 1986: ch. 2). Other distinctions have been made (Richards & Rogers, 1986, 'approach', 'design', and 'procedure'; Larsen-Freeman, 1986: p. xi, 'method', 'principles' and 'techniques'; and Stern, 1983, chs. 20, 21). Nunan (1991: p. 2) states:

> ... syllabus design is concerned with what, why and when; methodology is concerned with how. However, with the development of communicative approaches to language teaching, the traditional distinction between syllabus design and methodology has become difficult to sustain.

In light of such diversity in conceptualization of L2 teaching approaches, I will not attempt a definition here. A number of authors have reviewed L2 'approaches' in detail (e.g. Crandall & Peyton, 1993; Larsen-Freeman, 1986; Nunan, 1991; Richards & Rogers, 1986; Rodby, 1992; Stern, 1983), grouping them in various ways (see the review by Crandall). The following discussion is structured around: (1) three major perspectives on language

G.R. Tucker and D. Corson (eds), Encyclopedia of Language and Education,
Volume 4: Second Language Education, 95–104.
© *1997 Kluwer Academic Publishers. Printed in the Netherlands.*

as it relates to L2 teaching; (2) issues of age, language situation, and application of approaches in the classroom; and (3) future directions.

MAJOR CONTRIBUTIONS

From the point of view of their underlying concept of language, prominent approaches to L2 teaching are grouped here by their focus on: (1) language as (sentence) grammar; (2) language as communication; and (3) language as social practice. Although these perspectives have had separate historical periods of ascendancy, they are not mutually exclusive in their application to current practice. Theories associated with them and their implications continue to evolve for each. In association with perspectives on how learners learn L2, they appear in various ways in L2 teaching.

Language as grammar was the predominant perspective of L2 teaching for the first two-thirds of this century. From the time of the Second World War, the then popular L2 teaching approach, grammar-translation (Stern, 1983), which is implicitly founded on traditional concepts of language as grammar, was challenged by the audio-lingual method. Based on American structural linguistics (e.g., the work of Sapir and Bloomfield), it asserts the authority of the linguist (rather than the traditional grammarian) to reveal the grammatical patterns of the target language. The backbone of the L2 curriculum is carefully ordered grammatical material, even structured to maximize areas of greatest contrast with the learner's first language if possible. '[O]nly with sound materials based upon an adequate descriptive analysis of both the language to be studied and the native language of the student (or with the continued expert guidance of a trained linguist) can an adult make the maximum progress toward the satisfactory mastery of a foreign language' (Fries, 1945: p. 5). Partly in reaction to the emphasis on reading and writing and 'literary' language of the grammar-translation approach, audio-lingual methods discourage the use of reading and writing, at least until basic oral patterns have been established.

Using theory from behaviourist psychologists (e.g., B.F. Skinner), the audio-lingual teaching strategy aims at controlled, stimulus-response, rote learning. For example, *An Intensive Course in English for Latin-American Students*, as discussed in detail in Fries (1945), promoted drilled overlearning of productive language patterns (at the sentence level or below), and avoidance of error through careful control over grammatical content. In the early Cold War years with extensive post-war movements of people and cross-cultural contact, the formal teaching of second languages expanded rapidly to new groups of learners; many L2 teachers were rapidly recruited and hurriedly trained, if at all. The audio-lingual 'teacher proof' method, using linguist-prepared materials and strong control over learners, spread rapidly to many countries.

In the 1960s, Chomsky's work on the theory of language and its role in human development and functioning challenged earlier positions. Also, behaviourist assumptions about language learning were called into question (Stern, 1983). An approach, called cognitive code learning, reasserted the value of encouraging learners to use grammatical rules consciously through deduction as well as induction, in meaningful contexts, in reading and writing as well as listening and speaking, and by learning from mistakes. Links have been suggested between cognitive code learning and the earlier 'direct method' (Krashen & Terrell, 1983; Stern, 1983), but Chomsky's views on language and its psychology are evident. Although this approach was not wide-spread, it is noted here as a second example of an approach grounded in language as grammar.

Concerning the influence of psychological factors in language learning, a group of approaches to L2 learning are mentioned here for historical fit even though they do not take a strong stance on the nature of language. A number of approaches were developed which emphasize ways of reducing pressure on learners in the L2 classroom either through focussing on simple tasks (e.g., The Silent Way, Gattegno, 1972) or making the environment very comfortable (e.g., Suggestopedia, Lozanov, 1979). These approaches have been used mainly with beginning learners in widespread contexts, often in combination with other strategies. (See contributions by Shirai and by Crandall, this volume.)

The second perspective considered here is *language as communication*. From the early 1970s, the communicative approach, inspired by linguists such as Halliday, the linguistic anthropologist Hymes, and L2 theorists such as Widdowson, broadened the language base of L2 teaching from sentence grammar to a framework including semantic, discourse structure, and sociolinguistic components. General goals of communicative language teaching are grammatical competence, sociolinguistic competence, and strategic competence (Canale & Swain, 1980). Simplistically put, sociolinguistic competence concerns turning the various factors in the context and the purposes of the communicators into language that will accomplish the communicative intentions of the speaker/writer. Strategic competence involves verbal and non-verbal strategies that imperfect L2 speakers can use to create real communication in the L2 and to repair communication problems resulting from insufficient L2 skills. Written and oral language are considered important, and writing is not just speech written down since it has its own rules, constraints, and social meaning.

The major expansion of perspective on language in the communicative approach has generally meant reliance on a broader range of understandings of how learners learn language as well. Krashen and Terrell (1983), in the context of Chomsky's views on how L1 is learned and of a growing body of research on L1 and L2 acquisition in informal settings, proposed the 'natural approach' to L2 learning in classrooms. With a syllabus consisting of communicative language goals, the authors promote a learning environment that approximates that of child L1 acquisition. This includes involvement in immediate (rather than distant or abstract) content to lower anxiety about the L2, no pressure on learners to produce language until they are ready, no correction of errors which do not interfere with communication, and a rich L2 environment aimed just above the level that the learner can handle. The natural approach was evolving during the 1980s at the time when the communicative approach was gaining prominence. Although the natural approach has had considerable influence on a range of L2 programs, its strong theoretical claims to having universal application to L2 learning have been disputed. Communicative language teaching, as seen in the following examples, tends to favour and even require multiple perspectives on how language is learned rather than purportedly universal solutions.

One of the broadest applications of the communicative approach has been the development of a framework for foreign language teaching in the European Community (from van Ek, 1975, to Council of Europe, 1996). The framework starts with parameters for an analysis of needs of the learner and goes on to specify 'threshold' objectives for L2 learning. The framework, throughout its development, has featured detailed specifications of language functions (what is to be accomplished through language) and notions (basic concepts embodied in language). The 1996 version discusses not only communicative language competence but also general competence, language activity, text, domain, strategy, and task. The Council of Europe (1996: pp. 82–83) document explicitly takes no position on language learning/acquisition theory.

In addition to this role as a unifying factor in foreign language teaching in the European Community, the communicative approach is associated with many other sites of L2 teaching. For example, attention to the needs of particular learners has led to the specification of language forms and functions for L2 learners preparing to use the target language in academic programs or professions (e.g., English for Academic Purposes, English for Science and Technology) (Strevens, 1977). Other examples are programs for refugees in Asia destined for the United States which used a competency-based curriculum based on language-related life skills as selected and revised by curriculum developers and teachers (Ranard & Pfleger, 1995: p. 43), and the Canadian federal ESL program for adult immigrants which is structured around communicative competencies (Citizenship and Immigration Canada, 1996: pp. 12–16).

In a world where formal L2 training is increasingly used to address needs in social and economic contexts (travel, international business, vocational training, refugee settlement, and so on), the focus on learner needs of the communicative approach is useful in tailoring L2 programs for many situations. It also permits accountability frameworks to be built for the use of large organizations like the European Community. However, the broad nature of the concepts puts the onus on delivery agencies and ultimately on teachers to set immediate goals, create learning opportunities, and assess outcomes. This is particularly challenging for non-native speaking teachers and/or those in situations where 'authentic' L2 materials are scarce. Any communicative approach teacher needs considerable knowledge about the L2 grammar, sociolinguistic rules, and culture in order to facilitate activities and interpret learners' responses. Indeed, some (e.g., Nunan, 1991) argue that L2 teachers should learn to conduct research in the classroom. Since the prescriptive authority of one 'expert' can not provide ready-made answers for communicative classrooms, L2 teachers using this approach must become well informed about a range of aspects of language as well as their students' needs.

The third perspective for discussion is *language as social practice*. It is related to social concepts of 'discourse' from theorists like Foucault, and has been more directly influenced by work in adult literacy such as Freire's and Street's. The focus is on the empowerment of learners through critical analysis of social situations, language included, and the development of skills to address power differences. Because language standards and theory can be perceived as being created by the powerful, they too are scrutinized. Thus, language programs are challenged in which the (communicative) competencies and target situations in which these competencies are to be demonstrated are chosen without consultation with the learners. Current literature from this perspective generally focusses on language planning (e.g., Phillipson, 1992; Tollefson, 1991), but specific critiques of L2 approaches are also made (e.g., Pennycook, 1989; Rodby, 1992: ch. 1). In principle, in this approach learners define their own needs on their own terms rather than being fitted into a needs category as defined by the curriculum; in effect, they define the curriculum itself through a process of participatory research in which the teacher has no more power than the learners. The process is often one of problem-posing from the Freirean tradition (e.g., Wallerstein, 1982; McKay, 1993 and see the review by Auerbach in Volume 2). Regarding the specification of the target language, analyses (often participatory) of structures of language and literacy in L2 contexts have led to L2 teaching implications emphasizing valuation of other than 'standard' forms (e.g., Auerbach, 1992, Baynham, 1995; Rodby, 1992 and see the reviews by Corson in Volumes 1 and 6).

The 'language as social practice' approach in L2 is particularly associated with adult L1 literacy learning which, in turn, has significant connections to social practice analysis (e.g. Street, 1984: see the review by Street in Volume 2). Many would-be L2 learners attend adult literacy and basic education programs because L2 classes have no room for them (Chisman et al., 1993: p. 6). Also, as discussed above, L2 perspectives have generally treated the teaching of reading and writing as only two of several facets of language learning, often peripheral to oral language development (Rodby 1992: ch. 1) with the result that some L2 learners do not have their specific literacy needs addressed in programs. Such L2 practice frequently assumes that adult students are literate in their L1 and hence that they can transfer their literacy skills to the L2; students with little L1 literacy have been excluded from language classes (Klassen, 1992). For such learners and for learners who speak and read the L2 well beyond the survival level but who are held back in their potential for want of training in more sophisticated skills in the L2, the 'language as social practice' approach can be seen as addressing hitherto unserved populations by identifying systemic barriers to their access to learning and by working with them to specify goals that suit their own interests (McKay, 1993). Crucially, public pronouncements in favour of adult literacy are not necessarily to be understood, from a language as social practice stance, to be in the interests of L2 learners (e.g., Moore, 1996).

An important theme from the 'language as social practice' perspective is the difficult but essential position of teachers between the interests of the mainstream power structure and those of the students (Ricento & Hornberger, 1996). Wrigley (1993), Chisman et al. (1993), Burnaby (1992), McKay (1993), and others discuss the effects of power structures, especially government funding, on objectives, evaluation, and design in L2 programs. Shore et al. (1993) analyze factors in creating inclusive curricula for adult L2 and basic education programs. They express concern that the teacher not be left as the scapegoat when agendas of inclusivity conflict with conservative interests.

> While teachers are often seen as the key players in delivering the curriculum, it is our belief that this is an untenable position that leaves teachers in a vulnerable position, open to criticism about teaching outcomes that may be only marginally related to their input. 'Teacher as curriculum' beliefs draw attention away from the significant responsibilities of an individual organization, such as a neighbourhood house, or a system, such as Correctional Services. With the emphasis on the individual and often charismatic powers of teachers, educational theorising ignores organizational structures, decision-making procedures, and work practices that determine in part the possibilities of working towards an inclusive adult literacy, language, and numeracy curriculum for social justice. (p. 56)

From the 'language as social practice' perspective then, situations of difference, social friction, and conflicting interests are in full focus in L2 teaching. Grammar and the structure of communication are seen as embedded in contexts of social tension that must be considered if appropriate L2 learning is to be identified.

PROBLEMS AND DIFFICULTIES: INHERENT ISSUES

Although the topic for this review specified approaches for adult learners, I found that the age of L2 learners is not often included as a critical factor in language perspectives on L2 teaching. Some of the early examples of specific approaches were for adults (e.g., Fries, 1945, or van Ek, 1975). However, both of these approaches were soon transformed for use with children. Those approaches that rely on some level of intellectual maturity and/or L1 literacy (e.g., cognitive code, English for Science and Technology, grammar-translation, or 'language as social practice' programs focussed on adult social issues) are presumably used, at the earliest, with adolescents. Since the natural approach aims to reproduce in the L2 classroom the kinds of circumstances that young children have in L1 learning, it is constrained in theory with respect to age. Expanding identification of particular L2 needs have produced versions of approaches for specific age groups. Thus, Girard & Trim (1988) discuss specific applications of the European framework through occupationally-oriented language for young adults, for example. The basic program for adults in refugee Asian camps was extended and adapted for use with children and youth (Ranard & Pfleger, 1995). Although adult L2 literacy programs are by definition for adults, some literacy and ESL programs in the refugee camps (Ranard & Pfleger, 1995) and in the United States (as discussed in McKay, 1993) have been organized for families (see the review by Auerbach in Volume 2). In sum, it appears that L2 programs are developed to suit learners of various ages, but that the relevance of the learner's age is rarely central to *the conceptualization of language* in the approach.

For the language as grammar and language as communication perspectives, little significance appears to be attached to the language circumstances (i.e., foreign language, second language, or minority language) of the learner. For example, the European framework, designed for foreign language learning situations, is applied to migrant workers as well (Girard & Trim, 1988). Similarly, the program Fries (1945) described was for Spanish speakers learning English as a foreign language, but the audiolingual method has been widely applied in L2 learning and with minority language groups. However, proponents of 'language as social practice' approaches tend to focus on groups at the linguistic power periphery, including a wide variety of situations. For them, demographic distinctions among foreign, second, or minority languages are irrelevant in comparison with considerations of power relations between the learners' L1 and the target language. (See contributions by Schachter and by Singleton, this volume.)

Each successive perspective described here has incorporated facets of the one before and added dimensions. There continues to be rivalry among the perspectives, and theoretical positions in the various relevant academic disciplines are constantly being altered and extended. Meanwhile, there is room in a curriculum for only so many priorities, and those advocated from theory are only a few among many. Actual classroom practice tends to incorporate a wide selection of activities (Larsen-Freeman, 1986; Nunan, 1991). Although stressing the importance of clarifying the *ends* of L2 teaching, current perspectives on L2 teaching are highly accepting of many possible *means* as appropriate in the local environment. Crandall & Peyton (1993) outline five approaches to adult English as a second language literacy instruction, but note that 'In reality, programs often combine several of these approaches. ... The differences [between the approaches] are likely to reside in the basic philosophies upon which the programs are designed and the degree to which the learners are engaged in the overall direction setting' (p. 5). These authors (1993: pp. 4–5) and Savage (1993) point out that even the two perspectives often seen to be in competition, 'competency-based' (roughly, communicative) and 'participatory' (roughly, social practice), are not mutually exclusive. In this vein, Rodby (1992) discusses in detail a dialectic, in learners' desire and experience, between the universal value of the language of wider communication and the personal value of local language(s). Stern (1983: p. 517), summarizing his massive analysis of language teaching, says 'If any conclusion stands out from this study it is the multifactor, multidisciplinary, and multilevel character of language teaching theory.' Pennycook (1989: p. 613) advocates that 'we should either see practice and theory as informing each other, or, better still, do away with the distinction altogether.' (See the review by Pennycook in Volume 1.)

FUTURE DIRECTIONS

The discussion above suggests at least three likely areas of rising need for resolution. First, with respect to teachers, unrealistic pressures are accumulating in that: (1) teachers are theoretically expected to have significant knowledge about grammar, communicative theory, and language/literacy in social analysis; (2) teachers are to conduct research on learners' grammatical, sociolinguistic, and social needs and create unique curricula on this basis; (3) teachers are often at the centre of conflict between goals of inclusive teaching and conservative agendas of institutions and funders; and (4) economic and social pressures result in L2 teaching being increasingly put in the hands of volunteers and general social service workers. Second, the lines between L2, minority, and foreign language teaching may be redrawn in a struggle between the mainstream and the margins, and native and non-native speaker interests over priorities and resources for language training. Third, confusion needs to be addressed regarding real issues and impact of: (1) adult L1 literacy where the L1 is a mainstream language; (2) reading and writing in L2 learning for learners literate in their L1; and (3) literacy for learners in an L2 context who are not literate in their L1.

Ontario Institute for Studies in Education
Canada

REFERENCES

Anthony, E.M.: 1963, 'Approach, method and technique', *English Language Teaching* 17, 63–67.

Auerbach, E.R.: 1992, *Making Meaning, Making Change: Participatory Curriculum Development for Adult ESL Literacy*, Center for Applied Linguistics and Delta Systems, Washington, D.C. and McHenry, Illinois.

Baynham, M.: 1995, *Literacy Practices: Investigating Literacy in Social Contexts*, Longman, New York and London.

Belfiore, M.E. & Burnaby, B. (eds.): 1995, *Teaching English in the Workplace* (revised and expanded edition), Pippin Publishing and OISE Press, Toronto.

Burnaby, B.: 1992, 'Official language training for adult immigrants in Canada: Features and issues', in B. Burnaby & A. Cumming (eds.), *Socio-political Aspects of ESL in Canada*, OISE Press, Toronto, 3–34.

Canale, M. & Swain, M.: 1980, 'Theoretical bases of communicative approaches to second language teaching and testing', *Applied Linguistics* 1(1), 1–47.

Chisman, F.P., Wrigley, H.S., & Ewen, D.T.: 1993, *ESL and the American Dream: A Report on An Investigation of English as a Second Language Service for Adults*, The Southport Institute for Policy Analysis, Washington, DC.

Citizenship and Immigration Canada: 1996, *Canadian Language Benchmarks: English as a Second Language for Adults, English as a Second Language for Literacy Learners* (working document), Supply and Services Canada, Ottawa.

Council of Europe, Council for Cultural Co-operation, Education Committee: 1996, *Common European Framework of Reference for Language Learning and Teaching*, Draft 1 of a Framework Proposal, Council of Europe, Strasbourg.

Crandall, J. & Peyton, J.P.: 1993, *Approaches to Adult ESL Literacy Instruction*, Center for Applied Linguistics and Delta Systems, Washington, DC and McHenry, Illinois.

Fries, C.C.: 1945, *Teaching and Learning English as a Foreign Language*, The University of Michigan Press, Ann Arbor, Michigan.

Gattegno, C.: 1972, *Teaching Foreign Languages in Schools: The Silent Way*, Educational Solutions, New York.

Girard, D. & Trim, J.: 1988, *Learning and Teaching Modern Languages for Communication*, Project No. 12, Final Report of the Project Group, Council of Europe, Council for Cultural Co-operation, Strasbourg.

Klassen, C.: 1992, 'Obstacles to learning: The account of low-education Latin American adults', in B. Burnaby & A. Cumming (eds.), *Socio-political aspects of ESL in Canada*, OISE Press, Toronto, 253–264.

Krashen, S. & Terrell, T.: 1983, *The Natural Approach: Language Acquisition in the Classroom*, Pergamon Press and Alemany Press, Oxford, New York, Toronto, Sydney, Paris, Frankfurt, and San Francisco.

Larsen-Freeman, D.: 1986, *Techniques and Principles in Language Teaching*, Oxford University Press, Oxford.

Lozanov, G.: 1979, *Suggestology and Outlines of Suggestopedy*, Gordon and Breach, Science Publishers, New York.

McKay, S.L.: 1993, *Agendas for Second Language Literacy*, Cambridge University Press, Cambridge, New York, and Melbourne.

Moore, H.: 1996, 'Language policies as virtual reality: Two Australian examples', *TESOL Quarterly* 30(3), 473–498.

Nunan, D.: 1991, *Language Teaching Methodology: A Textbook for Teachers*, Prentice Hall, London, New York, Toronto, Sydney, Tokyo, and Singapore.

Pennycook, A.: 1989, 'The concept of method, interested knowledge, and the politics of language teaching' *TESOL Quarterly* 23(4), 589–618.

Phillipson, R.: 1992, *Linguistic Imperialism*, Oxford University Press, Oxford.

Ranard, D.A. & Pfleger, M. (eds.): 1995, *From the Classroom to the Community: A Fifteen-year Experiment in Refugee Education*, the Center for Applied Linguistics and Delta Systems, Washington, DC and McHenry, Illinois.

Ricento, T. & Hornberger, N.: 1996, 'Unpeeling the Onion: Language Planning and Policy and the ELT Professional', *TESOL Quarterly* 30(3), 401–428.

Richards, J.C. & Rogers, T.S.: 1986, *Approaches and Methods in Language Teaching: A Description and Analysis*, Cambridge University Press, Cambridge.

Rodby, J.: 1992, *Appropriating Literacy: Writing and Reading in English as a Second Language*, Boynton/Cook, Heinemann, Portsmouth, New Hampshire.

Savage, K.L.: 1993, 'What's wrong with CBE?' *TESOL Quarterly* 27(3), 555–558.

Shore, S., Black, A., Simpson, A. & Coombe, M.: 1993, *Positively Different: Guidance for Developing Inclusive Adult Literacy, Language, and Numeracy Curricula*, Department of Employment, Education, and Training, Canberra.

Stern, H.H.: 1983, *Fundamental Concepts of Language Teaching*, Oxford University Press, Oxford.

Street, B.: 1984, *Literacy in Theory and Practice*, Cambridge University Press, Cambridge.

Strevens, P.: 1977, 'Special-purpose language learning: A perspective', *Language Teaching and Linguistics: Abstracts* 10, 145–163.

Tollefson, J.W.: 1991, *Planning Language, Planning Inequality: Language Policy in the Community*, Longman, London and New York.

van Ek, J.A.: 1975, *The Threshold Level in a European Unit/Credit System for Modern Language Learning by Adults*, Council of Europe, Strasbourg.

Wallerstein, N.: 1982, *Language and Culture in Conflict*, Addison Wesley, Reading, Massachusetts.

Wrigley, H.S.: 1993, 'One size does not fit all: Educational perspectives and program practice in the U.S.' *TESOL Quarterly* 27(3), 449–466.

BRITT-LOUISE GUNNARSSON

LANGUAGE FOR SPECIAL PURPOSES

Language for special or specific purposes, *LSP*, is the traditional term for the various linguistic variants used in professional settings. The history of the field reveals an early theoretical interest in the description of various *sublanguages*, which are assumed to exist within the general language system in response to specific professional needs. Early studies were concerned with the written products – specific terminology, text types and registers. In recent decades, there has been a growing interest in the communicative processes involved and in their psychological and sociological dimensions, with a theoretical shift towards sociolinguistics, social constructivism and critical linguistics. Studies have dealt with spoken as well as written discourse and with the complex and diversified interplay between these media. The term *professional discourse or professional communication* is preferred to delineate this wider field.

LSP traditions developed mainly within foreign languages departments, with their orientation towards analysis of the language system. Practical problems relating to translation, standardization of terminology and design of technical and commercial documents were dealt with. This connection between the study of foreign languages and professional communication still exists, though the problems focused on have shifted somewhat. The earlier interest in language differences has made way for an interest in problems relating to language-in-context. In a gradually more international professional world, the cross-cultural dimension in all its social complexity is becoming more and more central.

EARLY DEVELOPMENTS

The use of language for special purposes is of ancient origin, stemming from the human need to moderate language to suit different types of activities. The systematic study of LSP and the establishment of LSP as a field of academic inquiry, however, has a much shorter history. The oldest branch is concerned with the study of terminology. In the early years of this century, German engineers elaborated lists of terms used within different fields, and the theoretical work of Eugen Wüster in the 1930s laid the foundations for international collaboration to standardize terminology (cf. Wüster, 1970).

It is not as easy, however, to determine when the study of texts for specific purposes began. We can find individual studies on business, legal and

G.R. Tucker and D. Corson (eds), Encyclopedia of Language and Education,
Volume 4: Second Language Education, 105–117.
© *1997 Kluwer Academic Publishers. Printed in the Netherlands.*

scientific language, for example, quite early on. The 1960s, of course, saw an increase in such work, as with other types of linguistic research. David Mellinkoff's famous book *The Language of the Law* appeared in 1963, and Charles Barber published his article 'Some Measurable Characteristics of Modern Scientific Prose' in 1962 (see Swales, 1988), to give just two examples. Interest in readability and document design also emerged in the 1960s, leading to the creation of 'document design centres'. As regards the LSP field in a more organized form, we have to go to the 1970s to find its starting-point. In the late 1970s, various activities were in progress which seem to indicate that LSP had become established as a field of its own. The first European symposium on LSP was held in 1977, the LSP journal *Fachsprache* was launched in 1979 and the journal *English for Specific Purposes* in 1981.

The early history of the LSP field is to a large extent connected with European scholars and European thinking. The study of language for specific purposes was undertaken in a language-based functionalist theoretical framework. The emphasis was on general characteristics at different levels (lexicon, syntax, style) of different sublanguages, such as the medical, economic, legal and technical sublanguages. The relevant knowledge base was fundamental to this differentiation into *sublanguages*, while functional aspects underlay a differentiation into *text types*.

Traditional, mainstream LSP research could thus be described as language-based and product-oriented, with the aim of describing and classifying different types of languages for specific purposes and of different types of texts (Kittredge & Lehrberger, 1982; Hoffmann, 1985).

In parallel with this Germanistic European LSP tradition, an Anglo-American tradition developed, following a largely different course. The ESP (English for Specific Purposes) field developed in the US and in Britain in English language departments, with their strong orientation towards literature and a more global and text-based analysis of different genres. It evolved within academic communities concerned with educational problems relating to teaching students how to write different types of English texts in a socially acceptable and also a competitive way. The study of ESP therefore came to be combined with an interest in rhetoric, the art of persuasion, and in sociology, the art of socializing and conforming.

This tradition, spread through a web of 'writing across the curriculum' courses in the English-speaking countries, focused on text patterns – argumentative and persuasive patterns – and the actual writing process, rather than on language structure and variation. The social dimension was also central. Writing was analysed as taking place within a *discourse community*, a sociorhetorical concept relating to the use of written texts for specialist professional purposes.

There is a clear connection between the concepts of *discourse community* and *sublanguage*; those using a particular sublanguage for specific purposes are thus assumed to form a discourse community. The interest of this group of scholars was directed not only towards the genre, but also towards the individual writers and their relationship to the discourse community (Bazerman, 1988; Swales, 1990).

MAJOR CONTRIBUTIONS

A characteristic feature of the LSP field as a whole, and in particular of its early history, is the disciplinary divide between studies of written and spoken discourse. The same domains – law, bureaucracy, technical writing, business discourse, medicine – have been studied in relation to both media, but there has been very little – if any – contact between the researchers in either camp.

Though as disciplines they are still distinct, there are important resemblances between these approaches to written and spoken discourse. The spoken discourse tradition, which draws on studies of interaction within anthropology, sociology, and sociolinguistics and analyses of discourse in institutional and professional settings, has used a multidisciplinary framework to elucidate the social and psychological factors constructing talk in the professions.

Among those studying written professional discourse, too, there has been a growing interest in the processes involved in the production and reception of texts and in the historical and contemporary construction of genres and registers. The objective of such studies has been to understand the psychological processes of writing and reading, the social processes behind the formation of written genres, and the social and societal dynamics behind the emergence and development of professional sublanguages. These process-oriented studies have been carried out in the borderlands between, on the one hand, the language-centred LSP field and, on the other, psycholinguistics, sociolinguistics, sociology and rhetoric.

The following discussion of major contributions will be arranged around different professional settings, and for each of these will be considered, where appropriate, studies of spoken as well as written discourse.

The Economic-Technical Setting

The 1970s and 1980s were the decades of the plain language movement. The idea was to formulate strategies and rules for writers which would improve documents of different kinds. Perhaps the most widespread and enduring result of this movement was what were called 'readability formulae'. Based on a mechanistic view of reading and comprehension, formulae were developed which could measure the difficulty – readability – of texts. Most of them were based on word and sentence length. The theoretical basis for these formulae is very weak, but they owe their popularity to their simplicity.

This movement, however, is much more than just readability formulae, and some work has been done under this umbrella which is of a good theoretical standard. Document design centres were set up, e.g. at Carnegie Mellon University in Pittsburgh. Linda Flower and John Hayes were among the researchers at this centre which was opened in 1978. Basing their studies on psycholinguistics and cognitive psychology, they managed to give their document design work a theoretical orientation. They conducted experiments with readers and writers, and came to develop their famous writing model (Hayes & Flower, 1980).

'Instructional science' was also used as a basis for document design work, for example in Europe. Instructional research centres on the development of procedures for optimizing learning in specific situations. Its aim is to establish rules that specify the most effective way of attaining knowledge or mastering skills. Another field which has contributed to document design work is that of 'human factors'. Here, methods and techniques are developed for the application of experimental procedures in real-life situations.

The plain language movement continues throughout the world. More recent studies have been oriented towards text linguistics and rhetoric with the goal of improving instructions, guidelines and technical reports, finding adequate strategies for the drafting of sales promotion letters and job applications, and also popularizing difficult documents.

From early on, translation of economic, technical and other professional texts was a key area of interest to LSP scholars, and special attention has been devoted to the linguistic basis for the translation of documents.

Legal and Bureaucratic Settings

Much work of interest has been carried out within legal and bureaucratic settings. The more purely descriptive work done on the characteristics of legislative language in terms of vocabulary, syntax and textual patterns (Mellinkoff, 1963; Kurzon, 1986; Bhatia, 1987) can be seen as forming the foundation for the more process-oriented studies. Other work had a sociological foundation, analysing the functions of laws and other legal texts (Danet, 1980; Gunnarsson, 1984).

One problem area focused on relates to the comprehensibility of legal language, that is, to the asymmetries in reading comprehension between lay people and professionals. Being undertaken with the aim of facilitating reading and comprehension for the ordinary man or woman, these studies have come to clearly reflect the theoretical situation within psycholinguistics. In the 1960s legislative texts were analysed and assessed in relation to their readability, which involved a mechanical way of analysing documents at a surface level. An analysis of jury instructions by Charrow and Charrow (1979) represented a step forward. Their ideas for reform derived from a number of linguistic factors, but they were not based on any theory of text comprehension or on a very searching analysis of the societal function of the texts.

Other studies have had a more theoretical foundation. On the basis of a critique of previous research, Gunnarsson (1984) rejected the concern with lexis or syntax, which went no further than memorization or ability to paraphrase, and developed a theory of functional comprehensibility focusing on perspective and function orientation (implications for action). The reading of laws and text comprehension is here viewed in a societal framework.

Difficulties due to asymmetries have also interested scholars of spoken legal discourse. Courtroom proceedings and police encounters etc. have been analysed by linguists, sociologists and ethnographers. Studies have focused on different types of content and argumentative features, in order to reveal how utterances are part of a prior and anticipated context. Cross-examination, question-answer patterns, topic progression and recycling, argumentative structure and story patterns have been analysed. This research has emanated from different traditions, ranging from speech act theory to an ethnomethodological tradition comprising micro-analysis of varying elements in dialogue (Atkinson & Drew, 1979; Drew, 1992).

Other studies have focused on the understanding and interpretation of utterances. Within a sociolinguistic theoretical framework, experiments have been carried out with different versions of utterances, in order to test powerful and powerless speech, gender differences etc. in style, self-presentation, tone of voice etc. (O'Barr, 1982; Adelswörd, Aronsson, Jönsson & Linell, 1987).

Important work has also been done on police interrogation. Cicourel (1968) analysed the part played by police questioning in the long bureaucratic judicial process. In this pioneering work, he studied the social construction of 'cases', particularly the formation and transformation of the images of young delinquents as the cases pass through the legal system (police, social workers, probation officers, prosecutors, courts). Jönsson (1988) focused on another problem associated with the bureaucratic routine. Her interest was in the interplay between police interrogation and the written police report, and she analysed to what extent police officers were influenced when interrogating suspects by the fact that they later had to write a report.

The Medical-Social Setting

Medical discourse has also been studied from a variety of angles. Here we find work done within a sociological tradition, such as more discourse-oriented studies. The problems that arise between doctors and patients have been seen to a large extent as interactional, and it has been assumed that it is possible to do something about them. The asymmetries between doctor and patient have been analysed in various ways. Mishler (1984) talked about the two different voices in doctor-patient interaction, the voice of medicine and the voice of the lifeworld, which represent different ways of conceptualizing and understanding patients' problems. The different perspectives in medical interaction have been the concern of Cicourel, one of the founders of doctor-patient research. By means of conversational analysis of extracts from doctor-patient encounters, he was able to reveal important sources of miscommunication (Cicourel, 1981).

Among the different medical specialities, psychiatric treatment has been of particular interest to linguists. A well-known example is Labov & Fanshel's work on therapeutic discourse (1977). Analyses have also focused on neurotic and psychotic language, interaction with aphasia and dementia sufferers, and talk to and about old people.

Science and the Academic Setting

Writing at the college and university level and the different academic genres of writing have attracted the attention of many researchers. As within the educational area, much research has been steered by the practical need to improve the teaching of writing in the college classroom.

The Freshman Writing Program in the US, which involves the teaching of academic writing to all college students, has led to a large number of studies on genres and on the writing process. The most recent trends within this field owe a debt to the Russian philosophers and sociologists Bakhtin, Leontev and Vygotsky, as well as to researchers within the sociology of science, such as Merton, Latour and Wolgaar. Flower, for instance, stresses in one of her books on the writing process (1994) the negotiative character of writing, in a truly Bakhtinian sense.

Within the American writing tradition, the learner's adjustment to the academic 'discourse community' is focused on from a sociological angle. Typical of this group of researchers, working in the competitive society of the US, is their interest in rhetorical (persuading) patterns (Swales, 1990; Berkenkotter & Huckin, 1995).

The European tradition, on the other hand, builds more on a text linguistic tradition, with a close analysis of texts at different levels: pragmatic, referential-cohesive, thematic, cognitive (Schröder, 1991; Gunnarsson, Melander & Näslund, 1994).

Academic genres have also been studied from a cross-cultural angle, with the aim of revealing differences and improving L2 writing. The contrastive rhetoric tradition, which has been influenced by the pioneering work of Kaplan in the 1960s, has led to many important studies on differences between the writing of scholars with different language backgrounds. In most cases, the basis for comparison has been the English language and Anglo-American culture (Kaplan, 1966; Connor, 1996).

WORK IN PROGRESS

The studies which will be discussed under this heading all relate to discourse in organizations, institutions or workplaces. With a theoretical orientation towards sociology and organization/network theory, social constructivism and critical linguistics, these studies try to grasp and understand problem areas relating to the complexity and diversity of communication in the professions. In many ways they can be seen as pointing towards the future.

Complexity in Relation to the Construction of Fact

The complexity of the construction of knowledge has been focused on by scholars dealing with scientific discourse. Proceeding from ideas within the social constructivist tradition, they have developed a methodology for the purpose of understanding how science is created through discourse.

Merton (1973) and others working within the sociology of science analysed the role of texts in the establishing of scientific fact. The scientific field is seen as a workplace, a laboratory in which social rules determine the establishing of facts and the rank order of the scientist. The writing up of results is seen as a process of tinkering with facts, rather than a knowledge-guided search. Latour and Woolgar (1986) described the social construction of scientific facts as an antagonistic struggle among scientists, leading to a deliberate diminishing of the results of others and a levelling up – to a generalized level – of one's own results. Scientific facts are regarded as mere works; rhetoric determines what become scientific facts.

Bazerman (1988) studied the rise of modern forms of scientific communication, focusing on the historical emergence of the experimental article. A social constructivist approach in relation to written texts is also found in Bazerman & Paradis (1991), which examines the important role played by texts in profession-building. Textual forms and definitions are found to impose structure on human activity and help to shape versions of reality. Texts are shown to play powerful roles in staging the daily actions of individuals, and to be important factors in the rise of actions.

The variety and heterogeneity of the discourse of mediation in court is analysed by Candlin & Maley (1997). Professional practice is shown to be a complex web of legal, therapeutic and counselling discourse. The construction of meaning is analysed from the perspective of intertextuality and interdiscursity. The focus here is on spoken discourse, but written legal texts are always present as a background to the negotiations.

Complexity in the construction of fact is also dealt with in two studies focusing on the interplay of verbal and non-verbal elements in discourse. Goodwin & Goodwin (1997) analyse the interplay between linguistic and non-linguistic means in the construction of the court discourse in the famous Rodney King trial in Los Angeles in 1992. Their analysis shows how the well-known scene on the video tape, showing the policemen beating the African-American man lying on the ground, is reconstructed in the trial by the defence lawyer focusing not on the policemen's actions, but on the movements of Rodney King. The lawyer deliberately places certain elements in the foreground and others in the background, using non-verbal as well as verbal means. Visually the body movements of Rodney King are highlighted, while the policemen's movements are toned down. The lawyer also breaks down the body movements into a set of small movements explicitly pointing to each one of these. Verbally, the lawyer focuses on the threatening character of each body turn. The purpose of this visual and verbal highlighting of certain parts of the scene is to construct and reconstruct the scene in such a way as to make the jury view it from the perspective of the accused policemen.

Complexity due to Organizational Structure

Another area of work in progress is the study of communication in organizations. These studies border in many cases on work on organization within sociology. The relationship between organizational structure and culture, hierarchy and writing activities is elucidated in a variety of studies, using methods ranging from pure survey to ethnographic observation (Odell & Goswani, 1985; Spilka, 1993).

Gunnarsson (1997) presents a study of writing with a theoretical base in sociolinguistics. The writing activities of a local government office are analysed in relation to its internal structure – hierarchies, clusters, role patterns – as well as to the external networks to which the actors-writers belong. Complexity is central in this study of writing in a non-academic workplace, a complexity which relates to the roles played by the writer, the network structure and also the intertwinement of spoken and written discourse. The collective character of writing in this workplace is demonstrated as is the continuous and varied interplay between talking and writing, and between formal and informal discourse.

Complexity due to the organizational structure in a medical setting, an out-patients' clinic at an Austrian hospital, is discussed in Wodak (1997). The actual discourse between the medical actors – doctor, nurse, patient and relatives – is analysed in relation to a macro description of the institution as a working organization, comprising an analysis of roles, routines and events. The research team found a clear relationship between the setting, the physical and mental state of the professionals and the actual conversation. The doctors' behaviour towards the patients, for instance the length of the conversation, the tone and the degree of mutual under-standing, varies with the degree of stress and tension caused by the events occurring. The Wodak study was carried out within the critical discourse analysis paradigm, and it has also found a direct application in that the research team have based courses for doctors on their results.

Complexity due to Social and Cultural Diversity

Encounters in working life have also been focused on from the perspective of the complexity of the social and cultural dimensions involved.

Negotiations are one of the subareas of interest in relation to the business world and organizations. The volume edited by Firth (1995) includes studies of negotiations in intraorganizational encounters, in commodity trading, and in professional-lay interactions. Negotiations are studied in the varied settings of the doctor's office, the welfare bureau, the travel agency, the consumer helpline, government, the university and business.

Considerable practical interest attaches to intercultural negotiations, and many studies have focused on negotiations between individuals from different cultures and with different mother tongues.

An adjacent area of concern is that of conflicts and misunderstandings in different working life settings. A special type of problematic talk is that relating to moral discourse, that is, discourse on shameful subjects such as alcoholism, abortion, theft and the like. Hall, Sarangi & Slembrouck (1997), for instance, studied moral construction in social work discourse. They analysed an interview with a social worker, in which he tells a former colleague about a case of child abuse – 'failure to thrive' – which he had been handling in an inner city public welfare agency in the UK. By analysing these interviews as narratives, the researchers were able to reveal the moral character of the decision making that occurred and the rhetorical character of its justification. They looked at the presence of institutionalized voice in the social worker's narrative, that is the voice which makes this narrative hearable as a social work story. They also studied how the case was established as a case of 'failure to thrive', and how the narrative makes it clear that the parents are responsible for the situation that has arisen. They found that the narrative seemed to derive its internal coherence and consistency from the point of view of the social worker's action-logic. The researchers' conclusion is that this narrative is a form of social practice, which is instrumental in reproducing social relations and realities within social work discourse, as in this case of child abuse.

PROBLEMS AND DIFFICULTIES

The first problem which should be considered is one touched on earlier. It relates to the historical disciplinary divide between studies of written discourse and work on spoken discourse. Studies of non-verbal communication and new technology, too, are often departmentally separated from studies of other types of discourse, as they are carried out in communication and technology departments, rather than in language and sociology departments. It should be said, however, that this problem can be solved, and that many steps have already been taken to bridge the gap, including conferences and joint volumes, and multiplex studies of real-life communication.

The second major problem in this field is the complexity of professional life and the variation from one environment to another. It is not always possible to generalize from one workplace to another, and even less from one culture to another. In addition, continuous – and often very rapid – changes take place in the various organizations and institutions, which means that painstaking studies, taking years to complete, are sometimes obsolete before they are finished and made known to the public.

A third and related problem has to do with establishing the right research contacts. It is not always easy for the researcher to gain access to the authentic workplace situation he or she wishes to observe. Many situations are too sensitive, which means that the presence of an outsider could ruin the outcome. Much of what happens in the business world is cloaked in strict secrecy, and many professionals are afraid to reveal their strategies to outsiders and, of course, to competitors.

A fourth problem concerns the acceptance of one's results, on the one hand among fellow researchers and on the other among practitioners. The researcher studying communication in the professions has to balance between two worlds – the academic and the practical – a task which is most certainly very complicated. Most of the studies presented in this chapter are accepted as solid research. It is probably safe to say, however, that most of this work is little known among the practitioners concerned.

One area of great importance, of course, is the dissemination of research results to teachers, not only to teachers of LSP and of writing in the professions, but also to all those who deal with spoken and written discourse in general. Although far from impossible, it has to be said that bridging this gap is sometimes also problematic.

Last but not least, I would lika to focus on the problems arising from the dominance of the rich parts of the world and their special languages in relation to research and teaching. Though important work was done as early as the 1970s on the development of course materials and textbooks specifically for use on English for science and technology courses in the developing countries (Swales, 1988), the rich world bias still prevails in the great flood of books that have spread around the globe. It is also to be regretted that, here as elsewhere, we know so little about studies on the smaller and less known special languages, in particular those used in the developing world.

FUTURE DIRECTIONS

To grasp the complexity and diversity of authentic situations in the professional world, theoretical and methodological integration must – and is likely to – take place within the field of professional discourse and communication. Such studies will need to adopt a holistic approach, that is, to include all kinds of communication – written, spoken, and new technology. Analysis of the interplay between written and spoken discourse is already underway, but much more needs to be done in order to grasp what is really happening. A few studies have dealt with new technology – e-mail, fax, telephone and video conferences etc. – but future research will have to explore these types of communication in greater detail. In particular, it will be necessary to analyse the new roles of and the interplay between traditional discourse types and this new technology in a changing professional world. What medium is used for what purpose, by whom and in what situation?

The use and function of different languages in the professions is another area that has been touched upon, but in which a lot more needs to be done. In a more and more internationally oriented professional world, language choice is a complex issue. In a multilingual professional community, the different languages are likely to serve different functions and also to have differing prestige. Translation issues are of course always central, but what is of growing importance in a rapid international interchange of information and ideas is the parallel production of discourse (spoken as well as written) in different languages.

In order to grasp the complexity of real life, it will be necessary to use a multiplex methodology, drawing on the traditional quantitative as well as qualitative traditions.

Uppsala University, Sweden

REFERENCES

Adelswärd, V., Aronsson, K., Jönsson, L. & Linell, P.: 1987, 'The unequal distribution of interactional space dominance and control in courtroom interaction', *TEXT* 7, 313–346.
Atkinson, J.M. & Drew, P.: 1979, *Order in court. The organization of verbal interaction in judicial settings*, Macmillan, London.
Bazerman, C.: 1988, *Shaping Written Knowledge. The Genre and Activity of the Experimental Article in Science*, The University of Wisconsin Press, Madison, Wisconsin.

Bazerman, C. & Paradis, J. (eds.): 1991, *Textual Dynamics of the Professions. Historical and Contemporary Studies of Writing in Professional Communities*, The University of Wisconsin Press, Madison, Wisconsin.

Berkenkotter, C. & Huckin, T.N.: 1995, *Genre knowledge in disciplinary communication. Cognition/Culture/Power*, Lawrence Erlbaum, Hillsdale, New Jersey.

Bhatia, V.K.: 1987, *Analysing Genre: Language Use in Professional Settings*, Longman, London and New York.

Candlin, C.N. & Maley, Y.: 1997, 'Intertextuality and interdiscursivity in the discourse of alternative dispute resolution', in B.-L. Gunnarsson, P. Linell & B. Nordberg (eds.), *The Construction of Professional Discourse*, Longman, London and New York.

Charrow, R.P. & Charrow, V.R.: 1979, 'Making legal language understandable: A psycholinguistic study of jury instructions', *Columbia Law Review* 79(7), 1306–1374.

Cicourel, A.: 1968, *The Social Organization of Juvenile Justice*, Wiley, New York.

Cicourel, A.V.: 1981, 'Language and medicine', in C. A. Ferguson & S. Brice Heath (eds.), *Language in the USA*, Cambridge University Press, Cambridge, 407–429.

Connor, U.: 1996, *Contrastive Rhetoric. Cross-cultural aspects of second-language writing*, Cambridge University Press, Cambridge.

Danet, B.: 1980, 'Language in the Legal process', *Law & Society Review* 14(3), 447–564.

Drew, P.: 1992, 'Contested evidence in courtroom cross-examination: the case of a trial for rape', in P. Drew & J. Heritage (eds.), *Talk at Work. Interaction in Institutional Settings*, Cambridge University Press, Cambridge.

Firth, A. (ed.): 1995, *The Discourse of Negotiation. Studies of Language in the Workplace*, Pergamon, Oxford.

Flower, L.: 1994, *The Construction of Negotiated Meaning. A Social Cognitive Theory of Writing*, Southern Illinois University Press, Carbondale and Edwardsville.

Goodwin, C. & Goodwin, M. Harness: 1997, 'Contested vision: The discursive constitution of Rodney King', in B.-L. Gunnarsson, P. Linell & B. Nordberg (eds.) *The Construction of Professional Discourse*, Longman, London and New York.

Gunnarsson, B.-L.: 1984, 'Functional comprehensibility of legislative texts: Experiments with a Swedish Act of Parliament', *Text* 4: 1–3.

Gunnarsson, B.-L.: 1997, 'The writing process from a sociolinguistic viewpoint', *Written Communication* 14.

Gunnarsson, B.-L., Melander, B. & Näslund, H.: 1994, 'LSP in a historical perspective', in M. Brekke, Ö. Andersen, T. Dahl & J. Myking (eds.), *Applications and Implications of Current LSP Research II*, Fagbokforlaget, Bergen, 878–918.

Hall, C., Sarangi, S.K. & Slembrouck, S.: 1997, 'Moral construction in social work discourse', in B.-L. Gunnarsson, P. Linell & B. Nordberg (eds.), *The Construction of Professional Discourse*, Longman, London and New York.

Hayes, J.R. & Flower, L.: 1980, 'Identifying the organization of writing processes', in L.W. Gregg & E.R. Steinberg, (eds.), *Cognitive Processes in Writing*, Lawrence Erlbaum, Hillsdale, NJ, 3–30.

Hoffmann, L.: 1985, *Kommunikationsmittel Fachsprache. Eine Ein-führung*, Zweite völlig neubearbeitete Auflage, Gunter Narr Verlag, Tübingen.

Jönsson, L.: 1988, Polisförhöret som kommunikationssituation, SIC 23, Studies in Communication, University of Linköping, Linköping.

Kaplan, R.: 1966, 'Cultural thought patterns in intercultural education', *Language Learning* 16, 1–20.

Kittredge, R. & Lehrberger, J. (eds.): 1982, *Sublanguage. Studies of Language in Restricted Semantic Domains*. Walter de Gruyter, Berlin and New York.

Kurzon, D.: 1986, *It is hereby performed. Legal speech acts*, Pragmatics & Beyond VII:6, John Benjamins, Amsterdam/Philadephia.

Labov, W. & Fanshel, D.: 1977, *Therapeutic Discourse. Psychotherapy as Conversation*, Academic Press, Orlando.

Latour, B. & Woolgar, S.: 1986 (1979), *Laboratory Life. The Construction of Scientific Facts*, Princeton, New Jersey.
Mellinkoff, D.: 1963, *The Language of the Law*, Little, Brown and Company, Boston and Toronto.
Merton, R.: 1973, *The Sociology of Science*, edited by N. Storer, University of Chicago Press, Chicago.
Mishler, E.G.: 1984, *The Discourse of Medicine. Dialectics of Medical Interviews*, Ablex Publishing Corporation, Norwood, New Jersey.
O'Barr, M.: 1982, *Linguistic Evidence: Language, Power and Strategy in the Courtroom*, Academic Press, New York.
Odell, L. & Goswani, D. (eds.): 1985, *Writing in Nonacademic Settings*, New York and London.
Schröder, H. (ed.): 1991, *Subject-oriented Texts. Languages for Special Purposes and Text Theory*, Walter de Gruyter, Berlin and New York.
Spilka, R. (ed.): 1993, *Writing in the Workplace. New Research Perspectives*, Illinois University Press, Carbondale and Edwardsville.
Swales, J.: 1988, *Episodes in ESP. A Source and Reference Book on the Development of English for Science and Technology*, Prentice Hall, New York, London etc.
Swales, J.: 1990, *Genre Analysis; English in Academic and Research Settings*, Cambridge University Press, Cambridge.
Wodak, R.: 1997, 'Critical discourse analysis and the study of doctor-patient interaction', in B.-L. Gunnarsson, P. Linell & B. Nordberg (eds.), *The Construction of Professional Discourse*, Longman, London and New York.
Wüster, E.: 1970, *Internationale Sprachnormung in der Technik besonders in der Eletrotechnik*, Dritte abermals ergänzte Auflage, Bonn.

Section 4

Focus on Professional Preparation

H.G. WIDDOWSON

APPROACHES TO SECOND LANGUAGE TEACHER EDUCATION

There are different views of what qualities and qualifications are required for language teachers to do their job properly, and these are reflected in the different terms that are used to refer to the kind of provision made to equip them for their task. The traditional term *teacher training*, for example seems to be solution orientated, and to carry the implication that teachers are to be given specific instruction in practical techniques to cope with predictable events, whereas *teacher education* seems to be problem orientated, and to imply a broader intellectual awareness of theoretical principles underlying particular practices (see Peters, 1977; Widdowson, 1990). The French term *formation* might be taken to cover both. All three terms can apply to the *pre-service preparation* of teachers and to their subsequent *in-service development*. The question arises as to whether the two orientations are equally appropriate in each case, and if so how they are to be reconciled. This applies to all teachers. The question also arises as to whether there is something specific to second language teachers that needs to be accounted for in their formation.

EARLY DEVELOPMENTS

The idea that teachers (of language or anything else) need to be instructed in *how* to teach seems to be relatively recent, and can be associated with a change in conception of the teaching role itself. If one thinks of the teacher as savant or sage (Buddha, Confucius, St Thomas Aquinas) the assumption is that what they had to say is directly transmitted, conveyed by the force of conviction. In this case the term teaching (or teachings) refers to content, not to the process of imparting it. This tradition of authoritative transmission finds expression in language teaching too. In the early part of the century the prevailing assumption was that the only essential qualification for language teachers was linguistic knowledge, and this was taken to mean declarative knowledge of the formal properties of the language, its phonetics and grammar. This defined the subject, and if teachers possessed this knowledge, they were deemed to be equipped to transmit it. The question of how teachers might themselves be educated to teach did not arise, for in transmission input is equated with intake. It only arises with the recognition that learning is not the simple reflex of teaching but needs to be engaged and directed in some way by taking the learners

G.R. Tucker and D. Corson (eds), Encyclopedia of Language and Education,
Volume 4: Second Language Education, 121–129.
© *1997 Kluwer Academic Publishers. Printed in the Netherlands.*

themselves into account. The emphasis then shifts from the teacher as sage, the source of authoritative knowledge, to teacher as pedagogue, expert in the inducement of learning. And the question then arises, of course, as to how this pedagogic expertise is to be provided.

One obviously relevant source of such expertise was the experience of those teachers who had grown wise in the practice of their craft, and the source therefore of authoritative know-how. And so the tradition of authority was continued but transferred to the pedagogic domain. Prospective and practising language teachers were given guidance in works like Palmer (1921/64), French (1948), Finocchiaro (1964), whose advice was generalised from particular pedagogic experience. Books like these, together with general courses in pyschology and education, became the staple diet on pre-service courses for the formation of language teachers, and especially of teachers of English as a foreign language.

This approach to language teacher education has been called into question on a number of counts over the past thirty years or so. One of these is the matter of the *theoretical validity* of such principles, based as they are on particular and localised experience. Another is the question of *practical alidation*, of how such principles can be realized effectively in circumstances other than those from which they originally derived. Educating teachers, in the sense of making them aware of principles does not necessarily transfer to training in the sense of being adept in the use of practical technique: teachers may acquire intellectual awareness, but not be able to act upon it. But even if the knowledge could be effectively acted upon, this approach still seems to presuppose a transmission view of teaching, with the teachers being better prepared to manipulate the conditions of learning without due regard to the particular circumstances of learners and what they bring to the learning process. Furthermore, the approach not only encourages a transmission view of teaching but is itself transmissive in design in that it casts the teacher in the dependent role of receivers of ideas, and gets them to conform to particular modes of thought and practice. One might argue that this is appropriate for pre-service preparation since novice teachers need to be initiated into the mysteries of their craft and have no experience of their own to refer to. But it may not be an appropriate model for in-service courses, since teachers in this case have already acquired professional experience and expertise, and with it the capability for initiative, which it would be impertinent to disregard. The central issue is that of the relationship between principle and technique, theory and practice (Widdowson, 1990), and more recent developments in language teacher education can be seen as different ways of resolving it.

MAJOR CONTRIBUTIONS

One way of resolving the issue is to dispense with theory altogether. There has been evidence of this tendency in recent years in pre-service teacher education of the kind provided (as in England and Wales, for example) by post-graduate courses, intended to be the pedagogic supplement to subject knowledge acquired in the main degree course. Thus the need for cheap teacher supply combined with a distrust of abstract thought can in some countries result in the policy makers adopting an apprenticeship concept of teacher preparation whereby prospective teachers pick up their expertise from practising teachers in schools, with minimal input from academic institutions. This constitutes a radical shift to a training orientation, and can lead to intellectual impoverishment and diminished prestige, with the teacher cast in the role of humble practitioner, trained to practise a trade rather than educated in a profession. Elsewhere, the theoretical side of pedagogy is maintained by having it incorporated into the language courses themselves at university level. Here the danger is that abstract ideas become detached from the practicalities of the classroom. In both cases there is a need to sustain teacher development by in-service provision, whereby the actual experience of teaching can be exploited to further the teacher's abstract understanding of the factors involved, and abstract understanding, conversely, made relevant to the contexts of actual classroom activity.

With regard to the question of theoretical validity mentioned above, the main contribution to in-service language teacher education has over the recent past come from applied linguistics, an area of enquiry which seeks to make explicit the abstract principles underlying the actual practice of language teaching and learning. As such, it has been the business of applied linguistics to point out to teachers the theoretical implications of what they do, and so to encourage this development of informed language pedagogy. Early examples of such work are Halliday, McIntosh & Strevens (1964), which emphasised the relevance of linguistics to language pedagogy and so focussed on what was to be taught, and Rivers (1964), whose emphasis was on pyschology and the learning process. Some years later, Allen & Corder (1973–75) provided wide ranging coverage of various aspects of language teaching set in theoretical perspective. Stern (1983) is a major attempt to draw up an integrated conceptual framework within which the different aspects of language teaching can be coherently related. This book might be compared with a similarly comprehensive work, Mackey (1965), and the comparison illustrates quite clearly the nature of the applied linguistic enterprise. For Mackey's work is essentially taxonomic, a descriptive compendium of factors, whereas Stern represents these factors as features of an integrated model. The difference is between descriptive and theoretical language teaching analysis.

The problem with this work in applied linguistics, however, is that those for whom it is, in principle, most relevant, often do not read it (see the review by Brumfit in Volume 6). Applied linguists have themselves debated at length the question of their own relevance (see Alatis, Stern & Strevens, 1983) but, generally speaking teachers themselves have not been consulted. That being so, practising teachers have generally seen the efforts in applied linguistics to establish the validity of pedagogic principle as remote from their immediate concerns. In these circumstances, theoretical validity has not been carried over into practical validation, and teachers have tended to look to other sources for assistance. They find it in collections of techniques and resource books which have proliferated over the past twenty years. These are attractive because they are essentially compendia of ad hoc solutions for immediate application. They are, in other words, basic training manuals with little or no explicit reference to principle. But other developments *have* been concerned with practical validation, and have tried to maintain a problem orientation to teaching, but in more immediate ways. These seek to involve practising teachers more directly, and to get them to participate in the exploration of ideas in relation to their practical concerns. This, for example, is the rationale behind the design of a scheme for language teacher education devised by Candlin & Widdowson (12 titles 1987–96) . Each title in this scheme first provides an explanation of the theoretical dimensions of a particular topic (grammar, pronunciation, reading, writing, classroom interaction, syllabus design etc.) and subsequently demonstrates the relevance of this theoretical perspective to the evaluation of actual teaching materials, and then provides activities based on this demonstration which teachers can undertake in their own classrooms. Throughout each book, tasks of various kinds are incorporated into the text to induce readers to participate in the exploration and application of ideas.

This scheme can be seen as an attempt to reproduce in print a less transmissive and more collaborative approach to language teacher education. Such an approach was particularly evident in the extensive programme of workshops organised by the Council of Europe between 1984–87, which were complementary to the design of the Theshold Level syllabuses for a range of different languages (van Ek & Trim, 1993). These did not specify any particular methodological approach to teaching, but with their emphasis on communication, carried implications for different kinds of activity in class from those associated with a structurally oriented approach. The workshops were exploratory and collaborative in spirit, and any suggestion that teachers were being directed was strenuously avoided: the people running the workshops were 'animators' not instructors. These workshops marked a change in orientation in teacher education, one which gave primacy to the role of teachers, denied the authority of theory imposed from outside, and recognised the validity of ideas generated from practical experience. This change has gathered momentum ever since.

WORK IN PROGRESS

The central issue in the formation of teachers (whether of language or any other subject) is the problem of the relationship between abstract principle and actual technique. You can educate people in an awareness of theoretical ideas in linguistics, pyschology, education itself, but there is no guarantee that they will act upon this awareness and transfer their knowledge into appropriate and effective behaviour. Conversely, you can train people in specific patterns of behaviour and so long as the situations they encounter more or less match (or can be *made* to match) those predicted they will be able to cope. But this training is necessarily based on past practice and allows for only a limited degree of change: old solutions do not fit new problems.

The assumption in the past has been that the relationship between theory and practice is essentially the same as the relationship between theorists and practitioners. Theorists have ideas, do research, produce findings, devise models, and pass them on to the practitioners who are meant to take note of them and apply as appropriate. Teachers are thus seen as the mediators not the initiators of ideas.

Proposals have been made over recent years for a redefinition of the teacher role and new ways of thinking of teacher education (Freeman & Cornwell, 1993). What is needed, it has been argued, is a recognition that pedagogy is not just a matter of deferential conformity to authority, no matter how prestigious this might seem. It is not an application of ideas from outside, not a patchwork of notions culled from disciplines like psychology, linguistics and the like, for it cannot be taken as self-evident that such notions have any necessary relevance to language teaching at all (Freeman, 1991). Instead, pedagogy should be seen as an area of enquiry in its own right which sets its own agenda, and has its own distinctive discourse. This is no doubt compounded of other influences and values (as all discourse are), but it has its own independent legitimacy. So instead of thinking of practice as as a derivation from theory, it would be more profitable to think of practice generating its own theory, and one which, by the very nature of its provenance, would necessarily be relevant to pedagogy. It is not a matter of making the classroom conform to some pattern established as effective by research from outside, but of making the classroom itself the locus of research (Allwright & Bailey, 1991). As such, it both provides the context of enquiry and sets the conditions of its own validity.

Such a view of research gives primacy to the beliefs, cognitions, attitudes and decision making processes of teachers themselves (Richards & Nunan, 1987; Woods 1996). The teacher assumes the role of 'reflective practitioner' and the activities which induce this reflection constitute research. These might take the form of informal observation or introspection, narrated as anecdote or recorded in a diary, with the emphasis on personal experience. It is commonly represented as teachers telling their stories. So teachers develop as they research (Edge & Richards 1995). As research it may not conform to standards conventionally adhered to in other lines of enquiry, but then why should it? It has its own standards of adequacy relevant to its own discourse. Typically it is qualitative rather than quantitative, giving weight to the affective rather more than the cognitive, and directed at subjective understanding rather than objective explanation. Nunan, 1991 gives guidance on how to do this kind of onsite reflective research, and Bailey & Nunan, 1996 and Freeman & Richards, 1996 are collections of examples of teachers learning through doing it.

Much of the stimulus for this move to teacher self-assertion and self-generated development comes from the literature of teacher education in general (eg Houston, 1990; Schoen, 1983), itself influenced by an ethos of distrust in the authority of established knowledge. Ideas about the reflective practitioner, self-generated awareness, and the legitimacy of local ethnographic research into the perceived realities of particular classrooms apply to the teaching of anything. These ideas can be, and have been, applied to second language classrooms, but there still remains the question as to whether there is anything distinctive about second language teaching which has implications for teacher preparation and development. In an earlier era the assumption was that all the teacher needed was a knowledge of the relevant subject matter. In recent work in language teacher education, the subject matter seems to be taken for granted, and the emphasis is on the ability of the teacher to explore the process of teaching. But these developments in language teacher education have coincided with developments in linguistic description, especially associated with the computer analysis of large corpora of actually occurring language (see Sinclair, 1991; Stubbs, 1996) which reveals patterns of usage generally inaccessible to intuition. Such analysis, it has been suggested, indicates radically different ways of defining the language subject, and, by implication, how it might be taught, and what expertise is required to teach it. At the same time, actual language data are now more readily available for reference in print, on disc, and on screen, and this inevitably reduces the teacher's traditional informant role. So developments in language description would seem to have a very obvious bearing on language teacher education, and it is relevant to ask how far they can be accommodated within the model of self generated teacher education currently in vogue.

Another issue that arises from all this which is uniquely specific to the second language classroom is the relative competence and status of native and non-native speaker teachers (see Medgyes, 1994). The common, and still prevailing, assumption is that since native-speaker teachers are to the language born, they have a special authority to teach it. But the logic of the current view of teacher education runs counter to this assumption. For if this is to be an ongoing process of self development, involving a critical appraisal of local pedagogic conditions, then it is obvious that the local non-native speaking teacher, as insider, who is in the privileged position. To the extent that these teachers share the cultural and linguistic background of their pupils, they have insights into what is likely to be pedagogically effective in class. But this also has a bearing on how the subject itself is to be defined, for these teachers know the language as a second language and have themselves been through the process of acquiring it. If one is to think of teacher education as a matter of local self development centred in actual classrooms, then one needs to consider how the language to be taught is locally conceived as a *second* language subject, and to accept that it might well be very different from how it is conceived as a first language. It needs to be noted that, as far as English is concerned at any rate, those who have been most prominent in proposing how it should be taught have had no experience of it whatever as a second language, and in that respect might be said to be ignorant of the subject (see the review by Christ in Volume 1). Similarly it is perhaps also worth noting that those who promote the notion of local teacher self-development are predominantly native speaker outsiders, and so, by the logic of their own argument, in no position to promote it. The voices we hear from the second language classroom (see Bailey & Nunan, 1996) seem often to be those of the ventriloquist.

PROBLEMS AND DIFFICULTIES

The major difficulties of current work in second language teacher education have already been touched upon. The recognition that teacher education, at least with reference to the in-service situation, should be a function of the teachers' critical reflection on their own pedagogic experience is a valuable corrective to a view of teacher education as the transmission of authoritative knowledge which teachers had simply to access and act upon. But the implications of this approach in respect to second language teaching remain relatively unexplored. There must also be the suspicion that this approach, while embracing the principle of local initiative, actually derives from values and beliefs which are themselves culturally specific, and expressive of a particular ideology which may be neither appropriate nor feasible elsewhere. The issues about the transmission of privileged knowledge and how it can be acted on remain unresolved. It is also worth making the related point that this account of developments in second language teacher education (or second language teaching generally) is restricted mainly to the activities of a small and prestigious group of people, for the most part concerned with the teaching of *English* as a second language, whose ideas appear in print. The stories we hear are their stories. It is salutory to think of all the developments in second language teacher education in different parts of the world which are taken by local initiative and which, by the very fact that they are local, often remain unrecognised.

University of London / University of Essex, England

REFERENCES

Alatis, J.E., Stern, H.H. & Strevens, P. (eds.): 1983, *Applied Linguistics and the Preparation of Second Language Teachers: Towards a Rationale*, Georgetown University Press, Washington DC.

Allen, J.P.B. & Corder, S.P. (eds.): 1973–75, *The Edinburgh Course in Applied Linguistics*, Oxford University Press, Oxford.

Allwright, D. &. Bailey, K.: 1991, *Focus on the Language Classroom*, Cambridge University Press, Cambridge.

Bailey, K. & Nunan, D. (eds.): 1996, *Voices from the Language Classroom*, Cambridge University Press, Cambridge.

Candlin, C.N. & Widdowson, H.G. (eds.): 1987–96, *Language Teaching: a Scheme for Teacher Education* (12 volumes), Oxford University Press, Oxford.

Edge, J. & Richards, K.: 1995, *Teachers Develop Teachers Research. Papers on Classroom Research and Teacher Development*, Heinemann, Oxford.

van Ek, J.A. & Trim, J.L.M.: 1993, *The Theshold Level 1990*, Council of Europe Press, Strasbourg.

Finocchiaro, M.: 1964, *Teaching Children Foreign Languages*, McGraw Hill, New York.

Freeman, D.: 1991, 'Mistaken constructs: Re-examining the nature and assumptions of language teacher education', in J.E. Alatis (ed.), *Linguistics and Language Pedagogy: the State of the Art*, Georgetown University Press, Washington DC.

Freeman, D. & Cornwell, S. (eds.): 1993, *New Ways in Teacher Education*, Teachers of English to Speakers of Other Languages, Alexandria, VA.

Freeman, D. & Richards, J.C.: 1996, *Teaching Learning in Language Teaching*, Cambridge University Press, Cambridge.

French, F.G: 1948, *The Teaching of English Abroad* (3 volumes), Oxford University Press, Oxford.

Halliday, M.A.K., McIntosh, A. & Strevens, P.: 1964, *The Linguistic Sciences and Language Teaching*, Longman, London.

Houston, W.R. (ed.): 1990, *Handbook of Research on Teacher Education*, McMillan, New York.

Mackey, W.F.: 1965, *Language Teaching Analysis*, Longman, London.

Medgyes, P.: 1994, *The Non-native Teacher*, Macmillan, London.

Nunan, D.: 1991, *Understanding Second Language Classrooms: A Guide for Teacher-Initiated Action*, Prentice Hall, Englewood Cliffs, NJ.

Palmer, H.E.: 1921/64, *The Principles of Language-Study*, Harrap, London. Republished 1964 edited by R. Mackin, Oxford University Press, Oxford.

Peters, R.S.: 1977, *Education and the Education of Teachers*, Routledge, London.

Richards, J.C. & Nunan, D. (eds.): 1987, *Second Language Teacher Education*, Cambridge University Press, Cambridge.

Rivers, W.: 1964, *The Psychologist and the Foreign Language Teacher*, University of Chicago Press, Chicago.

Schoen, D.: 1983, *The Reflective Practitioner*, Basic Books, New York.

Sinclair, J.McH.: 1991, *Corpus, Concordance, Collocation*, Oxford University Press. Oxford.

Stern, H.H.: 1983, *Fundamental Concepts of Language Teaching*, Oxford University Press, Oxford.

Stubbs, M.: 1996, *Text and Corpus Analysis*, Blackwell, Oxford.
Widdowson, H.G.: 1990, *Aspects of Language Teaching*, Oxford University Press, Oxford.
Widdowson, H.G.: 1993, 'Innovation in teacher development', *Annual Review of Applied Linguistics* 13, 260–275.
Woods, D.: 1996, *Teacher Cognition in Language Teaching*, Cambridge University Press, Cambridge.

UDO O.H. JUNG

THE USE OF MULTIMEDIA IN TEACHING

Educational technology has come a long way – from the language lab of
the 1950s and 1960s, which served, and still serves, as a 'convenient scapegoat in explaining why, even with a large infusion of money for equipment,
desired results were not achieved' (Otto, 1989: p. 14) to the 'multi-media
learning centers that deliver computer and video services to faculty and
students in addition to familiar audio resources' (Otto, 1989: p. 38; see
also Richardson & Scinicariello, 1989). In the 1990s, digital technology
helps to integrate the available resources into a convenient and manage-
able bundle (Hagen, 1993). Computers can nowadays deliver video and
sound in addition to text and graphics. The combination of these four
elements is usually called multimedia. To the minds of several the term is
unsatisfactory. This has something to do with its history. The picture is
further complicated, because multimedia has a rival term in hypermedia.
Hypermedia, in turn, is an extension of hypertext. Hypertext denotes an
associative mode of access to information. Whereas normal text is read
from beginning to end, in a piece of hypertext the reader clicks on an
unknown word or phrase, a so-called hot spot, and the software follows
the (previously established) route from this text element to its destination,
which may be a dictionary entry or a further piece of text detailing the linguistic, literary or cultural phenomenon in need of explanation. Hypertext
readers thus navigate through what is sometimes called hyperspace. If,
however, after clicking on one of the hot spots, the user is greeted with
an audio or video message instead of just another block of text, he or she
is in the presence of hypermedia. To all intents and purposes, multimedia
and hypermedia are identical twins, although useful distinctions between
them are occasionally made (Hill, 1994). A single computer platform is
nowadays capable of bringing about the 'seamless integration ... of any
of [sic] text, sound, still and animated images, and motion video' (Jacobs,
1992: p. 3).

ORIGINS AND EARLY HISTORY OF MULTIMEDIA SYSTEMS

Multimedia has a hyphenated predecessor, multi-media. PLATO (Pro-
grammed Logic for Automated Teaching Operation), the historians tell us,
'foreshadowed much of the newer multimedia technology' (Hart, 1995: p.

G.R. Tucker and D. Corson (eds), Encyclopedia of Language and Education,
Volume 4: Second Language Education, 131–139.
© *1997 Kluwer Academic Publishers. Printed in the Netherlands.*

35). When PLATO IV came into being, it boasted 'a graphic display device, a keyboard input, a random-access image selector, a random-access audio message selector as well as a device that allows touch input' (Ariew, 1974: p. 1). But PLATO sank into oblivion partly because a 'full system could run into the millions' (Hart, 1995: p. 31) and partly because it 'was an ideal vehicle for delivering the drill and practice emphasized in the audiolingual approach' (Hart, 1995, p: 32).

Multimedia also has a 'progenitor' (Jacobs, 1992: p. 2) in interactive video. Strictly speaking, there are two different formats of interactive video: tape-based and disc-based. In David Little's AUTOTUTOR system (Little 1988/1991) the computer drives a VHS-videorecorder and selects appropriate stretches of film to go with certain learning tasks. Locating information on a videotape can be a time-consuming ordeal. Programme authors must therefore have exercises at the ready on the computer screen, before the videorecorder can be started again. But the system is extremely cheap in comparison with its disc-based competitor.

The potential of the latter was first explored by American researchers. Their most famous example is MONTEVIDISCO, which simulates the visit by an intermediate learner of Spanish to a small Mexican village (Schneider & Bennion, 1983). At strategic points in the programme, the movie pictures freezeframe and the learner must make a forced choice. Depending on the answer the programme moves forward in a split-second to another branch. The learner can be treated to a tour of the village, but might equally well be 'dragged' to the police station after selecting a rude answer. Technically, the early programmes were extremely complex: There had to be two gender-specific discs. They had to be interfaced with the computer which displayed the multiple choice questions, whereas a separate color monitor was needed to show the scenes shot on location in Mexico. Attached to this configuration was also an audio cassette recorder to store student responses for later inspection by instructors.

In principle, then, programmes like MONTEVIDISCO can cater for all of the four skills. They are especially useful with respect to cultural aspects of language teaching. It is listening comprehension, however, that profits most from one or more run-throughs, because interactive video possesses two features which are very beneficial: a second audio track and intralingual subtitles. Students who for whatever reasons experience problems with the original sound track can choose to bring on a 'bowdlerized' studio version of the film script if earlier attempts to decode the spoken message with the help of subtitles have failed.

Useful as they may be, unilingual subtitles – either fully reproducing the spoken word or flashing a condensed version on the screen – are a deplorably underresearched aspect of educational technology. Foreign-language learners can avail themselves of the printed messages at the bottom of the screen, dump the decoded message in short-term memory and then return to the spoken signal with hindsight, as it were (Borrás & Lafayette, 1994). Meskill (in print) represents an inspiring scenario of how multimedia could support listening comprehension.

A count, in the early nineties, revealed that there were 72 interactive language discs (Rubin et al., 1990) on the market, with some of them as (technically) sophisticated as they were (methodologically) 'mouth-watering' and so expensive that the following verdict does not come as a complete surprise. 'Today,' Brian Hill says, 'it is clear that interactive video is unlikely to make any significant impact . . . ' (Hill, 1994: p. 221). This has something to do with the fact that video discs store signals in ana-logue fashion as opposed to the digital mode of storage on CD-ROMs. The same fact may also explain why early experiments to repurpose existing video discs (Davies, 1989) have not been followed up.

WORK IN PROGRESS

CD-ROMs, which can accommodate as much as 650 MB of digitized information, are about to replace analogue video discs. And even more capacious storage facilities are on the horizon. The new industry standard multimedia CD (MMCD) has a storage capacity of 7,4 gigabytes. MPEG (Motion Picture Expert Group) is a compression technique which expands the amount of video a standard CD-ROM can hold (not to mention the new MMCD) to such a degree that virtually unrestricted video storage room is now at the disposal of software developers.

Irrespective of technical solutions, however, a terminology is needed to describe the contributions such systems can make to language learning and teaching. Wolff (in press) introduces a distinction between closed and open multimedia systems. A characteristic feature of closed systems is their instructionist approach. Their authors take the learner by the hand, as it were, and guide him step by step to a predetermined goal. Whereas with closed systems the computer is reduced to an albeit highly sophisticated page-turning machine, in open multimedia systems students are given useful tools with which they can explore the world of languages. Wolff adduces as examples the *Oxford English Dictionary* on CD-ROM or the *Collins COBUILD Dictionary* and points to the possibilities inherent in encyclopedias. What the latter have to offer the learner, has been described by Peters (1993). The former allow the student to sort the dictionary entries according to semantic, formal or functional principles. Synonyms and antonyms can be brought up-screen and the path through the dictionary is sometimes recorded so that students can consciously attend to the learning process (see also Nesi, 1996).

Behind the distinction between closed and open multimedia systems, there lurks a philosophy of language learning and teaching. The proponents of open learnware believe that students must relate newly acquired items to their already existing knowledge store. This they can only do through creative interaction with elements in the learning environment. As a last resort, the cognitive psychologist says, learners must construct new knowledge themselves, and they must be given the freedom to do so.

Not all scholars subscribe wholeheartedly to the constructionist view of language learning. Some of them complain that the constructionists speak of the learner 'without identifying properly whom they have in mind. Or rather, they imply that "the learner" is by definition a creative adult, eager to enter an exploratory process on authentic texts and playing successfully with various integrated tools such as built-in dictionaries, thesauri or concordance-generators' (Decoo et al., 1996: p. 321). The critics are right in pointing out that characteristics of the target groups must not be lost sight of and should be taken into consideration when a decision is made as to whether a piece of software fits in with their previous path, present status, and targeted competence. A closer look at a few examplary programmes taking the learners' level of proficiency as our cue might therefore be a salutary experience.

Peters (1995a) has provided us with a compilation of available multimedia software on CD-ROM, giving shorthand information on 144 such pieces. Another useful source of information is the 1995 *CALICO Resource Guide for Computing and Language Learning* (Borchardt & Johnson, 1995). A quick survey of the subject areas covered by the Peters collection reveals that a large proportion of the available CDs was not originally made for use in the second language classroom. Foreign language teachers and their students are therefore best described as secondary users of the software.

It was Peters, too, who, pointed out and described a number of 'edutainment' books on CD-ROM for English-speaking children. His colleague Marianne Pemberger (1995) tried out a few of them on a class of second-year English students and reported that apart from noticeable accretions to their vocabulary, the interactive discovery procedures employed had led to improvements of the students' listening and speaking abilities. Motivation was high from the very beginning, because the pupils were confronted with and eventually mastered an extended piece of authentic language.

NICOLAS is an early example for intermediate learners of French based on *HyperCard* (Evans, 1993). Nicolas is the juvenile hero of a short story from the pen/paintbrush of French cartoonist Sempé. Together with a friend he plays truant one day. To reconstruct the incidents of this eventful day learners must perform a variety of tasks: clicking on the correct answer in a number of multiple choice questions to show that written and/or spoken questions have been correctly processed, selecting from among an assortment of objects the ones that were mentioned in the text or not mentioned at all, writing a postcard, solving a riddle, completing a cloze test, compiling a list of key words etc. Feedback of various forms is always provided, and students are given the option of looking up difficult words and phrases in an integrated dictionary. A certain amount of navigational control is granted to and exercised by the students. In the end, the book-keeping facility of the programme revealed that NICOLAS had probably stimulated a reading process which largely conformed to a model of reading that the author describes as involving 'pauses, reflection, reviewing earlier pages, absorption in the content, lapses of attention, skipping segments, making associations, formulating opinions, making predictions, learning new vocabulary, internalising dialogue, visualing [sic] descriptions' (Evans, 1993: p. 216). Thus, despite the fact that the computer has been reduced to a page-turning machine with only a limited degree of flexibility and intelligent interactivity, this HyperCard programme is almost half-way between closed and open systems.

Packed to the brim with data is a CD-ROM under the title of 'Romeo & Juliet', which houses not only the text and (synchronous) sound of William Shakespeare's play, but also a number of scenes from the 1978 BBC production of the Bard's best-loved creation. In addition, there are excerpts from TV documentaries and the BBC sound archives, which together with relevant information on the plot, the actors and acting, sets and scenery, costumes, music and musical adaptation as well as characters, language, themes and background (sources of the play, critical opinions, the life of Shakespeare) enable users to freely browse through a host of information, to research, save and print individual aspects of this master-piece of Elizabethan English play writing (Peters 1995b). At long last, learners can approach a piece of literature from a variety of angles. We are in the presence of an *open* multimedia system. The software no longer prescribes a way through the sequence of frames, but offers the student different routes of access to the data base to suit individual personality and learning styles. The influence of student personality on learning outcomes, it should be noted, has been researched in connection with CALL programmes (Jamieson & Chapelle, 1988), but not with multimedia so far.

A total of 49 such or similar multimedia applications for literature were reviewed by teams of teacher/reviewers under the leadership of Carla Meskill and Karen Swan in 1995. The research team set out to explore the contribution multimedia CD-ROMs can make to response-based literature teaching. Not surprisingly, the *Desiderata* chapter is the most voluminous. A clash between what a CD-ROM could do and what the teacher/reviewers actually found became noticeable: navigation through the software was not as transparent as one would wish; juxtaposition of text and images was not always available; notepad facilities may have been at the students' disposal, but the information created by them could not always be shared with other members of the group; accessing visual and/or auditory elements in the database in order to cut and paste material in support of one's understanding of a piece of literature was difficult, if not impossible; the programmes did not stimulate group discussion, because they were built with a single user in mind; the capability of CD-ROMs to induce student envisionment ('What does a Deep South cabin (that *leans* against a chimney) look like?') was not fully exploited.

The final verdict, therefore, on the majority of products is that 'most current applications treat the text as information, an object to be learned, parsed, and recalled' (Meskill & Swan, 1995: p. 19). Exceptions like *Romeo & Juliet or Mathilde Möhring* (Wittig Davis, 1995) only prove the rule.

Stand-alone computers with multimedia CD-ROM drives represent the classic case of an *off-line* system. Unfortunately, the information foreign-language learners can thrive on, is sometimes distributed across the world. To exploit the multimedia mines of the modern world, access to the information super highway is necessary. The information seeker can then surf through the INTERNET (Warschauer 1995) stopping here and there to search for and collect data, to discuss matters of importance with like-minded people, to collaborate with others on a project or simulation. This mode of use is called *on-line*.

Despite the warning issued by David Eastment (1996, p. 20) that 'for the average user, the Internet is still more of a dirt-track', the WORLD WIDE WEB (www) and its hypermedia-based information exchange system offers exciting possibilities. When clicked on, the hot spot of a www home page in Europe automatically reroutes the information seeker to another location whose URL (Uniform Resource Locator) may belong to an information provider as far away as Australia or the USA. An example is the 'European Virtual University' which, despite its name, is a relatively simple application, in which 9 European universities have banded together to benefit the hundreds of students who do *not* participate in EU exchange programmes. The 'European Virtual University' offers them a vicarious electronic experience, which includes 'profiles of the participating universities and the cities in which they are located, links to syllabi, courseware, bibliographies, research reports, project guidelines, CVs of staff, cultural resources and relevant "social" *Usenet* newsgroups, and pointers to European language resources, including electronic newspapers, journals, books, and dictionaries' (Hutchison, 1995: p. 68f.). Given the necessary technical infrastructure at all participating sites, the system could also deliver audio and video messages to provide the students with full multimedia instruction, but it depends in its present state for complete success on the students 'exchanging not only e-mail descriptions of themselves and their lives, but also, by postal mail, photographs, maps, sample course handouts (for non-core courses), for example, and specimen cultural artefacts such as bus tickets, theatre brochures, photocopies of student cards, and so forth' (Hutchison, 1995: p. 70). A video conference scheme to complement the largely text and/or graphics-based exchange system was foreseen

for 1995. Elsewhere video conferencing systems have already been successfully implemented in university language teaching experiments. The
most advanced system to date is probably the 'Multimedia Teleschool'
which relies on satellite broadcasts to the participating institutions and a
computer network to enable students to communicate with fellow students
and tutors. Live telephone and videophone messages complement this virtual classroom scenario (Fesl, 1994), which is so complex and expensive
that only large corporations can afford to participate. Schools and colleges
have only occasionally and at a less advanced level been able to exploit
the benefits of telecommunications. What is more, the warning, issued by
F. Marchessou (1993) that there is a 'nécessité d'un soutien continu aux
enseignements de langues reposant sur les multimedia', should be heeded
by the authorities.

FUTURE DIRECTIONS

The bottleneck in multimedia programmes is the same as in CALL software: unintelligent responses to student input. In the words of Melissa
Holland (1994: p. 95): 'Conventional CALL technology, such as interactive video and hypertext, often support beautiful designs and have
considerable popular appeal, but they accept only multiple choice, point-
and-click, and other nonlanguage responses'. However, the conclusion
she draws from this seems unwarranted: 'They are therefore limited to
exercising the receptive skills of listening and reading.' It has been observed time and again that in the process of exchanging e-mail messages a
hybrid form of communication develops: the distinction between spoken
and written language tends to disappear. One researcher observed that 'the
discourse flows like an oral conversation' (Kelm, 1992: p. 446) and another subtitled her paper 'conversation in slow motion' (Beauvois, 1992).
Written communication on a computer can thus make a contribution to the
development of the spoken language. We have reason to believe that this
observation is also valid if we move beyond e-mail and merely text-based
exchanges.

But multimedia programmes with fully functional artificial intelligence
components are certainly a long way in coming and the presently available software can be likened to so many islands dotting the CALLscape.
'Multimedia is . . . still very much in its infancy'(Briggs 1995, p. 30). The
integration of multimedia into a language teaching scenario based on sound
teaching principles and learning strategies is unquestionably a desidera-
tum. Until that moment in the future when blueprints become reality, the
practising teacher is well advised to try to make progress through retro-
gression. Jung (1994) has demonstrated how with the old-fashioned radio
at the centre and with a number of equally old-fashioned technical aids
(the language laboratory; the telephone) at the periphery, in conjunction

with computer technology and television, a virtual speech community, a community of discourse, can be created for native speakers and foreign-language learners alike. In his *omnimedia* approach to language learning intelligent multimedia products can replace outdated technologies as they become available in later years. But at the time of writing there are a number of technical aids of long standing which no multimedia invention can easily brush aside.

University of Bayreuth, Germany

REFERENCES

Ariew, R.: 1974, 'Teaching French on PLATO IV', *System* 2, 1–7.

Beauvois, M.H.: 1992, 'Computer-assisted classroom discussion in the foreign language classroom: Conversation in slow motion', *Foreign Language Annals* 25, 455–464.

Borchardt, F.L. & Johnson, E.M.T. (eds.): 1995, *CALICO Resource Guide for Computing and Language Learning*, Duke University, Durham NC.

Borrás, I. & Lafayette, R.C.: 1994, 'Effects of multimedia courseware subtitling on the speaking performance of college students of French', *The Modern Language Journal* 78, 61–75.

Briggs, J.: 1995, 'CD-I, CD-ROM and all that,' *TELL & CALL* 3, 28–30.

Davies, G.: 1989, ' "Repurposing" a videodisc for French language teaching', in I. Kecskés & L. Agócs (eds.), *New Tendencies in Computer Assisted Language Learning*, Kossuth University, Debrecen, 62–68.

Decoo, W. et al.: 1996, 'The standard vocabulary programms of DIDASCALIA: In search of external versatility and didactic optimization', *Computer Assisted Language Learning* 9(4), 375–384.

Eastment, D.: 1996, 'The internet for teachers and learners', *TELL & CALL* 2, 10–20.

Evans, M.: 1993, 'Nicolas: Using HyperCard with intermediate-level French learners', *System* 21, 213–229.

Fesl, G.: 1994, 'European foreign language learning in the multimedia teleschool', in H. Jung, & R. Vanderplank (eds.), *Barriers and Bridges: Media Technology in Language Learning*, Peter Lang Verlag, Frankfurt a.M., 25–29.

Hagen, S. (ed.): 1993, *Using Technology in Language Learning*, City Technology Colleges Trust in Association with CILT, London.

Hart, R.S.: 1995, 'The Illinois PLATO foreign language project', *CALICO Journal* 12, 15–37.

Hill, B.: 1994, 'Self-managed learning', *Language Teaching* 27, 213–223.

Holland, V.M.: 1994, 'Intelligent tutors for foreign languages: How parsers and lexical semantics can help learners and assess learning', in R.M. Kaplan & J.C. Burstein (eds.), *Educational Testing Service Conference on Natural Language Processing Techniques and Technology in Assessment and Education*, Educational Testing Service, Princeton NJ, 95–107.

Hutchison, C.: 1995, 'Online language support in the European virtual university or: "Europe on $10 a Day", in J. Colpaert et al. (eds.), *The Added Value of Technologies in Language Learning*, IBM International Education Centre, Brussels, 65–73.

Jacobs, G.: 1992, 'An interactive learning revolution?', *The CTISS File* 14, 3–5.

Jamieson, J. & Chapelle, C.: 1988, 'Using CALL effectively: What do we need to know about students?', *System* 16, 151–162.

Jung, U.O.H.: 1994, 'Experiential learning. What educational technology can contribute', in H. Jung & R. Vanderplank (eds.), *Barriers and Bridges: Media Technology in Language Learning*, Peter Lang Verlag, Frankfurt a.M., 1–14.

Kelm, O.R.: 1992, 'The use of synchronous computer networks in second language instruction: A preliminary report', *Foreign Language Annals* 25, 441–453.

Little, D. 1988/1991[2], 'The AUTOTUTOR. An interactive videocassette system for language learners', in U.O.H. Jung (ed.), *Computers in Applied Linguistics and Language Teaching*, Peter Lang Verlag, Frankfurt a.M., 71–77.

Marchessou, F.: 1993, 'De la Nécessité d'un Soutien Continu aux Enseignements de Langues Reposant sur les Multimédias', in J.P. Attal & M. Mémet (eds.), *Nouvelles Technologies et Enseignements des Langues*, TILV, Paris, 46–56.

Meskill, C.: 1996, 'Listening skills development through multimedia', *Journal of Educational Multimedia and Hypermedia* 5, 179–201.

Meskill, C. & Swan, K.: 1995, *Roles for Multimedia in the Response-based Literature Classroom*, University of Albany: National Research Center on Literature Teaching and Learning, Albany NY.

Nesi, H.: 1996, 'Review article: For future reference? Current English learners' dictionaries in electronic form', *System* 24.

Otto, S.E.K.: 1989, 'The language laboratory in the computer age', in W.F. Smith (ed.), *Modern Technology in Foreign Language Education: Applications and Projects*, National Textbook Company, Lincolnwood, IL, 13–41.

Pemberger, M.: 1995, 'Learning by playing: CD-ROMs im Englischunterricht einer zweiten Klasse', *TELL & CALL* 3, 14–22.

Peters, K.: 1993, 'Wissen auf Knopfdruck – elektronische Multimedia-Lexika im Vergleich', *TELL & CALL* 4, 28–35.

Peters, K.: 1995a, 'CD-ROM Update – eine Liste einsetzbarer Titel für verschiedene Fächer', *TELL & CALL* 1, 50–62.

Peters, K.: 1995b, 'To CD or not to CD, Is that the question? – Shakespeare auf CD-ROM', *TELL & CALL* 4, 36–45.

Richardson, C.P. & Scinicariello, S.G.: 1989, 'Television technology in the foreign language classroom', in W.F. Smith (ed.), *Modern Technology in Foreign Language Education: Applications and Projects*, National Textbook Company, Lincolnwood, IL, 43–74.

Rubin, J. et al.: 1990, 'Survey of interactive language discs', *CALICO Journal* 7, 31–47, 50–56.

Schneider, E.W. & Bennion, J.L.: 1983, 'Veni, vidi, vici, via videodisc: A simulator for instructional conversations', *System* 11, 41–46.

Warschauer, M.: 1995, *E-Mail for English Teaching. Bringing the Internet and Computer Learning Networks into the Language Classroom*, TESOL, Alexandria VA.

Wittig Davis, G.A.: 1995, 'The metamorphosed text: A multimedia approach to Theodor Fontane's Mathilde Möhring in text and film', *Die Unterrichtspraxis / Teaching German* 28, 132–145.

Wolff, D.: in press, 'Instruktivismus vs. Konstruktivismus oder können Multimedia die Schule verändern?'.

ELANA SHOHAMY

SECOND LANGUAGE ASSESSMENT

Second language assessment is concerned with procedures and techniques for measuring second language knowledge. Thus, the main focus of the field has been the definition of second language knowledge and the design of assessment procedures that match such definitions. While the field is generally known as 'language testing' it is also referred to as language assessment due to the recent trend to use multiple assessment procedures, and not just tests. Language testing/assessment is a dynamic field that holds annual conferences, including the Language Testing Research Colloquium (LTRC), publishes a journal, Language Testing, and many of whose practitioners belong to an international organization, the International Language Testing Association (ILTA).

Language testing addresses three inter-connected domains: theory, development and research. The theoretical domain attempts to define language competence so representative samples of language behaviors can be drawn based on these definitions; the developmental domain focuses on the construction of tests and scoring criteria for measuring language competence and the research domain examines the quality and use of language tests.

EARLY DEVELOPMENTS

Three periods, the discrete point, the integrative and the communicative, can be identified in the history of language testing. Each period reflects different definitions of second language competence and procedures for measuring those competencies; yet, features of earlier periods have been adapted in later ones.

In the discrete point period (beginning in the 1950s) attempts were made to view language testing as a scientific field. The tenets of structural linguistics were combined with psychometrically based testing in an attempt to find an objective method of measuring language (Lado, 1964). Thus, the test items focused on isolated and discrete elements, decontextualized phonemes, grammar and lexicon and used multiple choice, true-false, and other types of objective items.

In the integrative era that followed in the 1970s language was viewed in a holistic and contextualized manner so the tests sampled global language such as complete paragraphs and full texts. Much attention was given to a specific type of test, the cloze, in which words were deleted from longer

G.R. Tucker and D. Corson (eds), Encyclopedia of Language and Education,
Volume 4: Second Language Education, 141–149.
© 1997 Kluwer Academic Publishers. Printed in the Netherlands.

texts and test takers were expected to fill in those missing slots and thus mobilize their linguistic and extra-linguistic knowledge to reconstruct the meaning of the text. It was claimed that the cloze and dictation tapped such integrative language and that they represented a unitary notion of language that underlies the learner's pragmatic grammar of expectancy which was believed to be the chief mechanism underlying the skills of understanding, speaking, reading and writing (Oller, 1979).

The communicative era that followed, began in the 1980, mostly in Britain and later in the US and other parts of the world. It was based on the notion that language is interactive, direct and authentic. Thus, the type of tests developed required test takers to produce and comprehend language that replicated real interaction utilizing authentic oral and written texts and tasks and duplicating the setting and operation of real life situations in which proficiency is normally demonstrated. The Oral Proficiency Interview (OPI) developed by US government agencies for selecting candidates for various official tasks represented an example of a communicative oral test where test taker and tester interact in a spontaneous and direct manner (Clark, 1975). Other communicative tests included role plays, group discussions, reports, simulations (Shohamy, Reves, & Bejerano, 1986) and various types of situational tests. The emphasis on communicative language introduced a distinction between proficiency-type tests assessing language knowledge needed in future situations and achievement tests referring to language acquired in a specific course of study, usually in the past. The quality of the language samples obtained from communicative tests was assessed through rating scales which define hierarchical levels of proficiency. These scales range from beginning to advanced focusing on holistic and/or analytic criteria (e.g., grammar, lexicon, fluency). The American Council of the Teaching of Foreign Languages (ACTFL) adapted a number of existing scales and created rating scales which were accepted as the ACTFL Proficiency Guidelines used widely by US high schools and universities, creating a common yardstick of foreign language proficiency (ACTFL, 1986). Similar rating scales were developed in other contexts such as the Australian Second Language Proficiency Rating Scale (ASLPR) (Ingram & Wylie, 1984) for assessing language proficiency of adult immigrants.

In the theoretical domain, a framework for communicative competence consisting of grammatical, sociolinguistic, discourse and strategic competencies was proposed by Canale and Swain (1980) so that a valid assessment of communication would include these components. The framework led to a model of communicative competence introduced by Bachman (1990) (revised by Bachman & Palmer, 1996) which divides communicative language ability into language knowledge and strategic knowledge. The former consists of organizational knowledge referring to how utterances or sentences and texts are organized and the latter to how utterances or sentences and texts are related to the communicative goals of the language user and to the features of the language use situation. Organizational knowledge was further subdivided into grammatical knowledge (i.e., syntax and morphology, lexis, phonology and graphology) and textual knowledge (i.e., cohesion, coherence and rhetorical or conversational organization), while pragmatic competence consisted of illocutionary and sociolinguistic competencies.

MAJOR CONTRIBUTIONS

Communicative language testing dominates the field. However, performance assessment and alternative assessment are becoming more common. Performance assessment is based on the interaction between language knowledge and specific content, usually of the workplace or of professional preparation. Test takers perform realistic tasks which call for the application of skills to actual or simulated settings in an attempt to replicate the language needed in these contexts. Thus, performance tests are task-based, direct, functional, and authentic. Such tests were developed for a number of occupational areas such as health professionals (McNamara, 1990), university teaching (Wesche, 1992), business (Sajavaara, 1992) and court interpreters (Stansfield, 1996) (see also the review by McNamara in Volume 7). Alternative assessment is based on the notion that language knowledge consists of a variety of competencies and that tests alone cannot assess them all. Thus, multiple assessment procedures such as portfolios, self assessment, simulations, observations, peer assessment, and various types of performance tasks are needed so that a broader and more valid language perspective can be sampled (for more about self assessment see the review by Oscarson in Volume 7).

WORK IN PROGRESS

Current work in language testing continues to emphasize theory, development and research. On the theoretical level the language competence model of Bachman (1990) and Bachman and Palmer (1996) has been accepted as the definition of language competence used by testers that is often used as a basis for test construction (see the reviews by Bachman and Eignor and by Pollitt in Volume 7). Yet, there are those who claim that the model needs to be expanded to include variables that relate language with cognitive and affective areas, subject matter knowledge, communicative skills, personality and gender of the interactors, their attitudes and beliefs as well as variables which are part of the communicative process. There are also debates as to the appropriate statistical methods to use with language testing data. If communicative language ability is multidimensional, i.e., consisting of multiple elements, then most statistical methods of test analysis currently used are inappropriate as they assume that language is unidimensional, i.e., composed of one element (Henning, 1992). There is a need therefore for statistical procedures that are more appropriate for multidimensional constructs or for research to find out the degree to which these statistical methods violate statistical assumptions of unidimensionality (Buck, 1994).

In the development domain a large number of tests for multiple purposes have been developed by testing agencies, universities, and private companies. Examples include a revised computerized version of the TOEFL (Test of English as a Foreign Language) developed by Educational Testing Service (ETS) for measuring English language proficiency of incoming university students to the US, a test battery for assessing the English of incoming immigrants (the ACCESS test) developed in Australia, a number of semi-direct tests consisting of various tasks (e.g., giving directions, descriptions, role plays and simulations) where test-takers respond orally (on a tape) to an audio-recorded stimuli (Stansfield and Kenyon, 1988). A number of performance tests are being developed for various professions such as tour-guides, teachers, pilots and nurses.

Alternative types of assessment procedures are being designed for different contexts, Scharer (1996) reports on a life long portfolio used as part of a European certificate where learners collect and document their language experiences over a life time. Hamp-Lyons (1996) reports on different types of portfolios for assessing writing and Shohamy (1995) introduced an alternative assessment battery for immigrant children consisting of portfolios, self assessment, teachers' observations and tests, followed by an assessment conference where the test takers and assessors meet to discuss their language proficiency. A number of diagnostic tests are being developed for identifying specific language problems such as the one developed by Baker (1996) for diagnosing the linguistic problems of Alzheimer immigrant patients. New types of rating scales are being constructed and old ones are being revised. North (1994) reports on a rating scale for creating a common yardstick for evaluating language proficiency of foreign languages in Europe (See the review by Fulcher in Volume 7). A version of the ACTFL guidelines for school age children is being developed in the US and McKay (1995) reports on ESL proficiency descriptions for school contexts in Australia (see the review by McKay in Volume 7). A different way of describing language knowledge which is commonly used by national agencies for accountability, accreditation, certification and curriculum design is through 'language outcomes'. These refer to descriptions of proficiency levels as a result of a course of study and define explicit specifications of learning in the form of profiles.

Technology is getting special attention in test development (Burstein et al., 1996). Input devices for voice recognition, handwriting, gestures and eye movements are currently employed in restricted contexts. Output devices such as video, still and moving graphics, voice and other sounds are available for use in language assessment. Currently it is computerized tests which are mostly used for language assessment but this is likely to change in the near future.

The domain of research continues to be dynamic addressing diverse topics and issues. Current approaches employ quantitative and a variety of qualitative methods such as ethnography, discourse analysis and verbal reporting. Qualitative procedures are used mostly to analyze the discourse and interactions taking place on tests and to investigate cognitive processes involved in the test taking process. Studies that document the interactions of interviewer and candidate on oral interviews are common and focus on the type of interactions taking place on the these tests. Thus, Lazaraton (1996) documented the interaction of interviewer and candidate on oral interviews noticing specific type of linguistic and interactional support that the native speaker interlocutors provide the non-native speaker. Ross and Berwick (1992) showed that features of control (e.g., topic nomination and abandonment reformulation) and of accommodation (e.g., clarifications, requests, display questions and simplifications) are present in oral interviews concluding that oral interviews share features of both interviews and conversations. Shohamy (1994) compared the strategies and language samples obtained from direct vs. semi-direct oral tests showing that semi direct tests elicit more oral features while semi-direct tests elicit language that has more written or literate features.

Studies that examined the cognitive strategies were conducted as well. For example, Gordon and Hanauer (1996), using verbal reporting identified the strategies used by test takers in responding to different types of test questions on reading tests (see the review by Bensoussan in Volume 7). The extent to which background knowledge of the topic tested affects scores on reading comprehension has been widely examined. In spite of controversial evidence on this topic, a comprehensive study by Clapham (1995) did not find convincing evidence for such an effect. Research on the effect of the method of testing on test taker scores continues to be of interest showing such an effect to exist. For example, Riley and Lee (1996) demonstrate that using summaries and recalls result in different scores on reading comprehension tests in terms of main ideas and details (summaries contained higher percentage of main ideas). Validity of rating scales, their hierarchical levels and the extent to which the native speaker can be considered the top level criterion of language proficiency are becoming important topics of research as well as methods linking rating scales with scores obtained from objective items (Kenyon, 1995). (For more about the validation of rating scales, see the review by Fulcher in Volume 7.) The growing use of tasks on performance tests generates new research on the nature of tasks, their difficulty levels, and criteria for their analysis. A number of studies are being conducted on various types of alternative assessment focusing on different methods such as self and peer assessment, portfolio and the extent to which alternative procedures contribute to a more valid assessment; results often show that tests are still considered to be the most prestigious and frequently used procedure (Shohamy, 1994).

A relatively new area of research in language testing is the social and ethical aspects of tests and the effect of tests on teaching and learning. Washback effect of tests was examined by Alderson and Wall (1993) who found no convincing evidence for such an effect while Shohamy (1993) found that the introduction of three national language tests affected the teaching of the subject by narrowing the curriculum and producing teaching which was 'test-like', although such washback effect tends to vary depending on the type of test (e.g., high vs. low stake). Still bureaucrats use tests as power tools for introducing pedagogical changes. (See the review by Wall, in Volume 7.) Spolsky in *Measured Words* discusses the American and British institutional industrial contexts of test use and development emphasizing historical, sociological and political aspects. He documents the rise of the English testing industry demonstrating how the tests were used as gate keeping devices. Other studies shows how language tests are used for gatekeeping of immigrants and are biased for most foreign learners as they are based on cultural knowledge which is unfamiliar to adult immigrant learners (See chapters on Language Testing Standards, Accountability in Language Assessment and The Ethics of Language Testing in Volume 7).

PROBLEMS AND DIFFICULTIES

In spite of the dynamic and active nature of language assessment in all three domains, there are a number of problems and limitations. In the theoretical domain there is still no evidence for the validity of the Bachman model and its revised version in spite of its wide acceptability; some claim that the model is too complex to be used for actual test development, that it does not relate to language in more specific and well defined contexts and especially to the interaction among language users (McNamara, 1996). Lack of empirical underpinning is also a problem for the various rating scales used, especially with regards to the specific hierarchies. Thus Fulcher (1996) claims that rating scales are a priori measuring instruments based on descriptors constructed by experts using intuitive judgment concerning the nature of developing language proficiency. Young (1995) claims that while research on second language acquisition shows that language development is multidimensional showing patterns of discontinuity and U-shaped behavior, rating scales view language development as a linear process. Thus, there is limited information to provide descriptions of language abilities or performances that can be operationalized by language testers so that the results of rating scales are barely tenable as definitions of constructs. It is often stated that applied linguistics research and second language acquisition research are not feeding each other although there is much potential for such collaboration (Cohen & Bachman, in press). In the instructional domain, as well, it is often claimed that innovations taking place in language assessment lag behind their instructional counterparts so that assessment components of even very creative instructional programs remain unexciting. This is especially noticed in the use of computerized testing tasks which employ new media formats for responses but the tasks themselves differ little from paper and pencil tasks used in the past (Burstein et al., 1966). Other areas requiring much work are the development of criteria for constructing testing tasks, especially those used in performance tests and the development of psychometric criteria needed for examining the quality of such tasks. The domains of language testing need expansion; currently they address mostly English and not other languages, external tests, and not classroom tests; adults, and no children; higher education, and not learners in schools; foreign language learners and not immigrants and other second language learners; tests, and not enough alternative procedures; paper and pencil, not enough computerized and other technologies.

FUTURE DIRECTIONS

Expansion in the above areas is likely to guide language testing in the next few years in all three domains, theory, development and research. In the theoretical domain an expansion of existing models or the development of new ones which focus on additional features of the communicative, contextual and interactional use of language. Thus, such models are likely to be multidimensional, based on closer connection between language testing and second language acquisition research with a focus on the cognitive processes involved and drawing from quantitative and qualitative research methods. This can then be used to produce data for description of language use in rating scales through consideration of the linguistic meaning of constructs, rather than merely as post hoc enterprises. Along with this is a need for growing emphasis on understanding the cognitive processes involved in the test taking process, the type of interactions between tester and test taker as well as an examination of the type of discourse samples obtained in such interactions. With the increase in use of performance and alternative assessment there is a need for criteria for the development of assessment tasks as these are becoming commonly used devices for eliciting language samples. It is also likely that a variety of more innovative and creative procedures for assessment will be developed with the aid of advances in technology and with less emphasis on standardized tests in order to match the diverse societies in which assessment is needed and in which definitions of knowledge are controversial. These diverse definitions of knowledge are likely to lead to the development of different types of procedures and tasks to match such definitions in and out of the classroom. Thus a stronger differentiation between internal and external assessment procedures, each fulfilling a different purpose (i.e. classroom – as part of the instructional process, and external for selection and placement) will be developed. An integration of the two is likely to take place in certain contexts as well. A stronger emphasis on technological procedures (e.g. computers, distance assessment, interactive videos, etc.) which will be used for more efficient andaccurate assessment will take place as well relating to the varied assessment procedures. Within these different procedures there is going to be a new set of criteria for determining the psychometric qualities, validity and reliability, of such multiple assessment procedures.

Tel Aviv University, Isreal

REFERENCES

American Council on the Teaching of Foreign Languages: 1986, *ACTFL Proficiency Guidelines*, Hasting-on-Hudson, NY.
Alderson, C. & Wall, D.: 1993, 'Does washback exist?' *Applied Linguistics* 13, 115–129.
Bachman, L.: 1990, *Fundamental Considerations in Language Testing*, Oxford University Press, Oxford.
Bachman, L.& Palmer, A.: 1996, *Language Testing in Practice*, Oxford University Press, Oxford.
Baker, R.: 1996, 'Language testing and the assessment of dementia in second language settings: A case study', *Language Testing* 13, 3–22.
Buck, G.: 1994, 'The appropriacy of psychometric measurement models for testing second language testing' *Language Testing* 11, 145–170.
Burstein, J., Frase, L., Ginther, A. & Grant, L.: 1996, 'Technologies for language assessment', in W. Grabe (ed.), *Annual Review of Applied Linguistics. Technology and Language* 16, 240–260.
Canale M. & Swain, M.: 1980, 'Theoretical bases of communicative approaches to second language teaching and testing', *Applied Linguistics* 1, 1–47.
Clapham, C.: 1995, *The Effect of Background Knowledge on EAP Reading Test Performance*, Ph.D. Dissertation, Lancaster University.
Clark, J.L.D.: 1975, 'Theoretical and technical considerations in oral proficiency testing', in R. Jones & B. Spolsky (eds.), *Testing Language Proficiency*. Center for Applied Linguistics, Arlington, VA, 10–28.
Cohen, A. & Bachman, L.F.: in press, *Interfaces Between Second Language Acquisition and Language Testing Research*, Cambridge University Press, Cambridge.
Fulcher, G.: 1996, 'Does thick description lead to smart tests? A data-based approaches to rating scale construction', *Language Testing* 13, 208–238.
Gordon, C. & Hanauer, D.: 'The interaction between task and meaning construction in EFL reading comprehension tests', *TESOL Quarterly* 29, 299–325.
Hamp-Lyons, L.: 1996, 'Uncovering problems with portfolio assessment in the ESL context', Paper presented at the *18th Annual Language Testing Research Colloquium*, Tampere, Finland.
Henning, G.: 1992, 'Dimensinoality and construct validity of language tests', *Language Testing* 9, 1–11.
Ingram, D. & Wylie, E.: 1984, Australian Second Language Proficiency Ratings (ASLPR). Australian Government Publishing Service, Canberra.
Kenyon, D.: 1995, *Linking Multiple Choice Test Scores to Verbally-Defined Proficiency*

Levels: An Application to Chinese Reading Proficiency, Unpublished Ph.D dissertation, University of Maryland, College Park.

Lado, R.: 1964, *Language Teaching: A Scientific Approach*, McGraw Hill, New York.

Lazarton, A.: 1996, 'Interlocutor support in oral proficiency interviews: The case of CASE', *Language Testing* 13, 151–173.

McKay, P.: 1995, 'Developing ESL proficiency descriptions for the school context: The NLLIA ESL Bandscales', in G. Brindley (ed.), *Language Assessment in Action*, National Centre for English Language Teaching and Research, Sydney, Australia.

McNamara, T.: 1990, 'Item tesponse theory and the validation of an ESP test for health professionals', *Language Testing* 7, 52–75.

McNamara, T.: 1996, *Second Language Performance Assessment: Theory and Research*, Longman Publishers, London.

North, B.: 1994, 'Scales of language proficiency: A survey of some existing systems', *NFLC Occasional papers*, Washington, DC.

Oller, J.: 1979, *Language Tests at School: A Pragmatic Approach*, Longman Group Limited, London.

Riley, G. & Lee, J.: 1996, 'A comparison of recall and summary protocols as measures of second language reading comprehension', *Language Testing* 13, 173–187.

Ross, S. & Berwick, R.: 1992, 'The discourse of accommodation in 2 oral proficiency examinations', *Studies in Second Language Acquisition* 14, 159–176.

Sajavaava, K.: 1992, 'Designing tests to match the needs of the workplace', in E. Shohamy & R. Walton (eds.), *Language Assessment for Feedback: Testing and Other Strategies*, Kendall-Hunt. Dubuque, IA, 123–144.

Scharer, R.: 1996, 'Developing learner portfolio', Paper presented at the *18th Annual Language Testing Research Colloquium*, Tampere, Finland.

Shohamy, E.: 1993, 'The power of tests: The impact of language tests on teaching and learning', *NFLC Occassional Papers*, Washington DC.

Shohamy, F.: 1994, 'The validity of direct versus semi-direct oral tests', *Language Testing* 11, 99–124.

Shohamy, E.: 1995, 'Language testing: Matching assessment procedures with language knowledge', in M. Birenbaum & F. Dochy (eds.), *Alternatives in Assessment of Achievement, Learning Processes and Prior Knowledge*, Kluwer Acadmic Publishers, Boston, MA.

Shohamy, E., Reves, T & Bejarano, Y.: 1986, 'Introducing a new comprehensive test of oral proficiency', *English Language Teaching Journal* 40, 212–220.

Stansfield, C.: 1996, 'Description and analysis of tests for the certification of court interpreters in the USA', Paper presented at the *18th Annual Language Testing Research Colloquium*, Tampere, Finland.

Stansfield, C. & Kenyon, D.: 1988, 'Development of the portuguese speaking test. Year one project report on development of semi-direct tests of oral proficiency in Hausa, Indonesian and Portuguese', ERIC Document Reproduction Service, Alexandria, VA.

Spolsky, B.: 1995, *Measured Words: The Development of Objective Language Testing*, Oxford University Press, Oxford.

Young, R.: 1995, 'Discontinuous interlanguage development and its implications for oral proficiency rating scales', *Applied Language Learning* 6, 13–26.

Wesche, M.: 1992, 'Performance testing for work-related second language assessment', in E. Shohamy & R. Walton (eds.) *Language Assessment for Feedback: Testing and Other Strategies*, Kendall-Hunt Dubuque, IA, 103–122.

Section 5

Focus on Selected Regions of the World

CHRISTINA BRATT PAULSTON

UNDERSTANDING SECOND LANGUAGE EDUCATIONAL POLICIES IN MULTILINGUAL SETTINGS

The three main concepts in this entry, 'second languages', 'educational policies', and 'multilingual settings', can be given various meanings, so a delimitation of terms is called for.

The concept of 'second languages' is often defined as the non-home but official or dominant language of a nation which must be learned by its citizens for full social, economic and political participation in the life of that nation and so contrasts with 'foreign languages' which are studied as a cultural acquisition without similar tensions. Overlapping with this distinction are lingua francas of which today English is the most common language of wider communication, learned either as a second or foreign language depending on the context. It is always to the setting we have to look to understand educational policies.

Educational language policies, most often best seen as a sub-set of language planning, will be considered primarily at the national level and so will exclude private schools and practices of individual linguistic groups. Also excluded for reasons of space is any discussion of literacy, bilingual education, the signing deaf, teacher training as well as testing, textbook and materials writing (see reviews in Volumes 1, 2, 5 and 8).

The notion of 'multilingual setting' here refers to the prolonged contact of ethnic groups within a modern nation-state or country (political scientists disagree on the definition of nation-state so that *country* may be the preferable term). The main linguistic outcomes of such contact are language maintenance, bilingualism, or language shift, and an understanding of these phenomena and the social conditions under which they occur is a prerequisite to understanding educational language policies that seek to regulate the interactions of ethnic groups within a country.

EARLY DEVELOPMENTS

Multilingualism as a societal phenomenon is as old as our written records. The Sumerian-Akkadian Empire (third millennium B.C.) governed a multitude of peoples in two languages, and two millennia later the Bible attests to the prophet Daniel's bilingual education at the court of King Nebuchadnezzar for much the same administrative purposes. At the turn of the next millennium, Greek as the lingua franca of the civilized world gave way

G. R. Tucker and D. Corson (eds), Encyclopedia of Language and Education,
Volume 4: Second Language Education, 153–163.
© *1997 Kluwer Academic Publishers. Printed in the Netherlands.*

to Latin and later under the kings Louis to French. Not until the end of WWII, did English become the world language of wider communication.

The Romantic Movement in Europe during the nineteenth century coincided with the rise of nationalism and the idea of 'one nation-one language' and the consequent increase of some six-seven official languages in use to some one hundred twenty-five. Even so, the notion of one nation-one language remains mostly fictitious – only two countries in Europe are actually autochthonously monolingual (Iceland and Portugal), but undeniably nation and language had paired into the powerfully stirring concept of a national language (today, countries tend to use 'national' and 'official' interchangeably or one country will use 'national' to mean what another country designates as 'official' and vice versa, so no distinction is made between the two terms in this essay).

The twentieth century saw the development of two new academic disciplines, anthropology and linguistics, and in the latter part of the century, sociolinguistics of which language planning became an important branch.

In linguistics, Uriel Weinreich legitimized the study of bi/multilingualism with his dissertation on *Languages in Contact* (1953), named after a course taught at Columbia University by André Martinet. The topics he addressed were contact and interference, differences between languages, psychological and socio-cultural setting of language contact, and language contact and culture contact. This tradition still continues with titles like *Sociolinguistic Studies in Language Contact* (Mackey & Ornstein, 1979) and *Languages in Contact and Conflict* (Nelde, 1980).

Einar Haugen, one of the founders of sociolinguistics, wrote his dissertation on what was to become known as language planning in 1931 on 'The origin and early history of the New Norse movement in Norway', although never published. (*Language Conflict and Language Planning: the Case of Modern Norwegian* was published in 1966). In 1956, Haugen published the influential *Bilingualism in the Americas: a bibliography and research guide* and went on to a lifetime of writing about the ecology of language. Haugen joined the interests in multilingualism and in languages policies which became combined in the emerging field of language planning, triggered by real world problems and initially financially supported by the US government, as for instance the Airlie House conference in 1966 (Fishman, Ferguson, & das Gupta, 1968) and by the Ford Foundation as for example, the Dar es Salaam conference in 1968 (Whiteley, 1971), both on the language problems of the developing nations. This new academic field of language planning found itself consistently dealing with language policies for linguistic minorities.

Linguistic minorities do have to face the matter of language policies concerning them. Even the absence of explicit policy, as Heath points out (1976), is in itself an act of language policy. As far as education is concerned, the major issues typically are medium of instruction and the various combinations and implementations thereof, and to a lesser degree, literacy and choice of writing system. Much if not most of the research on the schooling of linguistic minority children is some sort of evaluation, usually involving medium of instruction, and throughout the world the results of such research are contradictory and confusing.

MAJOR CONTRIBUTIONS

What generalizations can be made about educational language policies in multilingual states and how can we predict success and failure? The possible linguistic outcomes of the prolonged contact of ethnic groups are basically three: language maintenance, bilingualism, or language shift. Bilingualism may also involve the spread of a lingua franca, a language of wider communication. An understanding of language maintenance and shift and the social conditions under which they occur constitutes a major means for understanding language policies which seek to regulate the inter-actions of ethnic groups within a modern nation-state. No language policy will be successful which goes counter to existing sociocultural forces. The difficulty lies in understanding and identifying the relevant social deter-minants of maintenance and shift. The corollary to this point needs to be stated: it is natural that educators concentrate on the immediate and overt linguistic problems of the children as the causal factor, the factor which leads to school failure, early drop out and alienation from society. Yet program after program, from the Canadian immersion programs to the Singaporean public schools, all demonstrate that children can be schooled happily and successfully in a second language *under certain social con-ditions*. Language problems in education are almost always corollaries of the social problems of ethnic groups in contact and competition.

The major point about multilingualism, which is not readily recognized in the literature, is that maintained group bilingualism is unusual. The norm for groups in prolonged contact within a nation-state is for the subordinate group to shift to the language of the dominant group, whether over three generations or over several hundred years. Where shift does not take place, there are identifiable reasons of which the major two are lack of incentive (usually economic) or lack of access to the dominant language.

The mechanism for language shift is bilingualism, often with exogamy. Groups will vary in their degree of ethnic maintenance and in the *rate* of shift of which one major influence is the origin of the contact situation. Voluntary migration results in much faster shift than does annexation or colonization. Other factors are, for maintenance, continued access to a standardized, written L_1 with cultural prestige and tradition in contradis-tinction to a non-standard, non-written language of little prestige. Sacred languages are also a factor. Ethnic groups also vary in their ethnic pride or ethnic stubbornness, so occasionally with what Spicer names persistent peoples we get internal (rather than social-external) factors working for language maintenance (Spicer, 1980).

Paulston posits a theoretical framework for explaining and predicting the language behavior of ethnic groups in contact within a contemporary nation-state (1994). The proposition is that linguistic groups form four distinct types of social mobilization: ethnicity, ethnic movements, ethnic nationalism and geographic nationalism which under certain specified social conditions result in differential linguistic outcomes of language maintenance and shift. Educational planning which goes counter to such social forces has very little chance of success.

What follows is a discussion of recent case studies of educational language policies concerning national languages and minority languages in a representative sampling of problems and concerns.

National Languages and Educational Concerns

The burning question at the national level of status planning has typically been the choice of national/official languages. For example, to this day the majority of African nations still have an ex-colonial language as the official national language precisely because of the politically sensitive nature of the problem.

There is an interesting case study from the U.S.A. to illustrate this point. Brown (1993) describes classic problems of language planning with Louisiana French. The Louisiana State Legislature declared French as official language of the state in 1968, and it established the Council for the Development of French in Louisiana (CODIFIL). The problem was which French to develop, Cajun French (from Acadia, now Nova Scotia), Haitian Creole, or international French, the standard prestige variety. As Brown notes, "On the one hand are the lawmakers, searching for a prestige norm; on the other are the local community members, learning that their mother tongue is incorrect and inappropriate" (1993: p. 77). It is a very real problem, repeated in many parts of the world. In Louisiana, as a result of the cultural revival movement and the bilingual education legislation, the question of the standardization of Louisiana French has become a major preoccupation in the educational domain (1993: p. 92). The study reflects – and discusses – the immediate implications for education which result from political decisions and legislation.

Another part of the world which faces choice of medium of instruction is southern Africa. Namibia, "Africa's last colony", attained independence in 1990 from South Africa. The language of administration and education had been Afrikaans. The constitution of Namibia prescribes that English shall be the official language but permits other mediums of instruction. Furthermore, provision is made for languages other than English for legislative, administrative, and judicial purposes in regions where other language(s) are spoken by a substantial proportion of the population.

Harlech-Jones (1990) provides a knowledgeable and pragmatic discussion of the implementation of English as a medium of instruction, based on survey results of teachers. Interestingly enough to the American and European reader who takes the importance of mother tongue teaching as axiomatic, this is not so in Southern Africa: "It may be inferred that, for many teachers, advocacy of a language of wider communication [English and Afrikaans] as a medium of instruction does not reflect contempt for, or denial of, their own specific backgrounds, but arises rather from an attempt to accommodate to the complexities and realities of a multilingual society" (Harlech-Jones, 1990: p. 24).

Cluver (1992) pursues problems similar to Namibia in a post-apartheid South Africa where English is now the only language of instruction in black high schools. He points out that any language planning model must remember the Soweto uprising of 1976 in which students rioted and were killed over the attempt to introduce Afrikaans as medium of instruction. Cluver concludes that the government's previous policies were determined partly by fear of English domination and partly by an attempt to promote Afrikaner nationalism and racial segregation. It is readily seen from these studies that Harlech-Jones is right when he says, "Education is thus a directly political activity, regarded and utilized by decision-makers as a major instrument of social policy" (1990: p. 68).

Another concern with implications for educational language policies is carefully outlined in Fierman's (1991) study of language planning in Uzbek. In particular, the choice of alphabet or writing system has great implications for social identity, protection of elite status, and national development to mention just a few concerns. Fierman relates this decision and its implications in Uzbekistan to choices made in independent Somalia. There, the vast majority of the population spoke Somali, but the government was unable to reach a consensus of choice of script, according to some because of clan rivalry, and continued to educate children in English and Italian, the languages of the former colonial administration. This decision severely limited participation by much of the population (1991: p. 17).

Fierman's study makes clear the crucial importance played by the writing system of a modern nation as well as the importance of the educational system in policy transmission. Following his study, the Turkic speaking nations of the former USSR, together with Turkey, met in 1992 and declared a return to the Latin alphabet (Chicago Tribune June 18, 1992). There is, at present, much costly corpus planning for education that needs to be undertaken in those countries.

Minority Languages in Education

Minority languages are the frequent object of language policies and legislation. The Latvian Language Law of 1992, the Slovak Language Law
of 1995 and the U.S. English-Only Movement all seek to restrict the use
of minority languages within their nation-states. However, most language
policies worldwide in regard to linguistic minorities probably concern the
educational problems of their children.

Linguistic minorities or minority groups, although the most commonly
used appellation, is actually a misnomer in that it implies that the problem
is one of number. Rather, the issue is one of power and of a super-
subordinate relationship between the groups, and as Lieberson (1981)
points out, a group enjoying both political and economic dominance is
in a position to ensure its linguistic position. A caveat is in order here:
frequently there is wider intra-group variation than intergroup (Lambert,
1997); the generalizations in this entry concern linguistic groups and do
not refer to individual differences within any groups.

Several typologies of minorities exist; for our purposes Schermerhorn's
emphasis on the origin of the contact situation is useful: voluntary (immigrant) and involuntary (slavery) migration, colonization and annexation
result in different degrees and rates of assimilation and thus accompanying
language shift. The third generation of European immigrants to the United
States (Ferguson & Heath, 1981) typically are monolingual in English and
so have no language problems in education in contradistinction to Chi-
canos and American Indians, in contact respectively through annexation
and colonization whose language shift has been much slower. Ogbu has
a very similar typology of minorities where his major emphasis is on the
difference between immigrants and involuntary minorities: "people who
were originally brought into the United States involuntarily through slavery, conquest or colonization" (1993: p. 92). As an anthropologist, his
major explanatory concept in explaining the school failures of the latter
lies in cultural differences between the minority group and the dominant
majority: "the children have difficulties in crossing cultural boundaries"
(1993: p. 106).

Most educational language policies concern medium of instruction and
consequent issues like teacher training, textbook materials, administration
and funding. The definition of the problem *per se* is usually determined by
the worldview and agenda of the political party in power, of the researcher,
and of the parents and so the interested parties are frequently at variance in
their orientation. The English-Only adherents see a different problem and
consequent policies than do the officials of the Center for Applied Linguistics (USA). Minority educational policies form a very controversial field,
partially because the perception of problems and solutions are so closely
linked to cultural orientation, partially because the thought of involun-

tary loss of the ancestral language reaches deep and emotional roots of being.

Canada represents an example of a language situation involving a large immigrant population. Educational programs, about 2 1/2 hours per week of original mother tongue language instruction, have long been in existence within the context of Canada's national policy of multi-culturalism, proclaimed in 1971. Studies have shown educational benefit for minority students from such programs (Cummins & Danesi, 1990). Swain and Lapkin (1991) also found highly significant differences in favor of those students with mother tongue literacy skills on both written and oral measures of French. As Cummins sums up, "In short, the research data suggest that there is considerable validity to the claim that promoting HL proficiency may enhance the educational development of the individual child" (1992: p. 286).

Since 1971 there have been dramatic increases in immigration levels so that in Toronto and Vancouver more than half of the school population comes from a non-English speaking background (Cummins, 1992: p. 281). With this increase has come opposition to the programs: "Opponents see heritage languages as socially divisive, excessively costly, and educationally retrograde in view of minority children's need to succeed academically in the school language" (Cummins, 1992: p. 285). Cummins concludes his article by pointing out that policies with respect to mother tongue teaching will be affected by the broader debate about Canada's multiculturalism policy itself, now under critical scrutiny.

New Zealand provides an important case of policy of a minority language, recognized as an official language, in the attempt at reversing language shift. Maori, the indigenous language of New Zealand, was by the late 1970s considered an endangered language. The Maori Language Commission estimates the number of fluent speakers at 50,000 but their greatest concern is the loss of speakers, as many as 10,000 during the last decade, and most fluent speakers today are aged over 55 (Nicholson & Garland, 1991: p. 394). The New Zealand Council for Educational Research estimates that less than one percent of Maori children aged nine or under were fluent speakers in 1986 (Waite, 1992: p. 32). In this situation of impending language death (Maori is not spoken elsewhere), there is a movement for language revitalization. The first Kohanga Reo or "language nest" was set up in 1982 for pre-school children and has now multiplied widely (over 500 by 1988 [Benton, 1991: p. 139]). The Maori Language Act of 1987 declared Maori an official language, and a Maori Language Commission was established.

In this situation, one finds some of the most interesting language-in-education policy and planning activities presently taking place anywhere (see the reviews by Durie in Volume 5; and by Watts in Volume 1 and in this volume). Benton (1990) provides an analysis of the various interpretations

and motivations which underlie the recommendations of the various actors
– the Government, the Ministries, the politicians, and the Maori interest
groups. The 1988 Picot Report on the reform of education states [highly
controversially], "It is clear that the revival of the Maori language and
culture is seen not as an end in itself, but as the key of lifting the educational
performance of Maori children" (Picot, 1988: para. 7.2.1.). (This is also,
although in other words, the U.S. government's own efficiency argument
for bilingual education.) Benton points out, however, that the major Maori
motivating force behind the cultural revival is an assertion of cultural
identity – as seen by the Maori people – because they are Maori, not
because they want to do well in a 'Pakeha' school system. Whether one
sees the solution as (1) improved educational performance through the use
of Maori or as (2) improved cultural identity through the use of Maori
depends on the reader's own ideology.

Western and Eastern Europe have also shown a considerable rise of
interest recently in minority languages, if for different reasons. Two problems of Western Europe which receive the major research interests, are:
(1) the question of maintenance of the ethnic language, and (2) the need for
education and literacy in the ethnic language (along with concurrent problems of standardization and materials (Jaespaert & Kroon, 1991). To these
major interests can also be added the concern for language revitalization,
for an obvious trend in European minority language communities is that
of language shift (Fase, Jaspaert & Kroon, 1992; Grin, 1993). Discussions
of language revitalization usually also suggest implications for education
(see also Williamson, 1991).

Tabouret-Keller (1992) discusses the documents of the European Charter
on Regional and Minority Languages and suggests that this policy is mostly
idealistic as "each state is left the responsibility of choosing its own policy
(1992: p. 277)". It seems obvious that the European Charter on Regional
or Minority Languages resolution will not have sufficient influence by
itself for setting any educational policies for minority languages.

FUTURE DIRECTIONS

A major concern for linguistics as well as for L2 policies is that of endangered languages and language loss (Hale et al., 1992; Robins & Uhlenberg,
eds., 1991). This concern has occasioned two others. One is the problem of language revitalization and how to stop language shift or death, of
reversing language shift in Fishman's (1991) words. One question, e.g.
about Maori, is whether education alone can manage language revitalization (Nicholson & Garland, 1991). Recently, because of the economic
situation, the government is selling some of the public broadcasting system to private interests and so the Maori are expected to lose their allotted

air time, and while this is of too recent a development to appear in the literature, the matter has been discussed over e-mail.

E-mail and internet will clearly have a substantial influence on the direction of research and practice, as e.g. in requests for information and help, for soliciting petition letter writing to officials, and the like; in offering counter argument and counter facts; and in scholarly discussion of ongoing work by researchers as well as pre-publication exchange.

The problem of language loss has also led to a concern for language rights of (in practice, primarily minority) groups, also at times referred to as Linguistic Human Rights (Skutnabb-Kangas & Phillipson, 1994). This notion as yet shows considerable conceptual confusion and disagreement, but as indicator of this interest trend can be cited the publications of two major journals on the topic for 1997: *International Journal of the Sociology of Language* (Hamel, 1997) and *Annual Review of Anthropology* (Paulston, 1997). (See the review by Skutnabb-Kangas in Volume 1.)

Other trends of interest to follow are Quebec's separatist movement and its possible reductionist effect on the highly successful Canadian immersion programs (in French for Anglo children); the Swedish school reform (Miron, 1993) with its decentralization of education and thus its national level support of mother tongue education of immigrant children relegated to local school authorities; this trend partially tied to downward economic trends; and the future course of the English Only movement in the USA and its consequences for bilingual education.

Also interesting are the language policies of the European Union and consequent educational policies (Baetens-Beardsmore, 1993; Ammon et al., 1994) and the recent interest in linguistic minorities of Central and Eastern Europe. The minorities have of course always been there, but have for ideological reasons of Marxism been ignored and repressed under the Soviet Union. Their newfound recognition will have implications for educational policies. There is yet little available in English on the subject but see *Current Issues in Language and Society* (ed. Wright, 1994) as well as a conference proceedings (State Language Centre), *Language Policy in the Baltic States* (1992).

But whatever the new trends and future directions of research and happenings in second language educational policies will be, the major concerns and problems are likely to remain the same (see Volume 1 passim).

University of Pittsburgh, USA

REFERENCES

Ammon, U., Mattheier, K.J. & Nelde, P.: 1994, 'English only? in Europe', *Sociolinguistica* 8.

Baetens-Beardsmore, H. (ed.): 1993, *European Models of Bilingual Education*. Clevedon, England: Multilingual Matters.

Benton, R.A.: 1990, 'Biculturalism in education: policy and practice under the fourth labour government', in M. Holland & J. Boston (eds.), *The Fourth Labour Government: Politics and Policy in New Zealand*, Auckland: Oxford University Press.

Benton, R.A.: 1991, 'Tomorrow's schools and the revitalization of Maori: Stimulus or tranquilizer?' in O. García (ed.), *Bilingual Education: Focusschrift in Honor of Joshua A. Fishman*. John Benjamins, Amsterdam/Philadelphia, 135–147.

Brown, B.: 1993, 'The social consequences of writing Louisiana French', *Language in Society* 22, 67–101.

Chicago Tribune: 1992, 'Republics reclaim Latin alphabet', June 18.

Cluver, A.D. de V.: 1992, 'Language planning models for a post-apartheid South Africa', *Language Problems and Language Planning* 16(2), 105–136.

Cummins, J.: 1992, 'Heritage language teaching in Canadian schools', *Journal of Curriculum Studies* 24(3), 281–286.

Cummins, J. & Danesi, M.: 1990, *Heritage Languages: The Development and Denial of Canada's Linguistic Resources*, Garamond, Toronto.

Fase, W., Jaspaert, K. & Kroon, S. (eds.): 1992, *Maintenance and Loss of Minority Languages*, John Benjamins, Amsterdam.

Ferguson, C.A. & Heath, S.B. (eds.): 1980, *Language in the USA*, Cambridge University Press.

Fierman, W.: 1991, *Language Planning and National Development: The Uzbek Experience*, Mouton de Gruyter, Berlin.

Fishman, J.A.: 1991, *Reversing Language Shift*, Multilingual Matters, Clevedon, Avon.

Fishman, J.A., Ferguson, C.A. & Das Gupta, J. (eds.): 1968, *Language Problems of Developing Nations*, John Wiley, New York.

Grin, F.: 1993, 'European economic integration and the fate of lesser-used languages', *Language Problems and Language Planning* 17(2), 101–116.

Hale, K. et al.: 1992, 'Endangered languages', *Language* 68(1), 1–42.

Hamel, R.E.: 1997, 'Linguistic human rights from a sociolinguistic perspective', *International Journal of the Sociology of Language* 127.

Harlech-Jones, B.: 1990, *You Taught Me Language: The Implementation of English as a Medium of Instruction in Namibia*, Oxford University Press, Cape Town.

Haugen, E.: 1956, *Bilingualism in the Americas: A Bibliography and Research Guide*, University of Alabama Press, Alabama.

Haugen, E.: 1966, *Language Conflict and Language Planning: The Case of Modern Norwegian*, Harvard University Press, Cambridge, Massachusetts.

Heath, S.B.: 1976, 'A national language academy?', *International Journal of Sociology of Language* 11, 9–43.

Jaspaert, K. & Kroon S. (eds.): 1991, *Ethnic Minority Languages and Education*, Swets and Zeitlinger B.V., Amsterdam.

Lambert, W.: 1997, 'Personal views on the beginnings of sociolinguistics', in C.B. Paulston & G.R. Tucker (eds.), *The Early Days of Sociolinguistics: Memories and Reflections*, Arlington, TX: SIL.

Mackey, W.F. & Ornstein, J. (eds.): 1979, *Sociolinguistic Studies in Language Conflict*, Franz Steiner Verlag, Wiesbaden.

Miron, G.: 1993, *Choice and the Use of Market Forces in Schooling: Swedish Education for the 1990s*, Stockholm University, Stockholm.

Nelde, P.H. (ed.): 1980, *Languages in Contact and Conflict*, Franz Steiner Verlag, Weisbaden.

Nicholson, R. & Garland, R.: 1991, 'New Zealanders' attitudes to the revitalization of the Maori language', *Journal of Multilingual and Multicultural Development* 12(5), 393–410.

Ogbu, J.U.: 1993, 'Frameworks – Variability in minority school performance: A problem in search of an explanation', in E. Jacob & C. Jordan (eds.), *Minority Education*, Norwood, NJ: Ablex.

Paulston, C.B.: 1994, *Linguistic Minorities in Multilingual Settings: Implications for Language Policies*, Benjamins, Amsterdam.

Paulston, C.B.: 1997,'Language rights and language policies', *Annual Review of Anthropology* 26.

Robins, H.R. & Uhlenbeck, E.M. (eds.): 1991, *Endangered Languages*, Oxford, Berg.

Skutnabb-Kangas, T. & Phillipson, R. (eds.): 1994, *Linguistic Human Rights*. Berlin: Mouton de Gruyter.

Spicer, E.H.: 1980, *The Yaquis: A cultural history*, University of Arizona Press, Tucson.

State Language Centre: 1992, *Language Policy in the Baltic States*, Conference Papers, Riga, Latvia. Dec. 17–18.

Swain, M. & Lapkin, S.: 1991, 'Heritage language children in an English-French bilingual program', *Canadian Modern Language Review/La review canadienne des langues vivantes* 47(4), 635–641.

Tabouret-Keller, A.: 1992, 'Some major features of the sociolinguistic situation in Europe and the European Charter', in K. Bolton & H. Kwok (eds.) *International Perspectives*, London: Routledge.

Waite, J.: 1992, *Aoteareo: Speaking for ourselves*, Wellington, Ministry of Education.

Weinreich, U.: 1953, *Languages in Contact*, Linguistic Circle of New York, New York.

Whiteley, W.H. (ed.): 1971, *Language Use and Social Change: Problems of Multilingualism with Special Reference to Eastern Africa*, Oxford University Press, Oxford.

Williamson, R.C.: 1991, *Minority Languages and Bilingualism: Case Studies in Maintenance and Shift*, Ablex, Norwood, New Jersey.

Wright, S., (ed.): 1994, 'Ethnicity in Eastern Europe: Questions of migration, language rights and education', *Current Issues in Language and Society* I: 1.

DONNA CHRISTIAN AND NANCY RHODES

INNOVATIVE SECOND LANGUAGE EDUCATION IN NORTH AMERICA

In second language education in North America, there has been a movement away from teaching language in isolation toward integrating language
and content instruction (Mohan, 1986; Enright & McCloskey, 1989). This
umbrella term encompasses instructional and programmatic approaches
where students are learning a second language as they learn content *through*
that language. Thus, integrated language and content (ILC) may be found
within the context of bilingual as well as monolingual programs, and it
may be applied with a primary goal of teaching either language or content.
When content is used as a vehicle for language learning and instruction
(i.e., language development is the primary goal), a term often used is
content-based language learning. In programs where instruction is entirely through a second language, the term *immersion* is typically used.
This review will consider the innovation of ILC in second language education, with primary emphasis on its realization at elementary and secondary
levels of education.

EARLY DEVELOPMENTS

In the traditional approach of second language instruction in elementary
and secondary schools, listening, speaking, reading and writing tasks were
not framed in the context of the regular curriculum. The integrated approach takes the real context of the regular curriculum and uses it to teach
all four language skills. This shift from the often contrived context of the
language classroom to the context of the full curriculum not only motivates
students (since they are performing meaningful tasks), but also promotes
broader development of language skills.

ILC instruction works toward both content objectives and language
objectives, with a focus on meaning rather than on form and little overt error
correction (although structural features may be reinforced in a meaningful
context). The language that is used is made comprehensible to the students,
through adjusted speech, controlled vocabulary, and use of multiple cues
to convey meaning (combinations of verbal, visual, and physical response
strategies) (Short, 1991).

The ILC approach is not new for language education; it has been used for
many years in adult education, in university programs for foreign students,

G. R. Tucker and D. Corson (eds), Encyclopedia of Language and Education,
Volume 4: Second Language Education, 165–174.
© *1997 Kluwer Academic Publishers. Printed in the Netherlands.*

and in language-for-special-purposes courses (for business or science, for example) (Brinton, Snow & Wesche, 1989), where the need to tie language instruction to academic or other real-world goals was clear.

The rationale for ILC comes from both general education and language acquisition research. Recent work on second language acquisition stresses natural acquisition of language, with minimal overt attention to language forms (Krashen & Terrell, 1983), even in classroom settings. There, the role of *comprehensible input* is critical for language development, as are authentic, interesting texts for reading and writing and authentic, meaningful interactions for speaking and listening (Krashen 1982). Swain (1985) emphasizes the need for opportunities to work toward *comprehensible output* as well to facilitate the development of proficiency.

Cummins (1981) and others provide evidence for two kinds of language proficiency – Basic Interpersonal Communication Skills (BICS) and Cognitive Academic Language Proficiency (CALP) – which vary in the amount of cognitive complexity and contextual support present. Research suggests that BICS may be acquired fairly quickly, in one to two years, but that CALP requires more time and experience, often taking from five to seven years or more to develop to native-like levels (Collier, 1987).

The ILC approach builds on these research foundations by promoting language development through relevant and comprehensible input and output. In school situations, language learning happens most effectively when students work toward communication in meaningful situations, because motivation is an important factor in language learning (Genesee, 1994). Authentic materials (realia) also contribute to more interesting bases for instruction. ILC instruction in schools helps students acquire academic language and specialized content area language 'registers' as in science and mathematics (Crandall, 1995). Saville-Troike (1984), in particular, has noted that vocabulary plays a key role in academic achievement, including the specialized vocabulary of various content areas. Corson (1995) cites and builds on the evidence for the centrality of vocabulary. He discusses a wide range of research and disciplinary perspectives on first and second language acquisition.

Language immersion programs illustrate an early application of ILC, where part or all of the regular curriculum is taught to students through a second language (Lambert & Tucker, 1972). The effectiveness of such programs in helping students achieve high levels of proficiency has been well documented (Harley et al., 1990) particularly for students who natively speak the majority language of the wider society.

MAJOR CONTRIBUTIONS

ILC has developed through expansions of implementation models for practice, of information about its current use, and of the knowledge base from research. The intersection of research and practice in the development of this approach has been a particularly close one, as social forces demanded improvements in second language learning.

Since the early 1980s, there has been considerable activity among researchers, teacher educators, administrators, and teachers to explore ILC in practice. The Center for Applied Linguistics conducted a series of projects to refine the approach, consider strategies for implementation in different contexts, and develop materials to present content-based language learning to a wider audience (Christian et al., 1990; Short, 1991; Crandall, 1995). Snow, Met and Genesee (1989) proposed a conceptual framework for ILC across multiple language education contexts. Investigations of language learning in particular content contexts, such as mathematics and science, also elaborated our understanding of ILC. For example, mathematics calculations and problem-solving are heavily dependent on technical vocabulary and language structures (Spanos et al., 1988). This line of work focused attention as well on thematic approaches to content-based language learning, where a theme (such as 'Migration') serves as the focal point for exploration of concepts and information from multiple content areas (science, geography, history) along with language.

The Cognitive Academic Language Learning Approach (CALLA), developed by Chamot and O'Malley (1994), is a model of instruction for English language learners at advanced beginning and intermediate levels of proficiency to help them make the transition from bilingual or English-as-a-second-language (ESL) instruction into grade-level content instruction. CALLA builds on ILC by incorporating content topics and academic language skills development, along with instruction in learning strategies, weaving insights from cognitive theory directly into the model. Since its initial conceptualization, CALLA has been refined and expanded through research in classrooms, development of text materials for students and teachers, and investigations of student assessment strategies.

A large-scale study of ILC programs in the United States (Sheppard 1995) reviewed pre-K through 12 programs to provide '... a descriptive analysis of the nature and scope of content-ESL classroom practices for LEP [limited English proficient] students, which are components of transitional bilingual education, pull-out, immersion programs or other programs' (p. ii). Using a broad definition of content-ESL (a program where one or more classes integrated ESL and subject matter), the study identified a sample of over 1,600 schools who reported operating this type of program and obtained detailed information about its implementation from 468 schools. Spanish was the predominant home language of students in content-ESL classes, with eighty-one percent of the programs reporting the presence of Spanish-speaking students. The students' home language was used for instruction in fifty percent of the programs. Approximately fifty-four percent of the programs had developed curricula specifically for content-ESL. Findings suggested that many content-ESL teachers have adopted methods and strategies associated with progressive trends in teaching (such as cooperative learning and discovery methods), consistent with current educational theory. There was little evidence, however, of a single methodology tailored specifically to content-ESL instruction. Rather, teachers appeared to draw eclectically on a variety of instructional practices from a variety of sources. In general, teachers and administrators have adopted practices that are consistent with broad trends in language instruction: away from discrete point ideas about language toward an interaction with general meaning, away from teacher-centeredness toward the learner-centered environment, and away from commercially-published texts toward the use of authentic and program-specific material (Sheppard, 1995: p. 123).

Among teachers in the sample who reported experience in teaching grammar-based ESL, seventy-nine percent said that their content-ESL students learned English skills faster than students in grammar-based classes, and eighty-nine percent felt that content-ESL students improved content area achievement faster as well (Sheppard, 1995: p. 96). While such teacher reports frequently testify to the effectiveness of content-based language learning, there has been little direct comparison of this approach to others in terms of student performance.

Although there has not been a systematic study of elementary and secondary school ILC programs in Canada, evidence from second language programs in Canada, comparing 'core French' (typically form-focused, or 'analytic', instruction in language as a subject for about an hour a day) and immersion (content-based, or 'experiential' instruction for a substantial portion of the day) yields some helpful insights about ILC (Harley et al., 1990). Investigators found that content-based instruction in immersion classrooms leads to high levels of fluency, extensive vocabulary knowledge, and well-developed discourse skills in the second language. They conclude that 'teaching that is *principally* meaning-based, learner-centered, experiential, and contextualized' (p. 90) is to be preferred, although some attention to language form (in meaningful contexts) is important to improve grammatical accuracy.

WORK IN PROGRESS

Our knowledge base on ILC continues to be built on information and evidence gathered from both research and practice (Genesee, 1987). Additional applications of ILC in different contexts are being constructed, and implications of ILC for language learning are being viewed from new perspectives.

A major area of activity has been program and curriculum development. One extension has been to the post-secondary level, where Brinton, Snow and Wesche (1989) note ongoing work on several models of ILC that differ in their focus on language and content. The adjunct model has gained attention for promise in promoting both language and content learning. In this model, a second language learning course is paired with a content course in the general curriculum (such as introductory psychology) which enrolls both second language learners and native English speakers. The content teacher covers the concepts in the subject area curriculum, and the language teacher in the adjunct course stresses language development related to that content, such as academic reading or writing. Collaboration between teachers and joint planning are essential. The adjunct model works best for students with high enough language skills to participate at a reasonable level in content instruction with English speaking students (Crandall, 1993 and see the review by Crandall in this volume).

Another manifestation of ILC that is gaining prominence is known as 'sheltered' instruction, in which content is modified to accommodate the proficiency level of second language learners (Kauffman, 1994). Such instruction may be offered by language or content area teachers and may or may not have specific language objectives (this may be distinguished from content-based language learning where language development is the primary aim). In sheltered instruction, content concepts and information are made accessible to students by using strategies to modify oral and written language input, provide additional contextual information, and give cues to meaning from multiple sources (graphic, auditory, print, and so on). As in immersion classes, improvement of language skills occurs, while concepts and content information are acquired. Investigators are currently examining what features of programs for second language learners such as sheltered instruction promote academic and/or language growth and how those features relate to local context (August & Pease-Alvarez, 1996).

In elementary and secondary contexts, more in depth investigations of ILC in particular content areas are extending our knowledge. In a classroom-based research project, Short (1994) looked specifically at the integration of language, culture, and social studies for English language learners in middle school social studies classrooms. Based on an examination of the academic language of American history classes, a series of lessons was designed to integrate language and content objectives with the development of critical-thinking skills and information about the cultural diversity of colonial America. An analysis of the implementation of these lessons showed that many of the successful strategies teachers use to facilitate students' comprehension of the subject matter and improve their academic language skills are adaptations of ESL techniques that have been applied to content-area lessons. These findings indicate that an integrated language and social studies course can assist English language learners gain academic language skills needed for participation in non-ILC content classes.

ILC has also surfaced in an increasingly popular program, two-way immersion (also known as bilingual immersion), which brings together students from two different language backgrounds, providing native and second language education for all. Majority language (in the United States, English) and minority language (most often Spanish) students work together in classes for most or all of their content instruction. As a result, each group of students experiences content-based language learning in the other's native language, and programs strive for bilingual proficiency and biliteracy for all students (Christian, 1996). These programs have produced promising results both in language and academic achievement, and they are increasingly being both implemented and studied. Christian and Whitcher (1995) profile two-way programs in over 180 schools in the United States, with elementary school level, Spanish-English programs by far the most numerous.

In two-way immersion and ILC programs, questions related to what instructional and programmatic strategies will lead to optimal language development continue to be addressed. The role of explicit teaching of language form, the value (if any) of certain forms of error correction, and the range of language domains that can be developed in a school setting are some of the topics being explored in ongoing studies (Swain, 1995 and see the review by Swain in Volume 5).

The recent development and ongoing application of national disciplinary standards in foreign languages and English as a second language promise to have a major impact on language teaching in the United States, giving a new perspective for examining ILC. These standards emerge in an atmosphere of educational reform in the U.S., where standards are seen as essential benchmarks for viewing student learning and accountability for programs (and for providing a framework for achieving a set of newly defined national education goals). As a consequence, the standards will likely play an integral role in curriculum and program planning.

The foreign language standards, released to the public in 1995, define standards for content – what students should know and be able to do – in foreign language education. Five goal areas were identified that encompass the purposes and uses of foreign languages: (1) communication – communicate in languages other than English; (2) cultures – gain knowledge and understanding of other cultures; (3) connections – connect with other disciplines and acquire information; (4) comparisons – develop insight into the nature of language and culture, and (5) communities – participate in multilingual communities at home and around the world (American Council on the Teaching of Foreign Languages, 1996). The standards proposed for ESL reflect goals related to communication in social settings, academic achievement in all content areas, and socially and culturally appropriate use of English (Teachers of English to Speakers of Other Languages, 1997).

Across Canada, various provinces are developing language standards for student outcomes or expected levels of achievement. For example, the Ontario Ministry of Education and Training (1995) specified outcomes for student achievement for English Language Arts and French (with a minor focus on ESL) at grades 3, 6 and 9, detailing outcomes for six modes (reading, writing, speaking, listening, viewing, and representation).

As schools and communities work to align their programs with local adaptations of the standards, ILC approaches are clearly compatible and will play a major role in providing the meaningful and effective language instruction that the standards call for. How the approaches are fashioned in different contexts and how language learning can be optimized (while working toward the full set of standards that will be in operation) are questions that are currently being investigated.

PROBLEMS AND DIFFICULTIES

Among the greatest challenges facing the implementation of integrated language and content programs is the preparation of teachers. Because of rapidly changing demographics in North America, increasing numbers of elementary and secondary school teachers have second language learners in their classes. Crandall (1993) suggests that in order to accommodate an increasingly diverse student population, language teachers need to learn how to better integrate academic language and content in their classrooms and content teachers need to learn how to facilitate second language development as well. Some teacher education and in-service programs are creatively addressing these issues, bringing together content and language teachers for collaboration. In some areas of the United States, legal actions have forced states and school districts to address the needs of language learners. In Florida, a consent order signed by the state education agency in 1990 had among its provisions a requirement for training content area teachers who teach second language learners in methodologies appropriate for the population (such as ILC).

Equally critical is the need for careful research to evaluate the effectiveness of program implementation. Are integrated language and content programs being implemented as designed? What adaptations are being made? Are students' needs being met by current programs? The findings reported in Sheppard (1995) underscore how variable and perhaps unsystematic implementation has been.

Tied into these issues are challenges related to the new standards for foreign languages and English as a second language in the United States. One challenge deals with the implementation of the standards. The national standards are designed to guide state departments of education and local school districts in developing their own curriculum frameworks. How can these standards best be used to help second language learners progress linguistically? State and local agencies will need to consider that question in the context of their schools, communities, and students as they adapt and implement the standards.

Another challenge deals with assessment issues. Although both foreign language and ESL content standards have been prepared, performance standards, dealing with the question of how well students perform, have yet to be developed. Both sets of standards include sample progress indicators, showing activities that students can perform in class to demonstrate progress toward meeting the standards. But more needs to be done to review long-term progress. ESL assessment guidelines are currently being developed that will help educators understand the purpose and audience of various assessment options and make connections with the standards. A major question that remains, however, for content-based language programs is how to treat language development and content mastery. With an increasing number of programs that integrate the teaching of language and content, there is a growing need to investigate the issues related to both adequately assessing language development and to separating language and content skills for assessment purposes where appropriate.

FUTURE DIRECTIONS

With general agreement that ILC promotes second language development, and growing popularity of programs that incorporate this approach, research and practice will continue to be closely intertwined. Future developments are likely to see refinements of the approach to fit more and varying contexts and to align it with other educational movements (such as standards) that unfold. As standards begin playing a more critical role in educational reform, their influence on ILC program models and the resultant curricular changes will be interesting to study. There is also a strong relationship between the ILC approach and language awareness, a contemporary movement in second language learning. Expanding language awareness is a key ingredient in preparing teachers to undertake ILC instruction and may benefit their students as well (see Volume 6 for more details on language awareness).

From a second language education perspective, it will be essential to pursue investigations of ways to strengthen the language development strategies in ILC. A number of investigators have raised the issue of the need for carefully designed explicit language instruction, to be embedded in a meaningful, content-based context (Harley et al., 1990; Swain, 1995) in order to promote optimal language development. Snow, Met and Genesee (1989) introduced the useful distinction between 'content-obligatory' (language that is required to understand a particular subject) and 'content-compatible' (language that fits naturally in a particular subject area) language. While the former must be developed for a given content area, the latter provides the flexibility to attend to students' second language needs in a meaningful context.

Attention is needed to implementation issues in general. As Sheppard (1995) discovered, teachers and program developers interpret the ILC approach in many ways. As refinements are worked through, such as the strengthening of language development, it will be essential to diffuse the findings widely in practice. In addition, there are a proliferation of second language education contexts in which ILC operates – content-based language instruction, sheltered content instruction, adjunct programs, immersion and two-way immersion – and the appropriate role and adaptation of ILC strategies needs to be sorted out. There is a need for more research on the effectiveness of ILC instruction in comparison with other instructional approaches. Work on implementation will also certainly touch on teacher development and assessment issues as well. See reviews by Brumfit in Volume 6; by Ricento in Volume 1; by Faltis in Volume 5; and by Widdowson in this volume.

Center for Applied Linguistics, USA

REFERENCES

American Council on the Teaching of Foreign Languages: 1996, *Standards for Foreign Language Learning: Preparing for the 21st Century*, ACTFL, Yonkers, NY.

August, D. & Pease-Alvarez, C.: 1996, *Attributes of Effective Programs and Classrooms Serving English Language Learners*, National Center for Research on Cultural Diversity and Second Language Learning, Santa Cruz, CA and Washington, DC.

Brinton, D.M., Snow, M.A. & Wesche, M.B.: 1989, *Content-Based Second Language Instruction*, Harper & Row, New York.

Chamot, A.U. & O'Malley, J.M.: 1994, *The CALLA Handbook: Implementing the Cognitive Academic Language Learning Approach*, Addison-Wesley, Reading, MA.

Christian, D.: 1996, 'Two-way immersion education: Students learning through two languages', *The Modern Language Journal* 80, 66–76.

Christian, D. & Whitcher, A.: 1995, *Two-Way Bilingual Education in the United States: A Directory of Programs*, National Center for Research on Cultural Diversity and Second Language Learning, Santa Cruz, CA and Washington, DC.

Christian D., Spanos, G., Crandall, J.A., Simich-Dudgeon, C. & Willetts, K.: 1990, 'Integrating language and content for second-language students', in A. Padilla, C. Valadez & H. Fairchild (eds.), *Bilingual Education: Issues and Strategies*, Sage, Newbury Park, CA, 141–156.

Collier, V.P.: 1987, 'Age and rate of acquisition of second language for academic purposes', *TESOL Quarterly* 21, 617–641.

Corson, D.: 1995, *Using English Words*, Kluwer, Boston and Amsterdam.

Crandall, J.A. (ed.): 1995, *ESL through Content-Area Instruction*, Delta Systems Co., McHenry, IL.

Crandall, J.A.: 1993, 'Content-centered learning in the United States', in W. Grabe (ed.), *Annual Review of Applied Linguistics* 13, Cambridge University Press, New York, 111–126.

Cummins, J.: 1981, 'The role of primary language development in promoting educational success for language minority students', in California State Department of Education (ed.), *Schooling and Language Minority Students: A Theoretical Framework*, Los Angeles, California State University: Evaluation, Dissemination and Assessment Center, 3–49.

Enright, S. & McCloskey, M.L.: 1989, *Integrating English: Developing English Language and Literacy in the Multilingual Classroom*, Addison-Wesley, Reading, MA.

Genesee, F.: 1987, *Learning Through Two Languages. Studies of Immersion and Bilingual Education*, Newbury House, Cambridge, MA.

Genesee, F.: 1994, *Integrating Language and Content: Lessons from Immersion*, Education Practice Report 11, National Center for Research on Cultural Diversity and Second Language Learning, Santa Cruz, CA and Washington, DC.

Harley, B., Allen, P., Cummins, J. & Swain, M. (eds.): 1990, *Development of Second Language Proficiency*, Cambridge University Press, Cambridge.

Kauffman, D.: 1994, *Content-ESL Across the USA*, ERIC Clearinghouse on Languages and Linguistics, Center for Applied Linguistics, Washington, DC.

Krashen, S.: 1982, *Principals and Practice in Second Language Acquisition*, Pergamon, Oxford.

Krashen, S. & Terrell, T.: 1983, *The Natural Approach: Language Acquisition in the Classroom,* Aleany, Hayward, CA.

Lambert, W.E. & Tucker, G.R.: 1972, *Bilingual Education of Children: The St. Lambert Experiment*, Newbury House, Rowley, MA.

Mohan, B.A.: 1986, *Language and Content*, Addison-Wesley, Reading, MA.

Ontario Ministry of Education and Training: 1995, *Language Standards of the Common Curriculum*, Ontario Ministry of Education and Training, Ottawa, Ontario (draft).

Saville-Troike, M.: 1984, 'What really matters in second language learning for academic achievement?', *TESOL Quarterly* 18, 199–220.

Sheppard, K.: 1995, *Content-ESL Across the USA. Volume 1. A Technical Report*. Center for Applied Linguistics, Washington, DC.

Short, D.: 1991, *How to Integrate Language and Content Instruction*, Center for Applied Linguistics, Washington, DC.

Short, D.: 1994, 'Expanding middle school horizons: Integrating language, culture, and social studies', *TESOL Quarterly* 28(3), 581–608.

Snow, M.A., Met, M. & Genesee, F.: 1989, 'A conceptual framework for the integration of language and content in second/foreign language instruction', *TESOL Quarterly* 23(2), 201–217.

Spanos, G.A., Rhodes, N.C., Dale, T.C. & Crandall J.A.: 1988, 'Linguistic features of mathematical problem solving', in R.C. Cocking & J.P. Mestre (eds.), *Linguistic and Cultural Influences on Learning Mathematics,* Lawrence Erlbaum, Hillsdale, NJ, 221–240.

Swain, M.: 1985, 'Communicative competence: Some roles of comprehensible input and comprehensible output in its development', in S. Gass & C. Madden (eds.), *Input in Second Language Acquisition*, Newbury House, Cambridge, MA.

Swain, M.: 1995, *Issues in Immersion Pedagogy*, Conference on Research and Practice in Immersion Education: Looking Back and Looking Forward, University of Minnesota (to appear in proceedings).

Teachers of English to Speakers of Other Languages, Inc. (TESOL): 1997, *ESL Standards for Pre-K-12 Students* TESOL, Alexandria, VA.

BERNHARD KETTEMANN

INNOVATIVE SECOND LANGUAGE EDUCATION IN WESTERN EUROPE

Second language education in the sense of foreign language teaching and learning has been a long established political priority in Western Europe and is now receiving increased attention triggered by the process of European integration.

A considerable amount of second language oriented research is being carried out and learning and teaching innovations are being tested in trial runs, some of which are being implemented in some countries. As a result, a number of new insights have influenced the present teaching practices in various ways and certain common trends can be observed all over Western Europe, despite the existing linguistic, cultural, political and social diversity.

First of all, language education in primary education (early learning) is increasing in importance nowadays. Secondly, language education in secondary education has seen some changes in the last few years and some of these will be referred to in this review, and thirdly, there will also be some co-ordination of second language education on the tertiary, or university level (by means of e.g. the EU-funded "SIGMA"-Project), and in other advanced adult language education, including vocationally oriented education and training, and teacher training.

Teaching some measure of communicative ability in a second language to a large proportion of the European population is important in order to facilitate free movement of people and ideas, to intensify cooperation in all sectors of society, to improve and widen access to information, to overcome prejudice and national (auto- and hetero-) stereotypes, to lay the linguistic foundations for a European citizenship and the preservation of cultural diversity. Communicative ability will therefore cover not only linguistic competence, but also e.g. social, cultural, discourse and compensatory competences.

EARLY HISTORY

During the Middle Ages the churches (Christian, Jewish, Muslim) were the institutions responsible for the educational system in Western Europe. Latin was taught systematically, with the help of classical grammar books, and used as a *lingua franca* in politics and education. Modern languages

G. R. Tucker and D. Corson (eds), Encyclopedia of Language and Education,
Volume 4: Second Language Education, 175–186.
© *1997 Kluwer Academic Publishers. Printed in the Netherlands.*

were not taught, classical Greek, which had been an important part of the Roman education system, was neglected, probably because unlike Latin it was of little practical use in the Catholic church (cf. Titone, 1986).

The expansion of trade in the late medieval and early modern periods necessitated some instruction in modern languages, yet unsystematic as needs arose, with the help of native or bilingual speakers (cf. Schröder, 1989–94). In the wake of the Renaissance, classical Greek was rediscovered and has formed an integral part of humanistic education ever since.

In the 16th century, following the reformation, the construction of national identities and the development of nation states slowly moved education from the churches towards the state. It also caused educational reformers like J.A. Comenius, Protestant bishop of Moravia (1592–1670) to emphasize the necessity for the additional teaching of the mother tongues, second and 'neighboring' languages. The common teaching method for these foreign languages was designed to meet basic communicative needs and therefore differed largely from the grammar-translation oriented approach used for the classical languages. In the absence of dictionaries and grammars, the instruction was usually carried out by native speakers using early equivalents of direct, communicative or natural approaches, with textbooks containing mainly exemplary dialogues. The first modern language to be taught systematically (to the upper class) in many European countries was French, the European *lingua franca* of the 17th and 18th centuries.

At the end of the 18th century, the educational ideals of Neoclassicism led to a neglect of utilitaristic aspects in language teaching, stressing the virtues of systematic grammar teaching and classical texts for the development of intellect and reason. Consequently, the grammar-translation method was used not only for Latin and Greek, but also for modern languages. While the choice of languages and the extent of foreign language teaching was very varied in the 19th century and up to the end of World War II, depending on the political, social and economic requirements of the respective period, region and political system, the grammar-translation approach was used all over Western Europe for over a century. Nevertheless, there were considerable differences in the style and organization of language teaching, not only between countries, but also between languages and institutions (cf. Stern, 1983).

In the last decades of the nineteenth century, a number of reform movements tried to emancipate modern language education from the classics (e.g., Berlitz & Viëtor, 1882; Jespersen, 1904). They were accompanied by the foundation of important new organizations (e.g., the MLA in 1883 or the IPA in 1886) and triggered an intensive debate on language teaching which has gone on ever since. After World War I, compromises were sought in the form of 'practical' solutions like the reading approach (West, 1926; Coleman, 1929), but these didn't improve the teaching practice substantially, and attention gradually turned towards new theoretical disciplines that could support the development of language teaching, like linguistics and psychology.

World War II effectively put an end to a number of attempts at a methodological reform during the interwar period and brought about a radically new approach which was then known (in the US) as the 'Army method'. In order to cope with the communication problems that arose in World War II, the U.S. Army had developed the audiolingual method, which focused on the needs of the learner rather than the skills of the teacher. This approach, which was later paralleled by similar developments in European countries, came to be influenced by two different theories: first, behaviorism, which saw language learning as a change in linguistic behavior that could be achieved in sequences of meticulously planned small steps, ultimately automatized by *pattern drills*, and secondly structural linguistics in its distributional variant, which provided the combinatory units and structural descriptions of language required for this method of language learning. Audiovisual presentation was later added as an effective way of presenting language patterns (cf. Macht, 1986–1990). In addition, new media (e.g. language labs) and new organizational patterns (e.g. 'immersion' courses) were developed, however, these innovations eventually failed to bring about the results that had been expected.

In the 1950s and 1960s, the economic boom of the post-war period increased the number of immigrants in Western Europe. This development created a need for tailor-made instruction in 'basic' language skills. One of the first attempts to develop a framework for this was the *Français fondamental* program (1954/1959). It resulted in a catalogue of fundamental linguistic means, containing 1,445 words and simple structures, selected by a French governmental commission according to their frequency and usefulness in everyday situations (cf. Pfeffer, 1964 *Grunddeutsch*, Caravolas, 1994). This led to the development of textbooks following these criteria, in France as well as in a number of other countries, and it prepared the way for a number of further developments of the learner-centered approach which have been co-ordinated by the Council of Europe since 1964, when the *Modern Languages Project* was initiated.

MAJOR CONTRIBUTIONS

Innovations in second language education in Europe are coordinated and mainly directed by the Council of Europe in Strasbourg within a common framework of reference as to the aims, methods and evaluation of language teaching in Europe. Major steps in the development of modern language teaching have been

Threshold level (1975, van Ek/Trim, 1991a) and Waystage (1977, van Ek/Trim, 1991b)

Communication in the modern languages classroom (Sheils, 1988)

Common European framework of reference for language learning (Trim, 1995).

The Threshold Level (van Ek/Trim, 1991a) provided a first specification of the minimum second language material a learner should be able to use for communication in a wide variety of everyday situations. Waystage is a still further selection of linguistic means from the Threshold level (van Ek/Trim, 1991b). The Threshold Level was warmly received by methodologists in the field because of its shift of emphasis from form to function. It was this "pragmatic turn" that marked the new curricula and in their wake the series of new textbooks initiating the communicative approach in Western Europe in the early eighties. This development was then taken one step further by introducing meaning (or intention) – based notional didactic grammars (e.g. Leech/Svartvik, 1975; Newby, 1989). This provided a new motivation for grammar teaching inside communicative language teaching (e.g. Jones, 1979).

At the same time communicative language teaching (e.g. Brumfit/Johnson, 1979) moved from the curriculum and the textbook to the classroom through a concerted effort in teacher training by series of workshops in Europe, cf. Communication in the modern languages classroom (Sheils, 1988).

WORK IN PROGRESS

The third and most recent innovation in second language education is the development of a common European framework of reference for continuing (secondary and adult) second language learning by providing transparency and coherence in language learning. This is to be achieved by agreeing on well defined reference points concerning the objectives, the procedures for assessment, and the systems of certification of certain degrees of communicative proficiency in Europe, cf. Trim (1992 and 1995).

The following represent what I consider the main innovative areas of major or general interest in second language learning and teaching in Western Europe. These are:

1. objectives specification

2. teaching methods and didactic principles

3. materials development, use of media and new technologies

4. bilingual teaching and the use of foreign language as the medium of content based instruction in other (non-language) subjects,

5. educational visits and exchanges, school links, twinnings

6. learner-centered teaching, learner autonomy, learning to learn

7. evaluation and assessment of communicative proficiency

8. initial and in-service teacher training

9. learning and teaching modern languages in primary schools

10. cultural competence and cultural (intercultural / multicultural) aware-ness, language learning for European citizenship

11. continuity in language teaching between primary and secondary schools

Each of these will now be reviewed briefly.

1. Objectives Specification

The objectives of second language education have been related to the needs, motivations, characteristics and resources of the learners, and to the socio-cultural dimensions. This is especially relevant for the teaching of heterogenous groups. At the moment a specification of objectives and evaluation criteria for vocationally-oriented language learning in upper secondary, vocational (age 15–20) and adult education are being developed (cf. Lampola, 1991).

2. Teaching Methods and Didactic Principles

Although a broad communicative, functional-notional approach underlies many modern textbooks in Europe, its introduction into all school systems is far from complete. There still are "pockets" of grammar-translation and the audiolingual methodology. It is clear that an innovation in curricula and syllabi does not necessarily imply a change in teaching habits. This is where teacher trainers still have to act as agents of change. Neverthe-less a strong tendency towards communicative teaching can be observed throughout Europe, which implies that grammar is introduced in the role of servant to and prerequisite for communication and not as a means to lin-guistic accuracy. On the other hand, there still are some problems with the introduction of the communicative method, as shortcomings of commu-nicative textbooks and other materials or constraints of evaluation systems. For additional information on teaching methods, see Stern (1983).

The Council of Europe has acted as a source of innovation in establishing a coherent system of language learning and teaching in Europe. Although several unifying measures, e.g. the Threshold level, have been widely accepted, there still are considerable differences between the curricula and syllabi for second language education in various countries. A general consensus seems to have been reached , though, on some didactic principles for second language education throughout Western Europe. Some of these are:

> motivate pupils and arouse their interest and curiosity, e.g. by authentic and topical material and an inductive approach

> refer to things that pupils already know before presenting new material

> use a variety of techniques and methods in single, partner, group and class work

> use a variety of media and materials, including multi-/hypermedia

> enhance input variety, opportunity for exploration, appropriacy and authenticity

> motivate pupils to perform well by positive feed-back

> reserve enough time for cyclic repetition

> establish links between subject matter and language and aim at interdisciplinary teaching

> include project work, practical work

> train pupils to work independently to gather information and to work co-operatively to share information

> prepare students for life-long learning

3. Materials Development, Use of Media and New Technologies

Several projects in Europe have been set up, e.g. information exchange networks, using the Internet. Materials and programs are being developed and momentarily needs and strategies for the successful use of information technologies as part of language training programs are being identified. Multi-media/hypermedia software is to be used in the teaching of foreign languages as well as computer/data show system in second language classrooms. As additional tools to enhance input variety, exploration, appropriacy and authenticity CD-Rom, the World Wide Web and the Internet are recommended to be used. Another newly developed means to enrich the teaching of foreign languages is the application of concordancing, which can be used for the inductive teaching and learning of vocabulary (collocations) and of certain grammar rules, cf. Kettemann (1995), IT Works (1994), Jung (1988), Jung (this volume), Hardisty/Windeatt, 1989).

4. Bilingual Teaching and the Use of the Foreign Language as the Medium of Instruction in Other (Non-Language) Subjects (or, Content Teaching)

Bilingual education, in the sense of the use of more than one language as the medium of communication and instruction in schools, both in bilingual areas with territorial and non-territorial ethnic minorities and in mainstream education in predominantly monolingual areas started in the late sixties and early seventies and at present is spreading in school systems throughout Europe (e.g. Lycée International, Lyon with five different language pairs, among them e.g. French/English, French/German, French/Japanese; Vienna Bilingual School and Graz International Bilingual School with Austrian German/English; there are more than 200 bilingual sections in secondary education in Germany with a wide variety of language pairs, e.g. German/French, German/English, German/Spanish, German/Italian, German/Russian, German/Dutch, German/Polish).

Educational concepts for multilingual countries and regions are being developed (cf. Baker, 1993). Multilingualism in migrant communities and education for children of highly mobile families are of interest. Materials to use a foreign language as medium of instruction in other non-language subjects are being developed and several projects are being carried out throughout Western Europe. For examples see Baetens-Beardsmore (1993), Paulston (1988) and reviews in Volume 5.

5. Educational Visits and Exchanges, School Links, Twinnings

There is a growing number of school exchanges in second language education which are arranged on the basis of individual pupils, groups of pupils or entire classes (cf. Savage, 1992; Haugen, 1995). These exchanges seem to have a positive effect as they increase the motivation of pupils to keep learning a foreign language. This positive effect clearly translates into emphasizing school exchanges and international links and twinnings in the future. This means the full curricular integration and exploitation of visits and exchanges of all kinds by means of developing international networks among all European countries.

6. Learner-Centered Teaching, Learner Autonomy, Learning to Learn

Learner strategies and learner autonomy in secondary education (age 10–19) and adult education are receiving increased attention (cf. Holec, 1980, 1988). This includes work on awareness of the learning process, learning to learn, learning strategies, reflective learning and learner independence. Communication in the classroom is seen as a necessary and integral part of the teaching and learning processes, which is viewed as a process of cognitive construction and reconstruction. Teachers should facilitate the learning strategies and cognitive processes, in short the activity of the language learner vis-à-vis the input. Recent findings in second language acquisition research suggest that the importance attributed to language input and general cognitive constructivist strategies of information processing and problem solving should be increased (cf. Oxford, this volume).

The problem the learner has to solve in language acquisition is "to crack the code" behind the input. This is achieved by the learner in a constant process of cognitive construction and restructuring, using his or her problem-solving capabilities as strategies to create order (by rule-formation) out of a chaos of information (the language input).

This clearly works best if the learner becomes personally involved by more exploratory and experiential tasks. As experience feeds into the construction of knowledge, it is hoped to facilitate this construction. Thus the pupils' ability to learn can be enhanced. Teachers should develop explicit objectives and practices to encourage methods of discovery and analysis. These are considered to be important skills for subsequent independent language learning in a move towards life-long learning.

7. Evaluation and Assessment of Communicative Proficiency

Attempts are made to locate evaluation, testing and assessment of communicative proficiency in the areas of comprehension, production, interaction (by e.g. information gap tasks, creative listening tasks) in a coherent and transparent system with fixed points of reference (cf. Green, 1987). Testing takes on an additional function as a means of providing feedback to all parties concerned with the learning process and its results. A more structured approach to the aspect of testing could feed into modular components comprising a personal document, comparable to a passport, a "European Language Portfolio", cf. Trim (1992), Shohamy (this volume) and reviews in Volume 7.

The International Association for the Evaluation of Educational Achievement's Language Education Study was supposed to provide a comparison and evaluation of the outcomes of different educational systems across Europe, but sofar only the political and social conditions in which the educational systems operate and language learning takes place have been analyzed, cf. Dickson/Cumming (1996) or Landsiedler (1997).

8. Initial and In-Service Teacher Training

As far as initial teacher training is concerned, there are considerable differences between countries, but attempts are made to coordinate issues relating to methodology (activities, techniques, tools), evaluation, organization and content in initial and in-service teacher training. Especially significant for encouraging innovations are internationally organized series of seminars and workshops for in-service training held regularly all over Western Europe by the various cultural institutes (e.g. British Council, Institut Français, Amerikahaus, Goetheinstitut), private language schools (e.g. Pilgrims, Eurocenters), and also on the local level by teacher trainer institutions. This includes the production, evaluation and selection of support materials in modular form, including e.g. hypermedia downloadable from the Interned at training centers.

9. Learning and Teaching Modern Languages in Primary Schools

A tendency to be observed in almost all Western European countries is the increasing stress on second languages in primary education (ages 6–10), after a certain period of neglect following the Burstall (1974) report. A number of different models can now be found. In some countries pupils start learning a second language at the age of eight (e.g. Austria, Germany, Italy, Spain), at the age of nine (e.g. Greece, France), at the age of ten (e.g. Scotland). In most European countries projects and trial runs of different models are being carried out and evaluated.

Generally speaking, the age of pupils learning the first second language in the European Union varies between the age of 8 and 11 years. In most countries English is the predominant language in the area of primary education. French can be chosen alternatively in some countries, e.g. Germany, Greece, Italy, Portugal, Spain, but English is nevertheless the most widely chosen language. In some cases pupils can choose between a number of other languages, but these other languages are very rarely chosen. The number of hours per week devoted to this early second language education generally ranges from two to three hours, although in some areas (like some parts of Belgium and Luxembourg) second language instruction in primary education ranges from five to eight hours per week.

10. Cultural Competence and Cultural (Intercultural/Multicultural) Awareness, Language Learning for European Citizenship

In addition to the development of the learners' communicative competence, modern language programs in schools now aim to develop their progressive independence of thought and action combined with social responsibility, as well as their acceptance of and respect for the histories and cultures of other peoples, historical and cultural empathy. This aim involves analyzing and where appropriate questioning the history and culture of the learners' own country as well as that of others (cf. Byram, 1989; Byram/Morgan, 1994; Kramsch, 1993; Tomalin/Stempleski; 1993).

11. Continuity in Language Education Between Primary and Secondary Schools

In all Western European countries the majority of pupils have the possibility of learning at least one second language when starting secondary school. In most countries pupils start at the age of 10 to 12 years. In most countries this first foreign language is a compulsory subject or at least as an optional subject till the end of compulsory schooling.

A second foreign language is a compulsory subject in some countries. At present proposals are being discussed to include two language subjects in secondary education until the school leaving examination (e.g. Netherlands). There are plans in Greece to introduce a compulsory second foreign language for their pupils. In some countries languages can be chosen as optional subjects and pupils can learn a third foreign language either on a compulsory basis (e.g. Luxembourg, Netherlands) or on an optional basis (e.g. Belgium, Germany etc.).

The most commonly chosen foreign language in Western Europe is English and the second position is held by French. There seems to be a tendency in many school systems towards an increased diversification of this choice. At present, it is impossible to say whether this move will be successful.

PROBLEMS, DIFFICULTIES AND FUTURE DIRECTIONS

The present developments (communicative approach, authenticity, topicality, new media) in second language teaching and learning call upon teachers to define new roles for themselves, which require additional skills and new attitudes. Teacher training will have to provide motivation and input to effect these changes. Teacher trainers and teachers and their students will have to act as agents of change.

There are additional problems with the low status of teachers in some countries, widespread cuts in educational funding, multilingual classrooms in focal areas of immigration throughout Western Europe and organizational problems with diversification (flexible interest grouping, streaming).

Evaluation in all its aspects, from the national curricula down to error classification still present as great a challenge for all educational systems as ever. Vocational language teaching, as well as offering opportunities for life-long language learning, the teaching of foreign languages in primary schools and the goal of a working knowledge of two foreign languages for every European citizen are new challenges that have to be met by the educational systems in Western Europe.

Universität Graz, Austria

REFERENCES

Baetens-Beardsmore, H.: 1993, *European Models of Bilingual Education*, Multilingual Matters, Clevedon.

Baker, C.: 1993, *Foundations of Bilingual Education and Bilingualism*, Multilingual Matters, Clevedon.

Brumfit, C.J. & Johnson, K. (eds.): 1979, *The Communicative Approach to Language Teaching*, Oxford University Press, Oxford.

Burstall, C. et al.: 1974, *Primary French in the Balance*, NFER, Windsor.

Byram, M.: 1989, *Cultural Studies in Foreign Language Education*, Multilingual Matters, Clevedon.

Byram, M., Morgan, C. et al.: 1994, *Teaching-and-Learning Language-and-Culture*, Multilingual Matters, Clevedon.

Caravolas, J.: 1994, *La didactique des langues. Précis d'histoire I*, Montréal/Tübingen.

Coleman, A.: 1929, *The Teaching of Modern Foreign Languages in the United States*, Macmillan, New York.

Dickson, P. & Cumming, A. (eds.): 1996, *National Profiles of Language Education in 25 Countries*, IEA, Amsterdam.

Fremdsprachenunterricht im Primar- und Sekundarbereich in der Europäischen Gemeinschaft: 1992, European Commission, Brüssel.

Français fondamental, 1er degré: 1954 (rev. ed. 1959), Paris.

Green, P.S. (ed.): 1987, *Communicative Language Testing*, Council of Europe, Strasbourg.

Hardisty, D. & Windeatt, S.: 1989, *CALL*, Oxford University Press, Oxford.

Haugen, O.: 1995, *The role of educational links and exchanges at secondary level (Council of Europe: Report on Workshop 18A)*, Council of Europe, Lillehammer/Strasbourg.

Holec, H.: 1980, *Autonomy and Foreign Language Learning*, Council of Europe, Strasbourg.

Holec, H. (ed.): 1988, *Autonomy and Self-directed Learning: Present Fields of Application*, Council of Europe, Strasbourg.

IT (Information Technology) Works: 1994, National Council for Educational Technology, Coventry.

Jespersen, O.: 1904, *How to Teach a Foreign Language*, Allen & Unwin, London.

Jones, L.: 1979, *Notions in English. A Course in Effective Communication for Upper-Intermedieate and More Advanced Students*, Cambridge University Press, Cambridge.

Jung, U.O.H. (ed.): 1988, *Computers in Applied Linguistics and Language Teaching*, Frankfurt/M.

Kettemann, B.: 1995, 'On the use of concordancing in ELT', *Arbeiten aus Anglistik und Amerikanistik* 20(1), 29–41.

Kramsch, C.: 1993, *Context and Culture in Language Teaching*, Oxford University Press, Oxford.

Lampola, R. (ed.): 1991, *"Learning to learn" languages in vocationally oriented education, (= Council of Europe: Report on Workshop 6A)*, Council of Europe, Tampere/Strasbourg.

Landsiedler, I., Kettemann, B., Kerschbaumer, M. & Cossée, M.: 1997, 'Foreign language education in Austria', *Language Learning Journal* 17 (in press).

Leech, G. & Svartvik, J.: 1975, *A Communicative Grammar of English*, Longman, London.

Macht, K.: 1986–1990, *Methodengeschichte des Englischunterrichts*, Augsburg.

Newby, D.: 1989, *Grammar for Communication*, Bundesverlag, Vienna.

Paulston, C.B. (ed.): 1988, *International Handbook of Bilingualism and Bilingual Education*, Greenwood Press, New York.

Pfeffer, A.: 1964, *Grunddeutsch. Basic (Spoken) German Word List*, Prentice Hall, Englewood Cliffs, NJ.

Savage, R.: 1992, *School Links & Exchanges in Europe. A Practical Guide*, Council of Europe, Strasbourg.

Schlüsselzahlen zum Bildungswesen in der Europäischen Union: 1995, European Commission, Brüssel.

Schröder, K.: 1989–94, *Biographisches und bibliographisches Lexikon der Fremdsprachenlehrer des deutschsprachigen Raumes*, University of Augsburg, Augsburg.

Sheils, J.: 1988, *Communication in the modern languages classroom*, Council of Europe, Strasbourg.

Stern, H.H.: 1983, *Fundamental Concepts of Language Teaching*, Oxford University Press, Oxford.

Titone, R.: 1986, *Cinque millenni di insegnamento delle lingue*, Brescia.

Tomalin, B. & Stempleski, S.: 1993, *Cultural Awareness*, Oxford University Press, Oxford.

Trim, J.L.M.: 1992, *Transparency and coherence in language learning in Europe*, Council of Europe, Strasbourg.

Trim, J.L.M.: 1993, *Action Programs 1990–1995: Report on the progress made during 1992 in Action Programs undertaken within the Project and their future prospects*, Council of Europe, Strasbourg.

Trim, J.L.M.: 1995, *Recent Developments on a Common European Framework of Reference for Modern Language Learning and Teaching*, Council of Europe, Strasbourg.

van Ek, J.A. & Trim, J.L.M.: 1991a, *Threshold Level 1990*, Council of Europe, Strasbourg.

van Ek, J.A. & Trim, J.L.M.: 1991b, *Waystage 1990*, Council of Europe, Strasbourg.

Viëtor, W. ('Quousque tandem'): 1882, *Der Sprachunterricht muss umkehren! Ein Beitrag zur Ueberbuerdungsfrage*, Henninger, Heilbronn.

West, M.P.: 1926, *Learning to Read a Foreign Language*, Longmans, Green & Co., New York.

PÉTER MEDGYES

INNOVATIVE SECOND LANGUAGE EDUCATION IN CENTRAL AND EASTERN EUROPE

For several decades, many people in the West were underinformed about life behind the 'iron curtain'. They viewed the countries of central and eastern Europe as look-alikes, with hardly any national or local traits worthy of note. This misconception seems to hold even today though the number of nation states has more than doubled since 1989–90, creating one of the most multi-faceted communities in the world.

This diversity is characteristic of language use too. Although Slavonic speakers form an overwhelming majority, other Indo-European languages (Albanian, Latvian, Lithuanian and Romanian) as well as languages of Finno-Ugrian origin (Estonian and Hungarian) are also represented in the region. However, with the exception of German and Russian, all the official languages are of limited currency beyond the national frontiers. Therefore, the knowledge of a *lingua franca* has always been considered a priority issue, and second languages have occupied a distinctive place in the school curriculum.

SECOND LANGUAGE EDUCATION DURING THE COMMUNIST ERA

The countries of central and eastern Europe may be divided into three fairly distinctive groups. The first group consisted of member states of the Soviet Union. Russian was the mother tongue of the majority of the population but even for non-Russian nationals a native-like command of the Russian language was a passport to a successful career.

The second group comprised five satellite countries (Bulgaria, Czechoslovakia, the German Democratic Republic, Hungary and Poland). After the communist takeover (1948–49), Russian became the compulsory language in all types of school. For forty years thereafter, every student received 8–10 years of Russian language instruction, followed by another 2–3 years at university. The low cost-effectiveness of Russian teaching was apparent, as were the political motives which maintained it in the curriculum. Whereas the teaching of western languages was banned or strictly curbed in the darkest period of Stalinism, from around the 1970s these languages made a gradual comeback, albeit never challenging the pride of place assigned to the Russian language. The most spectacular return of western languages was witnessed in Bulgaria; every major town

G.R. Tucker and D. Corson (eds), Encyclopedia of Language and Education,
Volume 4: Second Language Education, 187–196.
© *1997 Kluwer Academic Publishers. Printed in the Netherlands.*

ran special schools where certain curricular subjects were taught in Russian *or* in a western language (Radoulova, 1996).

The third group included the 'pariahs'. In Yugoslavia Russian was never a compulsory school subject while in Albania and Romania its mandatory status was suspended along with their political alienation from the Soviet Union.

In all countries of central and eastern Europe, however, the overall standard of instruction of western languages was not much higher than that of Russian. This was primarily due to the lack of learner motivation – most people only had limited opportunities to use these languages owing to restrictions on travel and access to the mass media. As Healey pointed out, 'until 1989, the learning of English and other "western languages" was treated as an intellectual and social accomplishment [. . .] comparable with playing a musical instrument, dancing the waltz and polka, or reading poetry' (1993: p.13). As regards the status of English specifically, it 'was low bordering on subversive' (Gill, 1993: p. 15).

The oppressive system nothwithstanding, second language education was not an arid land. For example, one of the most seminal innovations in second language education, Lozanov's Suggestopedia (1979), was conceived and piloted in Bulgaria. At the same time, there was a group of highly professional and erudite language educators in every country of the region; these experts were to be highly instrumental in jump-starting changes when the communist dictatorships collapsed.

STUDENT DEMAND AND TEACHER SUPPLY

In the past few years, second language education has made rapid progress. This may be chiefly attributed to the increased need for the knowledge of languages – English in the first place, followed by German, and at quite a distance by French and Spanish.

The generation brought up during the communist era is still suffering the consequences of 'second language illiteracy'. Since good communicative abilities in one or two second languages are a standard condition for application in an increasing number of jobs, millions of adults spare no time and energy in their efforts to learn languages (Kazaritskaya, 1996). Private language schools are full to bursting with customers even though, as Hartinger observes, 'many people have realized that it was easier to pull down the barbed wire on the border than it has been to cross the [. . .] language barrier' (1993: p. 33).

Young people are much better off. Since 1989–90 when the Russian language was stripped of its privileged status, they have enjoyed a free choice of second languages at school. Unfortunately, the system only works in theory because the sudden surge of interest in English and German has created an acute shortage of teachers. An aggravating factor is that thousands of qualified language teachers have been leaving the profession in favor of lucrative jobs in business, commerce, banking and tourism. Large numbers of teachers have also been syphoned off by private language schools offering much higher salaries than state schools.

To alleviate the shortfall, school principals are obliged to employ anyone who claims to have a smattering of English or German. The most obvious candidate is the Russian teacher whose work has suddenly become superfluous. Another possibility is to hire unqualified teachers; young native-speaking backpackers are a common sight in schools. As a last resort, principals may continue to impose Russian on the students simply because second language instruction is stipulated by law (Medgyes, 1993; Fisiak, 1994).

Meanwhile, governments have also been taking measures to ease the mismatch between supply and demand. One such undertaking, the Russian retraining program, helps teachers of Russian to become fully qualified teachers of another language. A project on a much larger scale has been the introduction of fast-track schemes.

THE FAST-TRACK PROGRAM IN POLAND

Although this innovative form of initial teacher education is vigorously expanding in several countries (Griffiths, 1995; Medgyes & Malderez, 1996), Poland seems to have created the most ambitious and firmly established system for the training of English teachers (Komorowska, 1991).

The fast-track program in Poland is run at 52 teacher-training colleges. These colleges are divided into eight clusters; each cluster is academically supervised by the nearest regional university and supported by the British Council. With a total output of around 1,500 graduates per year, this program has significantly contributed to the national goal of producing 20,000 English teachers by 2001. Upon graduation, 55 percent have found employment in state schools – an outstanding figure compared, for example, to the 10 percent ratio in Russia (Belyaeva, personal communication).

The fast-track program is different from traditional degree programs in two major respects. On the one hand, it is two years shorter in duration. On the other, practical methodology and teaching practice are granted a much larger scope than is customary in philology tracks. According to some estimates, fast-track graduates are superior to their university counterparts in terms of practical teaching skills, and are comparable in terms of language competence.

The success of fast-track programs has encouraged certain traditional university departments to give more weight to the teacher training components in their curriculum. Others have introduced practice-oriented civilization courses (Stone, 1993) and MA (even PhD) programs in Language Pedagogy and/or Applied Linguistics (Medgyes & Malderez, 1996). This indicates that second language education is beginning to be recognized as an academic discipline in some countries. In other places, however, fast-track programs are likely to be disbanded once the problem of teacher shortage has been solved.

THE TEACHING PRACTICE IN HUNGARY

The fast-track program in the Centre for English Teacher Training in Budapest has gained international acclaim mainly due to its teaching practice component (Bodóczky & Malderez, 1996). In this scheme, trainee teachers take over the responsibility for the teaching of one class in a secondary or primary school. Throughout this period, they are supported by a school-based mentor, their trainee partner and a university-based tutor.

This system displays at least three innovative features. The first one concerns the duration of the internship period. Instead of a few weeks, which is the standard length in most training systems, the Centre requires its trainees to teach for a full school-year. This mode of teaching practice is based on the assumption that an extended period of time is needed to gain self-confidence and learn the long-term aspects of a teacher's work.

Secondly, trainees are obliged to teach in pairs. The rationale is that working in close partnership with a peer not only provides additional support and fosters the idea of teacher co-operation, but also helps trainees guard against 'isolation stress' in their future career.

Finally, the school-based mentors receive special training before they are commissioned to look after the trainees. This mentor course is designed to develop an understanding of reflective practice and the necessary skills for its implementation. Reflective practice (Wallace, 1991) implies that, instead of internalizing the mentor's view and model of teaching, trainees are encouraged to teach on the basis of their own constructs and experience evolved prior to and during their internship period.

INSERVICE TRAINING SCHEMES

As well as establishing a new system of preservice training, second language experts have been concerned with problems of inservice teacher education. One of the most acute concerns is the high proportion of unqualified or underqualified teachers working in the state sector.

In Poland, where this figure stands at 41.2%, a program for unqualified teachers to obtain a license to teach has been launched (Bogucka, 1995). The candidates have to pass an internationally recognised language proficiency examination before they are allowed to enrol in a 280-hour methodology course. This model may be viewed as a bridge between preservice and inservice training (Komorowska, 1994). A similar integrative project is reported to be running in Albania (Drenova, 1995).

The inservice training program in Slovakia has been designed for fully-qualified secondary school teachers of English (Gill, 1993). Run by regional training centres, it consists of six meetings per centre per year. A characteristic feature of this scheme is that it is based on negotiations between trainers and trainees, and attempts to strike a balance between theoretical and practical issues. In the initial stage of the project all the facilitators were imported native English speakers, but even today local expertise is not harnessed in sufficient measure.

In contrast, the pan-Baltic Professional Development Programme relies exclusively on local expertise (Maguire, 1994; Giblin, 1995). In the first two years, each state delegated ten trainers, who would convene once a month to devise communicative materials and plan training sessions. The trainers would then go back to their own country to hold inservice sessions with groups of 15–20 local teachers. Meanwhile, the program has developed into a long-term venture, providing a framework for various forms of continuing education in the region.

In Hungary, a large-scale project has been commissioned by the Ministry of Education (Rádai, 1996). The two-year course for teachers of English consists of successive weekly seminars followed by intensive one-week blocks. Teachers may take one module per semester, each with a duration of 120 hours. After completing a compulsory methodology update module, the participants may choose three from a menu of seven modules.

A general problem that militates against widening the scope for teacher development schemes is the lack of enhanced career prospects. Except for a few countries (e.g. Belarus) where teachers are legally obliged to attend regular refresher courses, programs tend to run on goodwill. Unfortunately, few teachers can afford the luxury of long-term commitment if it means having to give up extra jobs which provide vital extra income. To make matters worse, the majority of school teachers are women who traditionally bear the brunt of household duties.

THE COURSEBOOK PROJECT IN ROMANIA

Before 1989–90, both teachers and learners were compelled to use locally produced teaching materials. Although these materials were usually drab in all respects, they were targeted at the needs of a relatively homogeneous audience.

As soon as the ban on imported books was lifted in 1989–90, the market was inundated by materials, nearly all of them soaked with the ideals of communicative language teaching. As they have a whiff of fresh air and a very attractive appearance, they sell in huge quantities, thus all but ruining capital-poor local publishing.

Among the attempts to create a home-made textbook series, the most comprehensive project has been set in motion in Romania (Bolitho, 1995).

Sponsored by the Ministry of Education, this series is being written for learners of English from grade 5 through grade 12. Apart from a couple of native-speaker advisors, the large team includes only Romanian authors, who are potentially more able to satisfy the specific language learning needs of the Romanian learner. Built around a topic-based, skills-integrated and culture-rich curriculum, every component of the series is being trialed, and teachers are receiving training in how to use it. This undertaking seems to have invigorated the whole English-language teaching profession in Romania, with ripple effects on the teaching of other languages as well.

TOWARDS SUSTAINABILITY

Throughout the area, second language education has been the beneficiary of sizable funds provided by national, bilateral and multilateral sponsoring agencies, including the World Bank, EU-offshoots, The British Council, the United States Information Service and the Peace Corps, the Goethe Institute, the Soros Foundation, as well as emigré organizations.

As a result, places of second language education have managed to procure up-to-date computers and audio-visual facilities, set up teacher's resource and self-access centers, as well as buy large stocks of books and teaching materials. Funds have also enabled local experts to participate in international conferences, workshops, training courses and attachments, and to pursue further studies in a target language country. At the same time, hundreds of in-country and visiting consultants from western countries have come to lend support – their contribution has been truly invaluable!

Nevertheless, heavy reliance on foreign expertise has produced undesirable side-effects. Komorowska (1994) points out, for example, that it was a mistake to involve short-term contractees in making long-term policy decisions; nor was it a good idea to adulate zealots of various trendy ideologies, who only had limited familiarity with local circumstances (Jacobson & Fletcher, 1996). Incidentally, the myth of native speaker superiority is still ubiquitous in the region, which may have something to do with the nonnative teachers' impaired self-esteem (Gill, 1993; Medgyes, 1994).

Worst of all, external support often fails to stimulate local initiatives and occasionally even stifles them. Therefore, it is becoming a general claim that a foreign specialist's work should be assessed primarily on the extent to which s/he has managed to empower local talent, thus contributing to the creation of a *sustainable* system of second language education. In this regard, it is worth considering Fisiak's warning:

> 'Each country can benefit from the experience of other countries. But each country must ultimately devise its own solutions compatible with its traditions. Innovations and modifications

coming from external sources must fit the existing system if they are going to succeed' (1994: p. 7).

PROJECT AND NETWORKING

For several decades, policy decisions had been made by top-level authorities and then passed down for implementation. As a consequence, when the 'project age' arrived in the early 90s places of second language education were in for a shock; even the word 'project' had an alien ring. However, the strict rules of application set by donor agencies forced institutions to adopt a more business-like attitude and seek opportunities to acquire basic management skills. In some countries, special training centers were set up to provide skills in project design, costings, development plans, job descriptions, etc. (Hall, 1995).

Lately, 'project' has become a buzz-word; to illustrate the situation, during the period of 1991–94 at least sixty new English-language projects were established by the British Council in the countries of the former Soviet Union alone (McGovern, 1995)! Although there are still a number of one-off projects, the ultimate aim is to build links and establish synergy between projects, institutions and people (Gough, 1995; Pearson, 1995).

The beneficiaries of support are keen to break old barriers down. Grassroots movements have led to the establishment of a plethora of teacher associations, journals and magazines, conferences, workshops and seminars, even in a country like war-torn Croatia (Jemersic & Krajski Hrsak, 1994).

National frontiers are also loosening up. 'Comradeship', which before 1989–90 consisted in little more than maintaining formal ties between respective ministry, university and trade union leaders, is taking on a new meaning. Erstwhile comrades are beginning to realize that in fact they have a lot to learn from each other (Yeo, 1995).

Numerous fora for networking and partnership have been created. National conferences are becoming international venues. While native speaker teachers have remained priority guests, an increasing number of central and eastern European colleagues are also represented at such gatherings. Professional journals adopt a similar policy: partners from the region not only get on their mailing list, but are welcome contributors as well.

FUTURE DIRECTIONS

This has been but a fragmentary account of the numerous innovative activities being pursued in central and eastern Europe at present. For example, no mention has been made about efforts aimed at:

* reforming national curricula;

* overhauling examination and testing procedures at both national and institutional levels;

* creating a system of teacher appraisal and program/course evaluation;

* providing inspector- and trainer-training courses;

* developing language programs for specific purposes;

* designing an accreditation system for private language schools.

In conclusion, it has to be reiterated that recent developments in second language education were fostered by political and economic forces. In the absence of such pressures, there would be less learner motivation, less involvement of foreign expertise, less monies around and, in turn, less progress. But with all these resources available, second language educators rose to the occasion and mobilized the creative energies which had lain dormant during the repressive years of communist rule. As a teacher from Romania remarked, 'If change is to be implemented, then second language classes are a propitious means of learning and developing democratic values'.

The most spectacular progress hitherto has been registered in countries situated on the 'western rim', which happened to be the first to undergo the historic changes. At the time of writing, it looks as though the wave of development is swiftly moving east. The next few years are likely to bring more news from countries of the former Soviet Union.

ACKNOWLEDGMENTS

I would like to thank all British Council officers who have assisted me in obtaining information and meeting key second language education experts in the region. My special thanks are due to *Yelena Belyaeva* (Russia), *Lutfie Cota* (Albania), *Maria Georgieva* (Bulgaria), *Tatiana Kazaritskaya* (Russia), *Hanna Komorowska* (Poland), *Michaela Pisova* (The Czech Republic), *Aldona Reksniene* (Lithuania), *Evi Saluveer* (Estonia), *Olga Shinkareva* (Belorus) and *Eva Tandlichová* (Slovakia).

Eötvös Loránd University
Hungary

REFERENCES

Bodóczky, C. & Malderez, A.: 1996, 'Out into schools', in P. Medgyes & A. Malderez (eds.), *Changing Perspectives in Teacher Education*, Heinemann English Language Teaching, Oxford, 62–78. (Hungary)

Bogucka, M.: 1995, 'Pilot INSETT Project Gdansk', in J. Greet (ed.), *ELTECS Fourth Annual Conference*, The British Council, Manchester, 46–48.

Bolitho, R.: 1995, 'Introducing the new textbook: a Time of change', *Together* 1(1), 5–13.

Drenova, K.: 1995, 'The role of the foreign language teacher', in J. Greet (ed.), *ELTECS Fourth Annual Conference*, The British Council, Manchester, 62–65.

Fisiak, J.: 1994, 'Training English language teachers in Poland: Recent reform and its future prospects', in C. Gough & A. Jankowska (eds.), *Directions Towards 2000.* Instytut Filologii Angielskiej, UAM, Poznan, 7–15.

Giblin, K.: 1995, 'PDP comes of age', *Prodess News* 9, 2–3.

Gill, S.: 1993, 'Insett in Slovakia: Past simple, present tense, future perfect?', *Perspectives* 2, 15–21.

Gough, C.: 1995, 'Developing synergy between projects', in J. Greet (ed.), *ELTECS Fourth Annual Conference*, The British Council, Manchester, 84–87.

Griffiths, M.: 1995, 'Keeping on track: Curriculum development on the three-year teacher training project in the Czech Republic', *Perspectives* 5, 5–13.

Hall, M.: 1995, 'Training teachers to do business: developing an INSETT mdel in a nw cntext', in J. Greet (ed.), *ELTECS Fourth Annual Conference*, The British Council, Manchester, 49–55.

Hartinger, K.: 1993, 'Why lnguage learning difficulties are not always linguistic', *Perspectives* 1, 33–5.

Healey, R.: 1993, 'The international working language of engineers: A new challenge for teachers of English in Czechoslovakia', *Perspectives* 1, 13–18.

Jacobson, J. & Fletcher, N.: 1994, 'Managing educational change in Romania', *ELT Management Newsletter* 16, 1–8.

Jemersic, J. & Krajski Hrsak, V. (eds.): 1994, *Hupe Newsletter*.

Kazaritskaya, T.A.: 1996, 'Will you be understood in Moscow?', *International Culture Forum Kosmopolit* 5, forthcoming.

Komorowska, H.: 1991, 'Second language teaching in Poland prior to the reform of 1990', in J.E. Alatis (ed.), *Georgetown University Round Table on Languages and Linguistics 1991*, Georgetown University Press, Washington, DC, 501–508.

Komorowska, H.: 1994, 'Curriculum development for in-service teacher education in Poland', *Studia Anglica Posnaniensia*, XXVIII, 113–121.

Lozanov, G.: 1979, *Suggestology and outlines of suggestopedy*, Gordon and Breach Science Publishers, New York.

Maguire, B.: 1994, 'Changes in the trainers', *Prodess News* 5, 2–3.

McGovern, J.: 1995, 'Changing paradigms – the project approach', *Prosper Newsletter* 4, 8–16.

Medgyes, P.: 1993, 'The national L2 curriculum in Hungary', *Annual Review of Applied Linguistics* 13, 24–36.

Medgyes, P.: 1994, *The Non-native Teacher*, Macmillan Publishers Ltd., Hammondsworth.

Medgyes, P. & Malderez, A. (eds.): 1996, *Changing Perspectives in Teacher Education*, Heinemann English Language Teaching, Oxford.

Pearson, I.: 1995, 'An English language teachers' resource centre as a Bbse for projects in staff, curriculum, materials and test development: How one thing leads to another', in J.Greet (ed.), *ELTECS Fourth Annual Conference*, The British Council, Manchester, 80–83.

Rádai, P. (ed.): 1996, *The Hungarian In-service Training Program for Teachers of English*, Centre for English Teacher Training, Budapest, Manuscript.

Radoulova, M.: 1996, 'Problems and prospects of foreign language teaching in Bulgarian schools', *Foreign Language Teaching* 1, 4–18.

Stone, L.A.: 1993, 'MA British studies: a new academic syllabus in Eastern Europe', *Perspectives* 1, 19–23.

Wallace, M.J.: 1991, *Training Foreign Language Language Teachers*, Cambridge University Press, Cambridge.
Yeo, S.: 1995, 'ESP in Slovakia and Romania: More similarities than differences', *Prosper Newsletter* 4, 39–40.

SAMIR ABU-ABSI

INNOVATIVE SECOND LANGUAGE EDUCATION IN THE MIDDLE EAST AND NORTH AFRICA

The region under consideration, the Middle East and North Africa, covers a vast geographical area which consists of over twenty independent nations whose populations represent diverse linguistic, ethnic, religious and historical backgrounds. The majority of people in this region are native speakers of Arabic with the exception of Iran, Israel and Turkey where the predominant languages are Farsi, Hebrew, and Turkish, respectively. The educational systems in the area run the gamut from the utilization of established traditional practices to the exploration and implementation of the most modern curricula and pedagogical approaches. Second language education, as it has evolved in the historical context of the region, is dominated by two languages, English and French, with English currently enjoying a definite advantage in terms of its increasing use. Since the scope of this review does not allow for any extensive coverage of the various situations, it is necessary to focus on certain areas which are representative of the complexity and diversity of the region.

EARLY DEVELOPMENTS

Since its early history, the Middle East has been a multilingual, multicultural region where ethnicity, language and religion have played central roles. In more modern times, the area has had close contact with the West which helped in shaping current policies and practices.

In North Africa, after a long period of French colonial rule during which Arabic was relegated to a secondary status, Algeria, Morocco and Tunisia had a long tradition of using French as the language of government and instruction. Following their independence, these countries opted for a policy of arabization which aimed at elevating Arabic to the status of an official language. Arabic is now the dominant language in a multilingual setting where Modern Standard Arabic is the official national language and French is the second language maintaining a special status as the predominant academic language, particularly in science (Ezzaki & Wagner, 1992). English, which is taught as a second foreign language, has acquired a high instrumental value.

Syria and Lebanon, which came under French Mandatory rule for a relatively short period of time, faced no significant problems in their drive for arabization. French continues to hold a special place as a second

G.R. Tucker and D. Corson (eds), Encyclopedia of Language and Education,
Volume 4: Second Language Education, 197–205.
© *1997 Kluwer Academic Publishers. Printed in the Netherlands.*

language in some parts of Lebanon, but English is the preferred first foreign language in many schools and university level education is available with either French or English or Arabic as the language of instruction (see the review by Shaaban, "Bilingual Education in Lebanon" in Volume 5 of this encyclopedia). In general, countries under British rule (e.g. Egypt, Iraq, Jordan) did not experience a great deal of linguistic and cultural turmoil and proceeded with arabization while keeping English as the preferred second language.

Israel is a special situation which presents unique problems and challenges. Under the British Mandate, Palestine had three official languages: Arabic, Hebrew and English. Although with the establishment of the state of Israel in 1948 English was dropped from the list of official languages, it has maintained a special status as a second language after Hebrew but ahead of Arabic (Hallel & Spolsky, 1993).

MAJOR CONTRIBUTIONS

The three areas highlighted in this section: Morocco, Jordan and Israel were chosen because they present unique problems and concerns while at the same time typifying the kind of scholarly activity taking place in other countries.

Morocco, a francophone country where French is in common use as a second language and where English is strengthening its status as a second foreign language, is somewhat typical of North Africa. One reason for choosing Morocco is the availability of scholarly publications in the form of journal articles and research reports written in English. There exists an active group of English language teachers and researchers, the Moroccan Association of Teachers of English (MATE), who publish a newsletter (*MATE Newsletter*) which contains short articles, interviews and announcements of interest to the profession. The association also holds in-service teacher training workshops known as *MATE Days* at various locations and sponsors an annual conference which culminates in the publications of *MATE Proceedings*.

Typical of the issues which are of concern to Moroccan teachers, textbook writers and policy makers are curriculum contents, teaching philosophy, pedagogical approach and teacher preparation. The issue of cultural content in English courses, which has received considerable attention in recent years, illustrates the kind of discussion which is taking place among educators.

One argument calls for keeping foreign cultural content in textbooks to a minimum. The criteria for limiting the selection are the officially stated aims of English language education and the estimation of the learners' future needs. The main reason given for minimizing exposure to foreign culture is the danger that a comparison between the native and foreign cultures could contribute to the students' discontent with their own culture. Additionally, it is argued, there may be certain patterns of behavior in English-speaking contexts that most Moroccans would prefer not to have presented as a model to their young people (Adaskou, Britten & Fahsi, 1990).

Another view raises the question of whether a language can indeed be dissociated from its culture. This question entails a discussion of nativization, i.e. the use of English materials with Moroccan cultural content, and ESP (English for Specific Purposes), which emphasizes the use of English as a purely functional or instrumental tool. It is argued that neither of these solutions are feasible and that the focus should be on the learner as an integrated whole person who needs to develop strategies for dealing with cultural pressures. The objective, impartial presentation of native and foreign cultures and the development of analytical thinking among students will enable the learners to evaluate their options and make informed choices (Hyde, 1994).

In Jordan, as in many other countries in the region, English is a compulsory school subject which enjoys popular support and official sanction. Under the auspices of the Ministry of Education, a national curriculum for the Basic Stage of Education was developed by a group of experts known as the English Language National Team. According to its authors, the new curriculum introduced various reforms described in the following quote (General Directorate of Curricula and Educational Technology, Curriculum Directorate, 1990: p. 1):

> It has delineated the general and specific objectives of teaching English in Jordan in explicit, realistic and functional terms within the rationale of an eclectic approach based on the findings of the psycholinguistic research. It has adopted a learner-centred approach with a notional-functional orientation, paying special attention to content and values, recommended methods and techniques for teaching English language skills to Jordanian learners and suggested methods of evaluation.

Based on this philosophy, the document described in significant detail various aspects of the English language curriculum. The aims and objectives were to be both educational as well as instrumental, enabling students to acquire a level of competence which would allow them to further pursue their education or to use English as a medium of communication with the outside world. To that end, specific objectives for each grade were drawn up for each of the linguistic skills: listening, speaking, reading and writing. Textbooks were to include a judicious blend of national and foreign culture with students beginning by learning in the foreign language about familiar things then gradually widening the coverage to aspects of other cultures. Although the content is primarily defined in terms of functions and notions to be covered in each grade, lexical and structural coverage is also described in some detail. The remaining parts of the curriculum deal with teaching methodology, educational media, co-curricular activities, evaluation, and recommendations for a teacher training program.

The Israeli situation, with its special problems and challenges, illustrates some of the complexities which are characteristic of a multilingual setting. With the establishment of the state of Israel, Hebrew became the national language and dominated Arabic, the other official language. Hebrew is the language of government and law courts and also the language of instruction in most schools. The majority of the population use Hebrew as a first language and it functions as a second language for Jewish immigrants and speakers of Arabic. Arabic is the language of instruction for Arabic-speaking students and a compulsory subject for Jewish students who take Modern Standard Arabic in grades 7–9. English is a compulsory subject between grades 5 and 12 and it is required for university study and has the status of a *de facto* second language, though not an official language. French, which used to be the main foreign language till World War I, continues to be taught as an optional additional foreign language. Other languages taught as optional subjects at various schools include Italian, German and Spanish. Languages which are recognized for examination by the Ministry of Education include Russian, Yiddish, Polish and Amharic (Hallel & Spolsky, 1993). In describing the various factors which influence language teaching policy, Spolsky (1996: p. 51) states:

> Language teaching policy in Israel continues to be dominated by the ideological role and practical value of Hebrew. It is further driven by the existence of non-Hebrew speaking groups, such as the non-Jewish minorities and the 70,000 new immigrant children who entered school in September 1991. It responds strongly to the instrumental claims for English as a world language, and is starting to recognise the political value of Arabic, and to a lesser extent, of French. Any limited recognition of other languages is a reflection of the linguistic complexity of the population.

WORK IN PROGRESS

Most of the work which has recently been done, at least that which has been published in English, was carried out by specialists trained at American or British universities. It is not surprising, hence, to discover that the research being conducted deals with some of the same issues that are of interest to Western scholars. Some of the areas which have received considerable attention include educational policy, teacher training, interlanguage development, material preparation and pedagogical approaches.

In matters of educational policy researchers have tackled the question of the appropriateness of curricular decisions for specific situations. For instance, Akünal (1992) investigated the effectiveness of English language content-based immersion programs in a Turkish university setting and discovered that such programs appear to be effective in improving students' receptive skills but not their ability to engage in meaningful communicative activity. A proposal to introduce the study of English in Saudi elementary schools concludes that early exposure to a foreign language is not detrimental to the students' acquisition of their native language or to their cultural and academic development (Abdan, 1991). The role of language, linguistics and literature in the Jordanian English-major curriculum is discussed by Bader (1992) and recommendations are given for placing more emphasis on language performance and the selection of appropriate literary texts which enhance the development of linguistic skills. In the Israeli setting, the teaching of Arabic as a second language, although officially sanctioned, has been negatively impacted by the students' attitude toward the language and its speakers and also by the inadequacy of teacher training (Brosh, 1993). Another issue which has a significant bearing on teaching Arabic as a second language is the implication of diglossia or the existence of two varieties of the language associated with writing or speech. Investigating this matter, Brosh and Ohlshtain (1995) conclude that previous exposure to the spoken language had no impact on the acquisition of the written variety, as had been assumed by policy makers.

A significant amount of research on reading has investigated strategies and approaches which are effective in the enhancement of reading comprehension. Working with Egyptian students of English, Amer (1992) found that using story grammar, i.e. identifying the internal structure of a story, had a significant positive effect on narrative text comprehension. He also discovered that the use of a knowledge-map, which is a graphic display of information showing the main ideas of a text and their relationships, is a more effective strategy than the use of outlining (Amer, 1994). A study of Omani students majoring in English revealed that they tended to employ two reading styles described as *analytic*, a text-based approach relying on word identification and detail, and *global*, a concept-driven approach relying on prior knowledge. None of them used the *synthetic* style which integrates appropriate aspects of the analytic and the global (Amer & Khouzam, 1993). The strategies used by Omani students studying chemistry for inferring the meaning of unknown words revealed that, while all of them used the context of the word and their knowledge of the world, the stronger students made use of contexts wider than the paragraph (Arden-Close, 1993). Concerns regarding the level of comprehension among Moroccan secondary students led to the identification of reading as well as language problems (Bouziane, 1993). In an effort to understand the lack of interest in reading among Moroccan students, the students were asked to report on their own reading behavior to make them aware of what strategies they used. The problem seemed to stem from their conception of reading as a classroom-oriented exercise rather than a pleasurable and intellectual activity (Oublal, 1994).

Exploring practices of grading written texts, Farghal (1992) found a tendency among English teachers at one Jordanian university to place emphasis on grammatical accuracy at the sentential level rather than on the use of cohesive devices to achieve coherence. Fakhri (1994) deals with the hypothesis that Arab students transfer Arabic text organization features into their writing in English. He finds no compelling evidence to support this contention aside from the use of *and* as a coordinating conjunction and he suggests that the notion of language transfer at the discourse level deserves more careful scrutiny.

Language transfer and interlanguage development among speakers of Farsi and Arabic are explored in various studies. Interlanguage use among Farsi-speakers studying English varied significantly according to the type of task (translation, picture description or grammatical judgement), suggesting that an accurate measure of interlanguage competence must take into account performance under different conditions and at various stages (Sajjadi & Tahririan, 1992). The strategic competence underlying interlanguage use among Iranian students was explored to determine what communicative strategies were used to handle problematic concepts (Yarmohammadi & Seif, 1992). For speakers of Arabic studying English as a foreign language at various stages and locations, the research includes topics such as: the placement of primary stress on English words and the establishment of hierarchies of difficulty based on syntactic, morphological and phonological criteria (Ghaith, 1993); the classification of spelling errors according to type and frequency (Haggan, 1991); the acquisition of English derivational morphology in order to determine the level of difficulty involved (Al-Qadi, 1992); a classification and analysis of errors involving lexical choice (Zughoul, 1991); and a study of errors related to the different uses of the present progressive construction (Al-Buanain, 1992).

Concerns regarding prospective teachers and their preparation are addressed by Fahmi and Bilton (1992) in an attempt to gauge the attitude of Omani undergraduate TEFL majors toward themselves and their exposure to a Western language and culture. Al-Arishi (1991) examines the quality of phonological input of Saudi English teachers to determine whether or not those trained in an ESL environment, i.e. in an English-speaking country, made fewer errors than those trained in an EFL environment. The question whether or not grammar should be taught explicitly in the foreign language class, rather than implicitly through the functional-notional approach, is explored by Cherchalli-Fadel (1993) in the Algerian context. Experimenting with the use of computers in an English language classroom, Stevens (1991) reports that Omani students expressed a positive attitude toward the use and usefulness of computer assisted language learning. Other work, which cannot be included here due to space limitations, adds to the richness of the literature dealing with the above topics.

PROBLEMS AND DIFFICULTIES

Considering the diversity of the region, one would expect that the problems and difficulties facing second language education would vary from country to country. While the oil-producing countries had traditionally sent students abroad for language training prior to commencing university study, they now tend to do most of this training at home. Although this was initially handled by importing language teachers from other countries, it is the expectation now that local teachers will assume this responsibility. Hence, there is a great deal of effort being placed on the development of teacher training programs, both pre-service and in-service, which would result in improving the linguistic and pedagogical skills of language teachers.

Another issue which is often mentioned in the literature is defining the aims of second language education in a manner which would have universal appeal among students. While most countries in the region encourage the study of French or English for academic purposes, there is a growing tendency to emphasize the instrumental and functional values of these languages, particularly English. This has resulted in a debate over curricular objectives and textbook contents with respect to an appropriate balance between language, literature and culture. The issue will be debated for a while as solutions are found which are appropriate for various situations.

FUTURE DIRECTIONS

The existing research, almost without exception, calls for further study and a continued examination of various issues related to pedagogical and policy matters. The issue of cultural content in foreign language teaching will continue to be debated, especially in those countries whose culture and traditions are perceived to be in conflict with Western values and culture. The extent to which cultural content in a foreign language course can be controlled will have to be answered locally.

More universal concerns deal with the nature of foreign language acquisition in terms of language interference and interlanguage developments. In this regard, the tentative conclusions reached by current research concerning the transfer of phonological, lexical, grammatical and discourse features will have to be verified and examined in more detail. Work will also continue on the use of reading strategies and the nature of communicative competence.

An evolving understanding of the nature of language acquisition gained from further research will entail a reexamination of the language curriculum and the development of new materials and appropriate pedagogical approaches to accompany them. This in turn could result in a modification of official language education policy, especially in multilingual settings where attitudes regarding minority languages play a significant role. The situation is dynamic, challenging and allows for rich research opportunities which would build on the solid foundation of the existing work.

The University of Toledo
USA

REFERENCES

Abdan, A.A.: 1991. 'An exploratory study of the teaching of English in the Saudi elementary public schools', *System* 19(3), 253–266.

Adaskou, K., Britten, D. & Fahsi, B.: 1990, 'Design decisions on the cultural content of a secondary English course for Morocco', *ELT Journal* 44(1), 3–10.

Akünal, Z.: 1992, 'Immersion programmes in Turkey: An evaluation by students and teachers', *System* 20(4), 517–529.

Al-Arishi, A.Y.: 1991, 'Quality of phonological input of ESL- and EFL-trained teachers', *System* 19(1/2), 61–74.

Al-Buanain, H.: 1992, 'Present progressive: suggestions for teaching this form to Arab students of English', *IRAL* 30(4), 329–350.

Al-Qadi, N.S.: 1992, 'The acquisition of English derivational morphology by Arab speakers: Empirical testing', *Language Sciences* 14(1/2), 89–107.

Amer, A.A.: 1992, 'The effect of story grammar instruction on EFL students' comprehension of narrative text', *Reading in A Foreign Language* 8(2), 711–720.

Amer, A.A.: 1994, 'The effect of knowledge-map and underlining training on the reading comprehension of scientific texts', *English For Specific Purposes* 13(1), 35–45.

Amer, A.A. & Khouzam, N.: 1993, 'The effect of EFL students' reading styles on their reading comprehension performance', *Reading in a Foreign Language* 10(1), 967–978.

Arden-Close, C.: 1993, 'NNS readers' strategies for inferring the meanings of unknown words', *Reading in a Foreign Language* 9(2), 867–893.

Bader, Y.: 1992, 'Curricula and teaching strategies in university English departments: A need for change', *IRAL* 30(3), 233–240.

Bouziane, A.: 1993, 'Toward an effective use of reading texts: An investigation', *Moroccan Association of Teachers of English: Proceedings of the 13th Annual Conference* 83–96.

Brosh, H.: 1993, 'The influence of language status on language acquisition: Arabic in the Israeli setting', *Foreign Language Annals* 26(3), 347–357.

Brosh, H. & Olshtain, E.: 1995, 'Language skills and the curriculum of diglossic language', *Foreign Language Annals* 28(2), 247–260.

Cherchalli-Fadel, S.: 1993, 'We don't feel we are doing grammar this year', *Moroccan Association of Teachers of English: Proceedings of the 13th Annual Conference* 113–118.

Ezzaki, A. & Wagner, D.A.: 1992, 'Language and literacy in the Maghreb', *Annual Review of Applied Linguistics* 12, 216–229.

Fahmy, J. J. & Bilton, L.: 1992, 'The sociocultural dimension of TEFL education: The omani file', *Journal of Multilingual and Multicultural Development* 13(3), 269–289.

Fakhri, A.: 1994, 'Text organization and transfer: The case of Arab ESL learners', *IRAL* 32(1), 78–86.

Farghal, M., 1992, 'Naturalness and the notion of cohesion in EFL writing classes', *IRAL* 30(1), 45–50.

Ghaith, S.: 1993, 'The assignment of primary stress to words by some Arab speakers', *System* 21(3), 381–390.

General Directorate of Curricula and Educational Technology, Curriculum Directorate: 1990, *English Language Curriculum and Its General Guidelines for the Basic Education Stage*, Economic Press Co.: Amman, Jordan.

Haggan, M.: 1991, 'Spelling errors in the native Arabic-speaking English majors: A comparison between remedial students and fourth year students', *System* 19(1/2), 45–61.

Hallel, M. & Spolsky, B.: 1993, 'The teaching of additional languages in Israel', *Annual Review of Applied Linguistics* 13, 37–49.

Hyde, M.: 1994, 'The teaching of English in Morocco: The place of culture', *ELT Journal* 48(4), 295–305.

Oublal, F.: 1994, 'Can we make our learners more interested in reading in the foreign language?', *Moroccan Association of Teachers of English: Proceedings of the 14th Annual Conference* 76–87.

Sajjadi, S. & Tahririan, M.H.: 1992, 'Task variability and interlanguage use', *IRAL* 30(1), 35–44.

Spolsky, B.: 1996, 'Prolegomena to an Israeli language policy', in T. Hickey & J. Williams (ed.), *Language, Education and Society in a Changing World*, Multilingual Matters Ltd.: Clevedon, 46–53.

Stevens, V.: 1991, 'A study of student attitudes toward CALL in a self-access student resource center', *System* 19(3), 289–299.

Yarmohammadi, L. & Seif, S.: 1992, 'More on communication strategies: Classification, resources, frequency, and underlying processes', *IRAL* 30(3), 223–232.

Zughoul, M.R.: 1991, 'Lexical choice: Towards writing problematic word lists', *IRAL* 29(1), 45–60.

J. VICTOR RODSETH

INNOVATIVE SECOND LANGUAGE EDUCATION IN SOUTHERN AFRICA

Much of second language (SL) education in Southern Africa concerns the use of a colonial language – English, French, Afrikaans, German or Portuguese – as the medium of instruction for first language (L1) African learners. This integrates SL studies in Southern Africa with policy issues (Volume 1), and with bilingual learning (Volume 5), in virtually all the literature on SL medium education.

The same overlapping does not apply to conventional SL teaching as subject, where innovation has striven to replicate methodological changes from grammar-translation through audio-lingualism to modern communicative approaches initiated elsewhere.

This section deals with innovation during the past 200 years in efforts by missionaries, education departments, non-governmental organisations (NGOs), publishers and educators, through curriculum planning, teacher training, materials development, assessment policies or the use of media to promote SL learning in unfavourable circumstances.

EARLY DEVELOPMENTS

The coincidental provision of SL education for South Africa's indigenous people by various missionary groups as a means to pursue evangelical and 'civilizing' ends is summarised in several general works, notable Harshorne (1992) and Lanham and Prinsloo (1978). A rich store of relevant primary sources on missionary education is housed in the Cory Library at Rhodes University, Grahamstown.

The policy of the Dutch East India Company at the Cape after 1652 – that indigenous people should learn Dutch, early British attempts to impose English on Cape inhabitants, and their later policy in missionary schools are described in Malherbe (1977) and Behr (1978). All the references above are useful on the promotion of Afrikaans both before the National Party came into power in 1948 and afterwards when its promotion became an aspect of apartheid policy, with implications for the SL learning of Afrikaans and English. Valuable research on early SL development in South Africa was also done by Lucket, Boshoff and Gough, unpublished in National Education Policy Investigation (NEPI) documents (1992).

Literature on other Southern African countries both before and after

G.R. Tucker and D. Corson (eds), Encyclopedia of Language and Education,
Volume 4: Second Language Education, 207–219.
© 1997 Kluwer Academic Publishers. Printed in the Netherlands.

independence, includes them in broader groupings such as sub-Saharan African countries, or according to colonial languages. Useful introductory works on early developments in other countries are Sebeok (1971), the Edinburgh University report on *Language in Education in Africa* (1985), and the World Bank Report *Education in Sub-Saharan Africa* (1988), Schmidt (1991), Bamgbose (1991) and Phillipson (1988). Articles on individual countries are found in these general works.

The early developments in adult literacy and the SL teaching which accompanied L2 literacy has been little studied, but French (1992) provides a readable and sympathetic overview of early and later struggles to establish adult literacy in South Africa, through the work of non-government organisations (NGOs) which were able and willing to function in a climate of suspicion and, later, hostility. Pioneering work was done by the Bureau of Language and Literacy and Operation Upgrade, both of which initially used the Laubach method. (See Vol. 2.)

MAJOR CONTRIBUTIONS

Apart from Kiernan (1991), Herbert (1992), Schmidt (1991), The World Bank Report, and Botha (1993), there are a few overviews of Southern African innovations; other sources are journals, government and project reports, conference proceedings and textbooks.

In the 1960's and 1970's, Publishers influenced ESL through textbooks and, sometimes, training support. *English Through Activity* (ETA) (Arnold and Varty, several dates) spread through Southern Africa because of a shift to activity methods and a strong training commitment from the authors.

The Molteno Project Report (Rodseth, 1978), from the Institute for the Study of English in Africa (ISEA), found ETA and other courses overreliant on audio-lingualism, weak in reading development and crosscurricular work. Drawing on overseas communicative work and Lanham's reading development project in Soweto, Molteno developed a language-experience-based model for teaching African L1's (*Breakthrough to Literacy*), and a phonics-with-meaning *Bridge to English* reader.

Associations such as the Linguistics Association of S.D.C.C. (Southern African Development Coordinating Conference) Universities (LASU), the Linguistic Society of South Africa (LSSA), the South African Association for Language Teaching (SAALT), the Southern African Society for Education (SASE), and the Southern African Applied Linguistics Association (SAALA) have affected change through journals, conferences and conference reports. Large organisations like MOLTENO and READ have made significant contributions through conferences.

The 1980's and 1990's Have Seen a Number of Innovative Initiatives.
In-service Teacher Training and Upgrading, and *Materials Development* have been a focus in many agencies, listed in directories like *Bridge, 1995; Profiles of NGOs Involved in Teacher Development, 1996; Prodder's Development Directory, 1992/3*. For example, in alphabetical order:

Centre for Cognitive Development (CCD)
English Language Education Trust (ELET)
English Language Teaching Information Centre (ELTIC)
Grahamstown Foundation Farm School Project
National Language Project (NLP)
Primary Education Upgrading Programme (PEUP, Lehobye, 1992)
Primary Science Project (PSP)
Project for the Study of Alternative Education in South Africa (PRAESA)
PROMAT (Pro Matric)
Read Education and Develop (READ)
Science Education Project (SEP)
South African Council for Higher Education Trust (SACHED)
South African Institute of Distance Education (SAIDE)
Teachers' English Language Improvement Project (TELIP)
UPTTRAIL Trust (Cognitive Development)

Some organisations and projects (acronyms explained above) are also concerned with:

- *Policy Development* (ELTIC, NLP, PRAESA);
- *Research* (CCD, ELTIC, NLP, PRAESA, TELIP, and *The Threshold Project* (MacDonald & Burroughs, 1991), which researched early-exit transition to English;
- *Language and Learning Across the Curriculum (LLAC)* and *Academic Support* (PSP, SACHED, SEP), Integrated Studies projects at various schools, and PROMAT;
- *Distance Learning* (ELET, ELTIC, NLP);
- *Organisations, Journals* and *Magazines* (African Language Association of Southern Africa (ALASA): *Journal of African Languages and Linguistics*, University of South Africa, Pretoria, *English Usage in Southern Africa*; ELTIC: *Eltic Reporter*; NLP: *Bua!*; *Per Linguam*; SAALA: *SAJALS Journal*; South African Association for Language Teaching (SAALT): *SAALT Journal*;
- *Reading Programmes* (CCD, READ, SACHED, THE LITTLE LIBRARY);
- *Provision of Resource Centres* (ELET, ELTIC, NLP);

- *Promotion of African Languages* (Languages in Contact and Conflict in Africa (LiCCA), Linguistic Association of S.D.C.C. Universities (LASU), (NLP);
- *Multilingualism* (ELTIC, LASU, LiCCA, NLP, READ);
- *Adult Basic Education and Training;*
- *Media Support Enterprises* (see Botha);
- *Schools-based Outreach Projects.*

An excellent Survey of Tertiary Bridging and Education Support Programmes (Agar et al., 1991) outlined problems, successes and potential in the field. The United States Information Service (USIS) and the British Council have contributed to a number of these initiatives.

Universities and colleges of education have contributed to ESL development in two distinct ways – firstly in developing bridging and academic support programmes for second language users of English, and secondly in making increasing provision for courses on applied linguistics and second language instruction. Government curriculum developers have produced syllabi (influencing publishers) which prescribe communicative approaches, the development of LLAC and Cognitive Academic Language Proficiency (CALP).

Efforts in literacy and SL for adults have been directed at the indigenous languages as L1, at Afrikaans as L1 and L2, and at English, which was and still is overwhelmingly the SL of choice of adult learners. SL literacy in South Africa is therefore mostly in English. It has been influenced by debates over the 'straight for English' model versus the 'L1 first' model, as well as by international trends in L1 and L2 teaching. These trends, issues and debates are discussed in Hutton (1992) and Aitchison et al. (1996). These overviews also provide reviews of the work of literacy agencies. Earlier work in support of policy debates is available in the published reports and unpublished working papers of the Adult Education and Adult Basic Education working groups of the *National Education Policy Investigation* (1992).

Many agencies have innovated in developing their own programmes and providing teacher training, in particular the English Literacy Project (ELP); Use Speak and Write English (USWE); and English for Adults (EFA).

Reading material for newly literate learners has come from newspaper supplements and adult learner newspapers, the Easy Reading for Adults (ERA) initiative and the New Readers Project. Electronic media, particularly television, have been used more for advocacy than for direct teaching, and computer based programmes are in their infancy.

Highlights in the Literature
- Initial literacy in African languages has been very weak. The Molteno Project's pioneering of successful L1 has helped establish a sounder base for early-exit bilingualism.
- Early-exit bilinguals are seriously under-equipped for a transition to SL medium of instruction. The Threshold Project's reports reveal most students not competent in L1 or L2 for cross-curricular cognitive tasks (MacDonald & Burroughs, 1991).
- Authoritarian transmission styles are entrenched in many schools. Development projects seek to foster mediated, learner-centred, task/text-based systems.
- The crucial role of reading has received attention from many agencies.
- LLAC has been tackled through using cross-curricular material in English courses (Molteno); 'language for science' – Science Education Project (SEP) and Primary Science Project (PSP); publications researched at universities, and the CCD's START (1995/6) programme.
- Education in multilingual societies has been examined by universities in training courses, by SAALA and NLP at conferences, in conference reports (Crawhall, 1992), and in the journal *Bua!*. The related concern of promoting African languages for their own sake has been debated at LiCCA, SAALA, ALASA and NLP conferences. ELTIC has developed two programmes: *Puo Dikolong* (Languages in Schools) and *Diteme Tsa Thuto* (Multilingual Learning), which address the challenges of multilingualism in classrooms.

WORK IN PROGRESS

Due to the virtual impossibility of gathering adequate data on many Southern African countries, the following description is selective.

The Molteno Project has gone to considerable scale. The Bridge ESL programme has developed up to Bridge Plus Three (the fifth year of school) and comprises comprehensive courses involving audio-visual aids, board games, book boxes, and L.A.C. materials, especially in the areas of Geography and Mathematics. According to the project's annual report for 1995, its courses are being used in about 10,000 classroom throughout Southern Africa. On any school day over 400,000 pupils learn from them. In-service teacher training consumes most of the budget. Evaluation studies (*Evaluations of the Molteno Project, 1995*) are overwhelmingly positive. A representative study, (Cunningsworth, 1990) describes Molteno as 'well in advance of anything currently available in South Africa, . . . it undoubtedly provides the best package to meet the increasing needs of black schools'. In 1996 the project received 3 of the 9 provincial Presidential Premier Education Awards. The English programmes are now up to the seventh year, and funding is being sought for extending the African L1s beyond the first year. *Breakthrough to Literacy* is now available in fourteen African languages.

The Bridge Materials were included in a comparative evaluation of available language courses by the Human Sciences Research Council (Kroes & Walker, 1987/8). The HSRC evaluators, who rated Molteno programmes as the best, noted that even superior materials fail in the hands of teachers who have not been properly trained to implement them. Molteno were already providing teacher-training to all their users, and the HSRC report persuaded the publishers of the two most widely used commercial courses (Macmillan Boleswa who publish *MacMillan Primary Education Project (MAPEP)* and Maskew Miller Longman who publish *New Day by Day*) to follow suit.

The University of Cape Town's school of Education, along with other units and departments, and with PRAESA, is seeking to deal with multilingualism's complexities through course work, a masters programme and a Further Diploma for practising teachers. The additive bilingualism lobby is being supported by research-based training of writers and publishing of books. These feature communicative language teaching and the development of creativity and literature-sensitivity in areas where a pervasive, instrumental ESL approach in the past tended to discourage the reading of literature and creative writing. Also, an inter-departmental project seeks to test the claims of the Additive Bilingualism lobby. All endeavours entail a complete re-think of established approaches to multilingual education.

The University of the Witwatersrand's Applied English Language Studies (AELS) department offers undergraduate and post graduate programmes featuring the study of English as social practice in a multilingual context, critical literacy, literacies, language and education and academic development (see the review by Janks in Volume 1). Materials are being developed for tertiary courses in academic literacy, and distance education materials for an in-service further diploma in English education. Texts for schools contributing to the multi-literacies position articulated by the *New London Group*, and to the *Critical Language Awareness* movement, are being produced. Language in Education research is being conducted and an inter-disciplinary MA is being offered.

Rhodes University's Department of Linguistics and English Language, working hand in hand with the Monument's Inset programme and MOLTENO, provide courses which are not purely 'English second language', but much more broadly focused on multilingual issues. They offer a coursework Masters collaboration with the Education Department and encourage the submission of innovative teaching materials (with a full theoretical and critical justification) as an alternative to purely academic theses for this course. L2 learner-dictionaries for various age-groups are being developed by the Dictionary Unit at Rhodes, now that their big Dictionary on South African English has been published.

The NLP and PRAESA continue to innovate in major theoretical, research and implementation endeavours, through projects and publications. Adding to the wealth in the *Bua!* journal is the seminal *Multilingual Education for South Africa* (Heugh et al., 1995). This work, a strong lobby for additive bilingualism, comprehensively deals with the whole theory-research-practice spectrum.

The USIS Regional Language Office (RELO) for Southern Africa (based in Pretoria) focuses its efforts on: Academic Development, Teacher Education, and Materials Development/Curriculum Reform/Policy. RELO concentrates on the role of English at all education levels, especially in maths, science and technical areas. To assist educators, 'programming tools' are used, including Academic Specialist Programs, Worldnet video interactives, Telepress conferences, USIS library facilities, Fulbright Exchanges, International Visitors and the English Teaching Fellows Program. Activities involving a wide range of educators include: designing curricula, courses and materials; establishing writing/reading centres; developing multicultural and LLAC approaches; organising conferences for returned grantees; collaborating in projects with organisations like ELET, ELTIC and MOLTENO; contributing to seminars; and promoting integrative curricula development.

The British Council is funded by the British Foreign and Commonwealth Office, which includes the Overseas Development Administration (ODA). The Council's activities focus on the management of change in education, support for teacher education initiatives at a policy and macro level, as well as supporting ODA education projects throughout the region. The Council backs positively-evaluated projects like MOLTENO, takes key educators to the UK for training, supplies consultants and evaluators to projects, contributes to teacher education, and maintains offices. The Council works both in Anglophone countries on ESL projects, and in Angola and Mozambique (Portuguese SL), in Madagascar, Mauritius and Seychelles where English is a foreign language. Mozambique, with her Anglophone neighbours, is a special focus. The ODA has launched a major project in English teaching at secondary level. The Council in Malawi has developed teacher training approaches for improving the use of English as medium after initial years of L1 medium. Expansion will take place through a national INSET system. Projects involve changing

very teacher-centred, rote-learning systems to more learning-centred, par-
ticipative approaches. Support mechanisms have been evolved for large
numbers of teachers, many unqualified, especially in remote areas. These
glimpses throw light on similar situations in other Southern African countries.

An additional influence from the UK is the use of University of Cambridge
examinations (International General Certificate of Secondary Education –
IGCSE – and the Higher Certificate – HIGCSE). These examinations are
used extensively throughout Southern Africa and their backwash effect on
classroom practice should not be underestimated.

The potential for the media, outlined in Botha (1993), is being realised.
Radio education in particular is being promoted, as it is the most penetra-
tive. The World Bank's excellent *Education in Sub-Saharan Africa* (1988)
comments on the potential of interactive educational radio in Kenya to
promote student interaction. A South African version, developed out of
a Lesotho adaptation of the Kenyan 'English in Action', is expanding
steadily and receiving generally favourable evaluations (Leigh, 1995).
    National broadcasters continue to develop programmes, often sub-
contracting work to experts.

Distance education courses are increasing, and now being coordinated by
the National Association of Distance Education Organisations of South
Africa (NADEOSA).

Matric-orientated courses, to compensate for inferior education, are mush-
rooming. Some involve television in the packages.

African language teaching is being highlighted (especially in South Africa
following constitutional enshrining of language rights). A very innovative
project, 'Transfer of African Language Knowledge' (TALK) pairs and
trains speakers of different languages to teach each other – and build
inter-group bridges.

ELET is developing cross-curricular courses with INSET, resource centres
and distance-teaching materials.

The CCD is implementing its high school and tertiary courses, and is
developing cross-curricular primary school texts. It hopes to adapt its
English academic reading and writing courses into African languages.

A major backwash effect on *ESL literacy* is resulting from the Independent Examinations Board's (IEB) pilot examinations (started in 1994) in communication in English at the first three levels of adult literacy. These examinations are based on broadly defined outcomes proposed by the National Qualifications Framework. Many literacy agencies are adapting their courses to prepare learners for these examinations, but funding cuts have shifted the emphasis from innovation to provision.

PROBLEMS AND DIFFICULTIES

There is a lack of systematic documentation (especially overviews), and many innovative projects are evaluated quite late in their histories. Also, project reports are selective of positive statements in their publications.

The situation is seriously fragmented. All resources will have to integrate far better.

Second-language teaching and learning problems often flow firstly from ideologically and politically-driven policies. Learners in Zambia, Namibia and Botswana have recently been faced with earlier transition to English medium (Heine, 1992: p. 28; Mkangwani, 1992: pp. 6–11) following policy decisions based on the belief that earlier and more English will improve ESL standards, empower learners in the major language of social and economic mobility, and contribute to nation-building through unification.

Negative attitudes are highly problematic. Colonial languages (especially English), though viewed positively by policy-makers, are seen by some segments of the population as promoting a privileged elite, and disempowering for the large excluded majority (de Klerk, 1995: pp. 8–14; Siachitema, 1992: p. 9).

There is a widespread ignorance of overseas research which points to the benefits of additive bilingualism (see Vol.5 and Ramirez, 1991). This lack is compounded by negative attitudes to indigenous L1's which are considered inadequate (Heugh & Siegrühn, 1992: p. 97; Siachitema, 1992: p. 9).

Bad environmental contexts, dwindling resources (Siachitema, 1992: 20–21), overlarge classes, under-qualified teachers, inadequate text-supply (especially in African languages), weak management infrastructures, demoralised teaching forces, staff attrition and mobility, all conspire to frustrate innovations. Aggravating bad contexts are experiences of IN-SET failure, and the lack of promotion and/or salary recognition following training.

Decades-long entrenchment of authoritarian transmission-teaching styles prevent the development of independent, thinking learners, capable of performing well in exams and later (Roets, 1991: 67–69; Ellis, 1985).

Consequently, innovators promoting learner-centred, task-based, mediated systems of learning have to struggle with teachers' disbelief that a non-authoritarian style can succeed (especially in large classes), and their belief that learner-centred and cooperative methods will create discipline problems and will not get everyone through the syllabus (*Speak Out!* articles).

More specific is the resultant neglect of CALP in cross-curricular academic reading and writing. There is a very long way to go before all teachers accept their role as academic reading and writing teachers.

In adult literacy and SL, the major problem is the chronic lack of funding, allied to pressure to deliver. Research and evaluation in L2 literacy have been neglected. Many teachers of ESL literacy are not themselves sufficiently competent in English and teacher training has also been skimpy. Demanding methodologies are not well applied. Old rivalries, now abating, have left a fragmented and incoherent field. Adult literacy specialist skills are scarce, although ESL is a growing industry in universities. The development of mother tongue literacies, while desirable, has been neglected.

FUTURE DIRECTIONS

There are at least ten streams for development: First, the movement towards bilingualism will radically change the context for second-language learning, modernise indigenous languages and equip them in terms of L1 and L2 teaching methodologies. The NLP, PRAESA, universities and SAALA will continue to follow and interpret overseas trends and provide local leadership. Government support for this will be coordinated by the Language Plan Task Group (LANGTAG) of the Department of Art, Culture and Technology.

Second, Outcomes-Based Education and Training (OBET) will, through the South African Government's commitment, the South African National Qualifications Framework (NQF) and the Independent Examinations Board (IEB) (together with related bodies in Southern Africa) drive policy and practice. The NQF aims to integrate education and training and bring coherence and portability to qualifications. Various bodies are developing standards for the NQF, and the IEB is piloting outcomes-based national examinations. *Ways of Seeing the National Qualifications Framework* (Burroughs, 1995) provides a readable insider view of the issues around policy and practice issues. If all national languages are to be assessed on specified outcomes and equivalent language credits are to be negotiated, it is possible that distinctions between first, second, third and foreign language assessment may disappear, with backwash effects on teaching.

Third, the use of media and distance-education will expand, become better coordinated and more adequately provide for the traditional have-nots. The 'promise' outlined in *The Role of the Media in Education* (Botha, 1993) and contained in the formation of a cooperative distance-teaching organisation (NADEOSA) will move closer to realisation.

Fourth, universities and colleges (substantially assisted by the USIS and the British Council) will develop theory and practice towards the 'state of the art'.

Fifth, the seminal influence of Cummins' hypothesis on the interdependency of L1 and L2 and the BICS (Basic Interpersonal Communication Skills) – CALP continuum will increase.

Sixth, (and related to 5), the LLAC movement will accelerate.

Seventh, trans-national bodies like LASU, LiCCA and SAALA will increase in their capacity to pool and disseminate information about SL in multi-lingual contexts.

Eighth, the disciplines of cognitive science and language-in-education will draw closer together. Cognition in language-teaching 'Cognitive Anti-Methods' (Brown, 1995) and Vygotsky-inspired language-in-cognition concerns will increasingly influence each other.

Ninth, participatory research in training will encourage practitioners to test theories, become involved in 'bottom-up' curriculum development (Heugh & Siegrühn, 1995: pp. 97–98), and be empowered to develop own materials.

Tenth, in adult literacy and SL, certification via the NQF is still to be negotiated. There is a danger that adult literacy may be dominated by the agendas of commerce and industry rather than those of adult educators and learners, and that a competency-based approach will be narrowly interpreted. There will be greater cooperation between those literacy agencies which survive. Support from university outreach will remain important.

Vista University, South Africa

REFERENCES

Aitchison, J., Harley, A., Land, S. & Lyster, E.: 1996, *Survey of Adult Basic Education in South Africa*, Maskew Miller Longman (in press).

Agar, D., Hofmeyr, J. & Moulder, J.: 1991, *Bridging Education in the 1990's: Learning from Experience*, Edusource, Johannesburg.

Arnold, L. & Varty, A.: Several dates, *English through Activity*, Shuter & Shooter, Pietermaritzburg, South Africa.

Bamgbose, A.: 1991, *Language and the Nation. The Language Question in Sub-Saharan Africa*, Edinburgh University Press, Edinburgh.

Barnard, D. (ed.): 1993, *Prodder's Development Directory 1992/3: An assessment and comprehensive survey of Southern African Development Agencies and Organisations*, Human Sciences Research Council, Pretoria.

Behr, A.L.: 1978, *Education in South Africa: Origins, Issues and Trends*, Van Schaik, Pretoria.

Botha, W.: 1993, *The Role of the Media in Education*, Edusource, Johannesburg.

Bridge 1995. A directory of organisations and conference centres in South Africa, 1995, Human Awareness Programme, Johannesburg.

Brown, H.D.: 1995, *Principles of Language Learning and Teaching (third edition)*, Prentice Hall Regents, Englewood Cliffs, NJ.

Bua! (formerly NLP Review), National Language Project.

Burroughs, E. (ed.): 1995; *Ways of Seeing the National Qualifications Framework*, Human Sciences Resources Council, Pretoria.

Centre for Cognitive Development (CCD): 1995/6, *START (Strategies for Academic Reading and Thinking) Levels 1–4*, Shuter & Shooter, Pietermaritzburg.

Crawhall, N.T. (ed.): 1992, *Democratically Speaking*, National Language Project, Salt River, South Africa.

Cunningworth, A.: 1995, 'The cunningworth evaluation' in *Evaluations of the Molteno Project*, The Molteno Project, Johannesburg.

de Klerk, G.: 1995, 'Slaves of English', in K. Heugh, A. Siegrühn & P. Plüddemann (eds.), *Multilingual Education for South Africa*, Heinemann, Johannesburg, 8–14.

Education in Sub-Saharan Africa: Policies for Adjustment, Revitalization and Expansion, 1988, The World Bank, Washington, DC.

Ellis, R.: 1985, 'Using the English medium in African schools', in *Language in Education in Africa: Seminar Proceedings No. 26*, University of Edinburgh, Edinburgh, 171–197.

ELTIC Reporter (The), English Language Teaching Information Centre, Johannesburg.

English Usage in Southern Africa, University of South Africa, Pretoria.

Evaluations of the Molteno Project, 1995: The Molteno Project, Johannesburg.

French, E.: 1992, 'Adult literacy in South Africa: past to present' in B. Hutton (ed.), *Adult Basic Education in South Africa*, Oxford, Cape Town, 48–85.

Hartshorne, K.B.: 1992, *Crisis and Challenge: Black Education 1910–1990*, Oxford University Press, Cape Town.

Heine, B.: 1992, 'Language policies in Africa', in R.K. Herbert (ed.), *Language and Society in Africa*, Witwatersrand University Press, Johannesburg, 23–35.

Herbert, R.K.: 1992, *Language and Society in Africa*, Witwatersrand University Press, Johannesburg.

Heugh, K. & Siegrühn, A.: 1995, 'Towards implementing multilingual education in South Africa', in K. Heugh, A. Siegrühn & P. Plüddemann (eds.), *Multilingual Education for South Africa*, Heinemann, Johannesburg, 91–99.

Hutton, B. (ed.): 1992, *Adult Basic Education in South Africa*, Oxford, Cape Town.

Journal for Language Teaching, SAALT (South African Association for Language Teaching).

Kiernan, E.T.: 1991, *The language policies of countries in Sub-Saharan Africa*, H.S.R.C., Pretoria.

Kroes, H. & Walker, G.: 1987/8, *Comparative Evaluation of Lower Primary English Courses in Black Education, Phase 1 & 2*, H.S.R.C., Pretoria.

Language in Education in Africa: Seminar Proceedings No. 26, 1985, University of Edinburgh, Edinburgh.

Lanham, L.W. & Prinsloo, K.D.: 1978, *Communication Studies in South Africa*, Oxford University Press, Cape Town.

LASU Linguistics Association for SACCD (Southern African Development Coordinating Conference) Universities. Reports.

Lehobye, S.M.M.: 1992, *An Evaluation of the Primary Education Upgrading (PEUP) Programme*, Institute of Education, University of Bophuthatswana.

Leigh, S.: 1995, *Changing Times in South Africa: Remodelling Interactive Learning*. Case Studies No.8, LearnTech, Washington, DC.

LiCCA Languages in Contact and Conflict in Africa Research Development Programme. Reports, University of Pretoria, Pretoria.

MacDonald, C. & Burroughs, E.: 1991, *Eager to Talk and Learn and Think* (Consolidated report of 'The Threshold Project'), Maskew Miller Longman, Cape Town.

Malherbe, E.G.: 1977, *Education in Southern Africa* (Two volumes), Juta, Cape Town.

Mkanganwi, K.: 1992, 'Language planning in Southern Africa', in N.T. Crawhall (ed.), *Democratically Speaking*, National Language Project, Salt River, South Africa, 6–11.

National Education Policy Investigation (NEPI): 1992, *Adult Basic Education*, Oxford, Cape Town.

National Education Policy Investigation (NEPI): 1992, working papers (unpublished) available for inspection at the Education Policy Unit, University of the Witwatersrand, Johannesburg.

Per Linguam: Journal of Language and Learning, University of Stellenbosch, Stellenbosch, South Africa.

Phillipson, R.: 1988, 'Linguicism: Structures and ideologies in linguistic imperialism', in T. Skutnabb-Kangas & J. Cummins (eds.), *Minority Education Multilingual Matters*, Clevedon, Philadelphia.

Profiles of NGOs Involved in Teacher Development 1996: Addendum to the National Teacher Education Audit (NGO sector): 1996, Joint Education Trust, Johannesburg.

Ramirez, J.D., Yuen, S.D., Ramey, D.R. & Pasta, D.J.: 1991, *Final Report: Longitudinal Study of Structured English Immersion Strategy, Early-Exit and Late-Exit Transitional Bilingual Education Programmes for Language Minority Children*, Aguirre International, San Mateo, California.

Rodseth, J.V.: 1978, *The Molteno Project Report*, I.S.E.A., Rhodes University, Grahamstown, South Africa.

Roets, N.: 1991, 'Language for academic purposes', *Journal for Language Teaching 25 No. 4*.

SAALA South African Applied Linguistics Association. Annual Conference Proceedings.

SAJALS Journal, Southern African Journal of Applied Language Studies.

Seboek, T.A. (ed.): 1971, *Current Trends in Linguistics, Vol. 7, Sub-Saharan Africa*, Mouton, The Hague.

Siachitema, K.: 1992, 'When nationism conflicts with nationalist goals', in N.T. Crawhall (ed.), *Democratically Speaking*, National Language Project, Salt River, South Africa, 17–21.

Schmidt, J.: 1991, *English in Africa: An Introduction*, Longmans, New York & London.

Speak Out! A Forum for Transformative Education. Magazine of the Centre for Cognitive Development, Centurion, South Africa.

ANNE PAKIR

INNOVATIVE SECOND LANGUAGE EDUCATION IN SOUTHEAST ASIA

Southeast Asia, located between India and China, represents approximately six per cent of the world's population (450 million), but more than fifteen per cent of the world's languages. With a heritage of over 2,000 years, Southeast Asia contains all the religions and cultures of the world, giving it a distinctive character of cultural diversity and plurality. Modern Southeast Asia can be considered along two demarcations: the seven countries belonging to the regional organization called the Association of Southeast Asian Nations (ASEAN) formed in 1967 and the three currently outside ASEAN: Laos, Kampuchea (Cambodia), and Myanmar (Burma). A recently published book (Thumboo, ed., 1996) provide country studies of each ASEAN nation in terms of their rich cultures and the likely directions of their development.

Among the seven ASEAN countries comprising Brunei, Indonesia, Malaysia, the Philippines, Singapore, Thailand, and Vietnam, four will be examined in terms of the research on the status and role of the second language and on innovative teaching/learning strategies employed in the instruction of the second language. The four countries – Brunei, Malaysia, the Philippines and Singapore – have had a long internal history with English, a natural second language because of an extended formal association with Britain (till 1984 in the case of Brunei), with British colonialism (till 1957 in the case of Malaysia; till 1963 in the case of Singapore), and with American colonialisation (till 1946 in the case of the Philippines). The fifth, Indonesia, went through a Dutch colonization period (lasting till 1949) but in recent decades has turned increasingly to English as an additional language especially with independence in 1949. In Thailand (which was never colonized) and Vietnam (which attained national independence from France in 1954) English is considered a foreign language, albeit an important one.

English is taken to be the 'second language' in all of the four 'English-associated' nations although its status and role will differ from country to country. The first point to note in this survey of innovative second language education in Southeast Asia is that all of the nations in focus here are multiracial, multilingual, and multicultural; the diversity of population in each and its geographical distribution affect the patterns of language acquisition and use among the young school going populace. The second point is that these ASEAN countries have, in recent years, undergone impressive eco-

G.R. Tucker and D. Corson (eds), Encyclopedia of Language and Education,
Volume 4: Second Language Education, 221–230.
© *1997 Kluwer Academic Publishers. Printed in the Netherlands.*

nomic growth and rapid socio-cultural transformation through the use of English, a language which enables these newly industrializing economies to continue plugging into the international grid of finance and industry but at the same time seems to threaten their national identity. The experiences and practices of second language education in such multilingual communities provide new perspectives, whether one focuses on language policy and development, curriculum planning and practice, materials and media development, teacher training or language learning.

Research on the topic of how English language education has been handled in the four ASEAN countries, and some innovative practices are reviewed below. A statement at the end will highlight future developments for these member countries and the remaining ASEAN countries of Southeast Asia which are not covered in this review.

EARLY DEVELOPMENTS

Preliminary discussion of the English language education in Southeast Asia started with a series of SEAMEO RELC publications (a well recognized acronym in the region, which stands for Southeast Asian Ministers of Education Organisation (SEAMEO) Regional Language Centre (RELC). The early editors of monographs and anthologies selected and published papers presented at the Regional Language Centre (RELC) annual seminars on themes such as language education in multilingual societies (Yap, 1978), language teaching issues in multilingual environments in Southeast Asia (Noss, 1982), and varieties of English in Southeast Asia (Noss, 1983). Most of the papers concentrated on the learner in the context of language learning in multilingual societies, and on the relationship between language and identity.

Halliday's paper (1978) looked at language largely as a resource (a 'meaning potential' for serving a range of different functions) and the value that is placed on this resource in the educational process. Halliday argued that 'If the context is a multilingual one, the principle of 'learn language, learn through language' applies with no less force ... Teachers and educators who recommend teaching school subjects in a second language are applying the same principle; they want to use that language as a window on new realities. This is what lies behind the view that if we want primary school children to learn a new language, we should use that language for teaching a school subject' (1978: p. 110). This suggestion has been followed in many Southeast Asian countries, where English is recognized as a valuable resource and used for teaching school subjects.

On a societal level, Llamzon (1978) presented the view that language education in Southeast Asian countries should have two crucial concerns: the learning and use of English and the national language in relation to their cultural underpinnings. In the same volume, Sibayan (1978: p. 23) posed the question 'When can all subjects in the curriculum be taught in Pilipino?', expressing the hope that eventually Pilipino could replace English in practically all domains. Gonzalez (1982: p. 89) raised the issues connected with English, an official language of the Philippines, vis-à-vis 'its association with a colonial past and its maintenance in Philippine society'.

Although in these early deliberations there was a deep appreciation of the importance of national languages in building a cohesive society, by the time of the 1983 RELC publication, the focus had shifted to varieties of English in Southeast Asia. Already in 1980, Platt and Weber had discussed the sub-varieties of English in Singapore and Malaysia in terms of their features, functions and status. Five papers on Southeast Asian varieties of English are found in the RELC volume. Three of the varieties described – from Malaysia (Wong, 1983), the Philippines (Gonzalez, 1983), and Singapore (Tay & Gupta, 1983) – fit the category of 'new varieties' in that they were used for intra-national communication and have some native speakers, who were usually bilingual. Two other papers, one on the Indonesian variety of English and the other on the Thai variety discussed the complexity of the description and interpretation of a foreign variety of English.

Such a discussion in the early 1980s soon gave rise to several publications on the developments in the roles, functions, status and features of English in Southeast Asia and the possible pedagogical implications. Among the Malaysians working in this early period were Asmah Haji Omar (1982) and Asiah Abu Samah (1984). In Singapore, Mary Tay was active (see the volume published in 1993, a collection of ten essays from this period), and David Bloom (1986). Gonzalez (1983) and Llamzon (1983) called attention to a new variety called Philippine English.

While most of these early developments were exciting, the next decade was to see significant contributions to innovative second language learning and teaching in some ASEAN contexts, based on their specific circumstances.

MAJOR CONTRIBUTIONS

Overall, most research has focused on understanding second language educational policies in multilingual settings, especially with regard to the status and function of English in the countries as well as the attitudes towards it; e.g. in Singapore, English is one of the four official languages (the others being Mandarin, Malay, and Tamil) and the working language of the country. In the Philippines and Singapore, English is the medium of instruction in schools and universities. Where English is used so centrally in education, we would expect to find new research and theory that could inform educators coming from monolingual situations who view second language education from another perspective.

In the area of reading and writing, two recent anthologies have been published, both edited by M. L. Tickoo (1994, 1995). The 1994 Southeast Asian collection, especially is informative. Attempts were made to explain patterns in bilingual reading among students in Singapore and reading comprehension ability of bilingual primary 5 and 6 children in Brunei. Reading initiative programs in Malaysia, Singapore and Brunei took new directions. For example, the Singapore experience with a successful model called the Reading and English Acquisition Programme (REAP) employed a modified Language Experience Approach to reading in Singapore classrooms. The implementation of REAP in 1985 resulted in effective teaching for lower primary classes in 183 schools (P1–P3) which prepared the way for effective teaching in the upper primary classes with a follow-up program called Active Communicative Teaching (ACT), introduced in 120 schools in 1986, the year when the first group of pupils in Phase 1 REAP reached the ACT level (Mok, 1994). The results were encouraging: evaluated formatively and summatively each year, the program came under external scrutiny after a three year experimentation. The conclusion was that 'there were clear differences between REAP and non-REAP pupils'. For instance, REAP children were found to be ahead by over 7 months in their reading comprehension in P3. Attracted by the success of REAP in Singapore, the Brunei Ministry of Education commissioned an adaptation for local primary schools. The version developed by Ng (1994) was named RELA (for Reading and Language Acquisition) and introduced in 1989 (see the review by Jones in Volume 5).

An attempt to gather material on composition research in Malaysia revealed that only two major endeavors have really been made: the Process Writing Project of the Curriculum Development Centre of the Ministry of Education and the University of Malaya Project on academic and professional writing. This is not surprising in light of the fact that Malaysian educators have taken the view that English is needed only as 'a window on the world'; thus reading rather than writing has been emphasized (Chitravelu, 1994: p. 100).

On the other hand, in Singapore, much more experimentation has taken place in terms of the theory and practice of writing. Working with the centrally controlled English Language Syllabus, departmental handbooks, and textbooks, teachers are often requested to give feedback. Constant appraisals of textbooks, class instruction, and implementation records, all give rise to a dynamic educational practice which emphasizes reading and writing. The process paradigm of the 1980s has not yet given way fully to the meaning constructivist approach of the early 1990s in Singapore classrooms (see Varghese, 1995: p. 72, for a brief discussion of the different approaches in the teaching of writing). On the contrary, there seems to be some evidence of the necessity to see both as one integrated 'cognitively oriented, process-based approach' (Varghese, 1994: p. 311). Varghese's later study of six top percentile students led her to conclude that good writers are reflective writers, who deliberate 'metacognitively about the task and their goals in writing' (1995: p. 82).

In a sophisticated discussion on writing and the process of knowledge creation, Abraham (1995) looks at the effect of new technologies (e.g. the printing press and the word processor) on conceptualizations of writing, knowledge and of education. The paper offers a theoretically coherent argument for equating writing with thinking, but ends with the perplexing question of whether it is pedagogically possible to teach writing/thinking as a skill.

In the middle of the 1990s, several new books on language, society and education in Singapore, Brunei, Malaysia and the Philippines were published. Jones and Ozog's (1993) volume on bilingualism and national development, and the Khoo et al. (1993) volume on European models and Asian realities in the movement towards global multilingualism dwell on the languages in contact phenomenon and its implications for teaching and learning.

Gopinathan et al. (1994) had seven chapters on language in education in Singapore. Three were on English, and among those, Ho (1994) examined at a macro-level how much of English language teaching in Singapore drew on theories and practice of researchers from abroad. But, he noted that in the movement of such ideas from one culture system to another, modifications and adjustments take place naturally, fitting into the needs of the recipient country, its goals and targets in education, and the local institutional structures as well as existing infrastructure. Ho's excellent chapter argues persuasively that the English language curriculum in Singapore has maintained 'a balance between extreme swings of the language pedagogy pendulum' keeping clearly within sight the core-periphery distinction and the necessary process of indigenisation within the practice of curriculum planning.

Pakir (1992, 1993a), and Pakir and Low (1995) highlighted the notion that English in Singapore was rapidly moving from a much used second language in the country to an institutionalized first school language, affecting changing language acquisition and use patterns. Pakir (1993b) suggested that the conceptual framework, the strands in pedagogy, curriculum planning, and syllabus design, must take cognizance of the fact that the English language has indigenised, and there has been a shift in orientation from language form to language use. It was further suggested that definitions of 'first language', 'second language' and 'mother tongue' be re-examined in such a multilingual context as Singapore's. The sociolinguistic trends and prospects were deemed to be exciting as the dynamic language situation would give rise to different teaching strategies and processes, unique to the country.

English and language planning in Southeast Asia (Kandiah & Kwan-Terry, 1994) are described in a volume designed to be of interest to those who are involved in planning for English for other countries of the world wherever the language, as an additional second language, interacts with other indigenous languages. Two papers dwell on the macro- and micro-perspectives in the language management of English and education. The country papers on the role and status of English in the Philippines, on visible and invisible second language planning in Singapore, and on the typology and roles of English in Malaysia, examine the basis upon which the whole enterprise of innovative second language education is based in each of these countries.

Saran Kaur Gill (1995) published the proceedings of a conference which considered international English language education covering the internationalization of the language and its practical implications. Some focus was given to varieties of English and their appropriateness for international communication, as well as to English for cross-cultural communication. The development of language skills at various levels, the design and development of curriculum, teaching methods, texts, teaching aids, and innovations in testing and evaluation, were discussed in the context of English as an international language and a language for cross-cultural communication. Some of the interesting presentations touch on socio-pragmatic factors in learner discourse, semantic mapping in the teaching of reading and writing in Malaysian secondary English classrooms, cross-cultural differences in using English as an international language, designing materials with local color and feel, and giving reading support to weak readers in rural areas. The volume makes for an interesting foray into national and international responses to the challenge of international English language education.

From these publications it is clear that second language contexts characteristic of these countries give new perspectives on language learning as new language teaching situations obtain.

WORK IN PROGRESS

Assessing the kinds of papers published in recent years within the Southeast Asian region, one notes that much of the research effort at the present time concentrates on teaching English without myths. Issues such as the ownership of the English language, identity issues, 'native' versus 'non-native' speaker-teacher, listener-student, notions of correctness, and empowerment through English as an international language for cross-cultural exchange, are constantly raised. Projects especially those which use the technology headed for the twenty first century such as that used for corpus linguistics are currently being undertaken. The Department of English Language and Literature at the National University of Singapore, for example, has a Corpus Studies Unit which among other things looks at English in terms of large computerized databases collected locally. The profiles of Singapore-based English are being undertaken in order to enhance research and teaching of English in such multilingual contexts as Singapore. A dictionary of English in Southeast Asia is being planned (by the Australian Macquarie dictionary group), and several conferences on language and knowledge, with the subtitle of 'the unpacking of text' have been organized. An 'English in Southeast Asia' conference held in Singapore in late 1996 reports on current work in progress in the area of educational research and applications.

PROBLEMS AND DIFFICULTIES

Intense concentration on the social contexts of second language learning has led to innovations in English language teaching in Southeast Asia. However, the diffusion of innovations in second language education can only depend on the change process itself. Implementation difficulties arise, for example, when the resistance to change is not overcome. It is well known that curriculum development does not automatically lead to program implementation.

Program implementation in English Language teaching in the ASEAN countries is not uniformly successful. Where the incentives are greater (for example in Singapore, Brunei, Malaysia, the Philippines) and where there are innovating persons or groups, or institutional support, fewer problems would be envisaged in implementing new targets, objectives, curricula, methodologies, material designs, and in using new technologies.

For innovation to spread there must be a framework for analyzing and applying the program for change. These are especially crucial in the other ASEAN nations where second language education lags behind.

FUTURE DIRECTIONS

The determination and implementation of language policy is observable in Brunei (*dwibahasa*, promoting Malay and English), Malaysia (the promotion of Bahasa Malaysia and English), Singapore (the promotion of English and one other official language), Indonesia (the promotion of Bahasa Indonesia and English as an additional language), and the Philippines (the promotion of Filipino and English). Because Singapore publicly acknowledges English as the working language of the country, it has invested heavily in the training and development of teachers of English; so has the Philippines, relatively speaking. In the former, theory is given less emphasis than practice. However, the implications for second language teaching and learning are carefully studied.

As increasingly more is known about the second language situation in the countries listed above, so will more light be shed on the situation in the other ASEAN countries. In recent years conference papers and articles on the second language situation in Cambodia, Laos, Myanmar, Vietnam, Thailand and Indonesia have been on the increase. However, data on Laos, Cambodia and Myanmar in terms of second language education are not as easily available as those of Thailand and Indonesia.

ASEAN scholars who have been devoting their research and practice to English as an important second language in the English-associated ASEAN countries may well begin paying some attention to the less researched regions such as Cambodia, Laos, Myanmar, and Vietnam (which joined ASEAN only in 1995) (also see reviews by Jones, and by Wong and Ho in Volume 5).

National University of Singapore, Singapore

REFERENCES

Abraham, Sunita A.: 1995, *Writing and the Process of Knowledge Creation*. Topics in Language and Literature, Occasional Papers Series. Number 3, September 1995. Department of English Language and Literature, National University of Singapore, Singapore.

Asiah Abu Samah: 1984, 'The English language (communicational) curriculum for upper secondary schools in Malaysia: Rationale, design, and implementation', in J.A.S. Read (ed.), *Trends in English Language Syllabus Design*, SEAMEO Regional Language Centre, Singapore.

Asmah Haji Omar: 1982, *Language and Society in Malaysia*, Dewan Bahasa dan Pustaka, Kuala Lumpur.

Bloom, D.: 1986, 'The English language and Singapore: A critical survey', in Basant Kapur (ed.), *Singapore Studies*. Singapore University Press, Singapore, 407–458.

Chitravelu, Nesamalar: 1994, 'Composition research in Malaysia: some observations', in M.L. Tickoo (ed.), *Research in Reading and Writing: A Southeast Asian Collection*, Anthology Series 32, SEAMEO RELC, Singapore, 100–108.

Gonzalez, A.B.: 1982, 'The Philippines: Identification of languages in the country', in R.B. Noss (ed.), *Language Teaching Issues in Multilingual Environments in Southeast Asia*, Anthology Series 10, SEAMEO RELC, Singapore, 78–136.

Gonzalez, A.B.: 1983, 'When does an error become a feature of Philippine English?', in R.B. Noss (ed.), *Varieties of English in Southeast Asia*, Anthology Series 11, SEAMEO RELC, Singapore, 150–172.

Gonzalez, A.B.: 1994, 'English and education in the association of Southeast Asian nations (ASEAN) region: Past, present and future', in T. Kandiah & J. Kwan-Terry (eds.), *English and Language Planning: A Southeast Asian Contribution*, Times Academic Press, Singapore, 92–105.

Gopinathan, S., Pakir, A., Ho, W.K., & Vanithamani S. (eds.): 1994, *Language, Society and Education in Singapore: Issues and Trends*, Times Academic Press, Singapore.

Halliday, M.A.K.: 1978, 'Some reflections on language education in multilingual societies', in A. Yap (ed.), *Language Education in Multilingual Societies*, Anthology Series 4, SEAMEO RELC, Singapore, 103–119.

Ho, W.K.: 1994, 'The English language curriculum in perspective: Exogenous influences and indigenization', in S. Gopinathan et al. (eds.), *Language, Society and Education in Singapore: Issues and Trends*, Times Academic Press, Singapore, 235–266.

Jones, G. & Ozog, C. (eds): 1993, *Bilingualism and National Development*. Special issue, *Journal of Multilingual and Multicultural Development* 14, 1 & 2.

Kandiah, Thiru & Kwan-Terry, J. (eds.): 1994, *English and Language Planning: A Southeast Asian Contribution*, Times Academic Press, Singapore.

Khoo, R., Kreher, U. & Wong, R. (eds.): 1993, *Towards Global Multilingualism: European models and Asian realities*. Special issue, *Language, Culture and Curriculum* 6, 3.

Llamzon, T.A.: 1978, 'The dimensions of cultural pluralism in language education', in A. Yap (ed.), *Language Education in Multilingual Societies*, Anthology Series 4, SEAMEO RELC, Singapore, 80–91.

Llamzon, T.A.: 1983, 'Essential features of new varieties of English', in R.B. Noss (ed.), *Varieties of English in Southeast Asia*, Anthology Series 11, SEAMEO RELC, Singapore, 92–109.

Mok, R.: 1994, 'Reading and English acquisition programme (REAP)', in M.L. Tickoo (ed.), *Research in Reading and Writing: A Southeast Asian Collection*, Anthology Series 32, SEAMEO RELC, Singapore, 30–40.

Ng, S.M.: 1994, 'Improving English in language learning in the upper primary levels in Brunei Darussalam', in M.L. Tickoo (ed.), *Research in Reading and Writing: A Southeast Asian Collection*, Anthology Series 32, SEAMEO RELC, Singapore, 41–54.

Noss, R.B.: (ed.): 1982, *Language Teaching Issues in Multilingual Environments in Southeast Asia,* Anthology Series 10, SEAMEO RELC, Singapore.

Noss, R.B. (ed.): 1983, *Varieties of English in Southeast Asia*, Anthology Series 11, SEAMEO RELC, Singapore.

Pakir, A.: 1992, 'Issues in second language curriculum development: Singapore, Malaysia and Brunei', *Annual Review of Applied Linguistics* 13, 3–23.

Pakir, A. (ed.): 1993a, *The English Language in Singapore: Standards and Norms*, Uni-Press, Singapore.

Pakir, A.: 1993b. 'Making bilingualism work: developments in bilingual education in ASEAN', in R. Khoo et al. (eds.), *Towards Global Multilingualism: European models and Asian realities*, Special issue, *Language, Culture and Curriculum* 6(3), 209–223.

Pakir, A. & Low E.L.: 1995, 'The teaching of writing in Singapore', *Journal of Asian Pacific Communication* 6(1/2), 103–115.

Platt, J. & Weber, H.: 1980, *English in Singapore and Malaysia*, Oxford University Press, Kuala Lumpur.

Saran Kaur Gill (ed.): 1995, *INTELEC '94 Proceedings: International English Language Education*, Language Centre, Universiti Kebangsaan Malaysia, Kuala Lumpur.

Sibayan, B.P.: 1978, 'Views on language and identity: Limited metro Manila example', in A. Yap (ed.), *Language Education in Multilingual Societies*, Anthology Series 4, SEAMEO RELC, Singapore, 3–53.

Tay, M.W.J. & Gupta, A.: 1983, 'Towards a description of standard Singapore English', in R.B. Noss (ed.), *Varieties of English in Southeast Asia*, Anthology Series 11, SEAMEO RELC, Singapore, 173–189.

Tay, M.W.J.: 1993, *The English Language in Singapore: Issues and Development*, Uni-Press, Singapore.

Thumboo, E. (ed.): 1996, *Cultures in ASEAN and the 21st Century*, UniPress, Singapore.

Tickoo, M.L. (ed.): 1994, *Research in Reading and Writing: A Southeast Asian Collection*, Anthology Series 32, SEAMEO RELC, Singapore.

Tickoo, M.L. (ed.): 1995, *Reading and Writing: Theory into Practice*, Anthology Series 35, SEAMEO RELC, Singapore.

Varghese, S.: 1994, 'Reading and writing instruction in Singapore secondary schools', in S. Gopinathan et al. (eds.), *Language, Society and Education in Singapore: Issues and Trends*, Times Academic Press, Singapore, 296–312.

Varghese, S.: 1995. 'Reflectiveness in text composing', in M.L. Tickoo (ed.), *Reading and Writing: Theory into Practice*, Anthology Series 35, SEAMEO RELC, Singapore, 72–83.

Wong, I.F.H.: 1983. 'Simplification features in the structure of colloquial Malaysian English', in R.B. Noss (ed.), *Varieties of English in Southeast Asia*, Anthology Series 11, SEAMEO RELC, Singapore, 125–149.

Yap, A. (ed.): 1978. *Language Education in Multilingual Societies*, Anthology Series 4, SEAMEO RELC, Singapore.

NOEL WATTS

INNOVATIVE SECOND LANGUAGE EDUCATION IN THE SOUTH PACIFIC

The South Pacific comprises numerous small islands together with larger land masses such as Australia, New Zealand and Papua New Guinea which are dispersed over a wide geographical area. It is also linguistically and culturally one of the most diverse regions in the world.

In view of these factors it is not surprising that second language education in the South Pacific region has developed in distinctively different ways to meet the specific needs of language learners.

This review of innovative developments in second language education in the South Pacific will attempt to identify the more significant of the initiatives that have been taken in Australia, New Zealand and other Oceanic countries.

EARLY DEVELOPMENTS

In South Pacific countries the first schools were established by the missionaries. It was in these small mission schools that not only were pioneering efforts made to develop literacy in the vernacular but also, in a number of cases, an introduction was given to second language learning.

This was the situation in New Zealand where a mission school was opened as early as 1816. The mission schools placed emphasis initially on developing literacy in Maori. English was included in the curriculum in the 1840s.

An important influence on English language learning as elementary schooling developed later in the nineteenth century was that of James Pope, the first Inspector of Maori Schools, who introduced English readers based on situations familiar to Maori students. Pope may also be seen as ahead of his time in advocating in the 1880s a modified form of bilingual schooling (Benton, 1981).

Early New Zealand secondary schools sought to provide a traditional English education for the children of the colonial elite including in the curriculum languages such as French, Latin and Greek. George Hogben, the Inspector General of Schools at the turn of the century, showed foresight in endeavouring to introduce "natural" methods into foreign language teaching. However, Hogben's influence was short-lived and the grammatical methods of language teaching that Hogben criticised were to prevail for more than half a century (Watts, 1974).

G.R. Tucker and D. Corson (eds), Encyclopedia of Language and Education,
Volume 4: Second Language Education, 231–239.
© *1997 Kluwer Academic Publishers. Printed in the Netherlands.*

The Australian experience in the nineteenth century has some parallels with that of New Zealand. Gale (1990) suggests that in view of the missionary efforts in the early nineteenth century Australia could be considered one of the pioneers of vernacular programs for pre-literate societies. In 1838 the Lutheran missionaries Teichelmann and Schuermann began to establish schools in South Australia for Aboriginal children which taught reading and writing in the vernacular, though these schools were, in many cases, short-lived. Much of the teaching in Aboriginal languages languished after the middle of the nineteenth century and the period up to the 1940s is marked by sporadic attempts to provide western education for Aboriginal children through the medium of English (McConnochie, 1982).

However, there were significant developments in secular and religious schools that catered for the sons and daughters of new settlers from the United Kingdom and Europe. Clyne (1991) notes that bilingual approaches to education were followed in many Australian schools from the 1850s. Most bilingual schools were designed to cater for families from non-English speaking backgrounds (Gaelic, German, Hebrew) while a few were intended for a predominantly English-speaking elite who wanted their children to gain skills in another language.

In other South Pacific countries the early missionaries also contributed to vernacular education in the early nineteenth century. However, while vernacular teaching would continue strongly in the eastern region of the South Pacific where children came mainly from homogeneous language backgrounds (Baldauf, 1990), in the western areas of the South Pacific in countries with a multiplicity of languages, such as Papua New Guinea or Vanuatu, the trend once formal schooling became more established in the twentieth century was towards providing education through a colonial language (English or French).

MAJOR CONTRIBUTIONS

The post World War II period has seen a number of innovative developments in second language education emerge in the South Pacific region as countries have responded to the need to provide language learning opportunities for rapidly increasing numbers of learners. The development of competence in English or other languages of wider communication has been seen as a priority area. But there has also been growing recognition that the development of competence in a second language should not be at the expense of an indigenous or heritage language.

The New Zealand experience reflects these concerns. The use of Maori declined sharply in the twentieth century resulting in only a small minority possessing native fluency in the language by the 1970s (Benton, 1979). A number of initiatives have since been taken to support Maori. In 1976 a bilingual Maori-English school was opened at Ruatoki and this was followed by other bilingual programs (Cazden, 1989). However, the most far reaching development has been the establishment of *kohanga reo* centres and their extension to *kura kaupapa Maori*.

The first *kohanga reo* (language nest) was set up in 1982 with the aim of providing total immersion in Maori language and culture for pre-school children in an environment that attempts to replicate traditional Maori home life. The success of these *kohanga reo* centres can be attributed to the involvement of the local Maori community and the ways in which programmes are closely integrated with and supported by the community in all areas of activity from development of resources to overall management (Government Review Team, 1988). Pressure to continue Maori immersion education from pre-school to primary school levels and beyond has led to the establishment of *kura kaupapa Maori* (schools based on a Maori philosophy of learning) as an alternative to the European-style school system (see the review by Durie in Volume 5).

In Australia, since the 1970s, bilingual and immersion programs for Aboriginal and Torres Strait Islander people have also been mounted (Mills, 1982, see the reviews by Harris and Devlin, and by Gibbons in Volume 5). However, whereas in New Zealand attention in bilingual education has mainly focused on Maori and to a lesser extent Pacific Island languages, Australian bilingual and immersion programs have been developed in a wide range of LOTEs (Languages other than English), particularly languages spoken in ethnic communities, such as Italian and Modern Greek, following large-scale migration from non-English speaking countries in the post-World War II period. Studies of the features of immersion and bilingual programs at different levels of schooling have been made, amongst others, by Rado (1991), and Berthold (1995).

Literacy has been a key area of attention in all countries in the South Pacific region. A number of curriculum initiatives have taken place to enhance literacy development of second language learners of English. Amongst the notable contributions one might signal the work of Clay (1985) whose work on whole-language reading approaches, early detection of reading difficulties and reading recovery techniques has had a major influence on reading methods in Pacific countries as well as further afield. Other significant work in the area of English literacy includes the Book Flood conducted in Fiji rural schools in the late 1970s (Elley & Mangubhai, 1983) which was based on the premise that second language learners of English who followed an extensive book-based program with daily shared reading would experience considerable gains in language development. The success of this venture led to the development of reading programs using shared book methods in other Pacific Island countries (De'Ath, 1980).

Distance education has been strongly promoted in the South Pacific region to provide language learning opportunities for people in remote areas as well as those who are prevented from attending learning institutions because of work or other commitments. In Australia, for example, distance education is well established as a mode of pedagogical delivery for language learning with a large range of language programs offered by different providers using new technologies such as videotext, electronic mail, audioconferencing, interactive video, satellite dishes and telematics. Cunningham (1992) noted that 200 government schools in Victoria were conducting or receiving curricular offerings via networked computers supported by voice links and faxed documents. Distance education has also played an important part in promoting language learning in New Zealand and Fiji. The New Zealand Correspondence School, for example, offers foreign languages as well as English as a second language and Maori and employs a wide range of media resources. The University of the South Pacific in Suva also makes extensive use of satellite broadcasts in its distance education network (Matthewson, 1994).

WORK IN PROGRESS

Most of the developments referred to in the preceding section are currently being advanced. In New Zealand, for example, as part of the revival strategy for the Maori language increased funding is being provided for *kohanga reo* centres and for *kura kaupapa Maori*. It has been recognised that the supply of competent teachers is the key to further development of Maori-medium programs and this is being addressed by recruitment of larger numbers of Maori teachers and expansion of opportunities to upskill the language competence of practising teachers through Maori immersion inservice courses. The publication of resources written in Maori has been another priority area particularly to assist teaching in content areas such as science and mathematics.

In Australia work continues in developing programs in schools to extend awareness of the languages of Australia's indigenous peoples (Aborigines and Torres Strait Islanders) as well as in expanding bilingual programs in English and Aboriginal vernaculars particularly in the Northern Territory where many Aboriginal children live in traditionally oriented communities (Willmett, 1993).

Initiatives are being taken in both Australia and New Zealand to improve the quality of ESOL (English for speakers of other languages) instruction through teacher training and the provision of additional resources for schools in areas with high concentrations of migrants. In New Zealand, for instance, the Ministry of Education is supporting school-based teacher development programs to provide additional training for primary and secondary teachers of students from non-English speaking backgrounds. Language Australia (formerly the National Languages and Literacy Institute of Australia) through its National Office in Canberra and its centres in different states is playing a major role in co-ordinating language projects and disseminating information on language and literacy education. A recent initiative in this respect is the NLLIA ESL Development Project which has involved development of bandscales for reporting on the proficiency development of second language learners of English in the school context, together with exemplar assessment activities and observation guides (McKay, 1994).

As far as LOTEs (Languages other than English) in Australia or LOTEMs (Languages other than English or Maori) in New Zealand are concerned, the current developments focus on expansion of second language learning at all levels. In Australia increased levels of participation in the learning of languages are a key objective of the Australian Language and Literacy Policy (ALLP) which was endorsed by the Federal Government in 1991 (see the review by Clyne in Volume 1). This builds on the National Policy on Languages (Lo Bianco, 1987). The ALLP identified 14 priority languages – Aboriginal languages, Arabic, Chinese (Mandarin), French, German, Modern Greek, Indonesian, Italian, Japanese, Korean, Russian, Spanish, Thai and Vietnamese but allowed each State and Territory to nominate its own priority list. Profiles of key languages in Australia, their importance culturally and economically and the ways in which they are being taught at secondary and tertiary levels may be found in Stanley et al. (1990), Marriott et al. (1993) and Djité (1994). Clyne et al. (1995) provide a comprehensive examination of primary school language programs in the state of Victoria which since 1983 has embarked on a ambitious program to develop and expand the teaching of LOTEs at the elementary level.

Current activities in the teaching of LOTEMs in New Zealand include extending support for community languages through Government funding of early childhood Pacific Islands language centres and bilingual programs at the primary and secondary levels. As far as other languages are concerned, while the support for foreign languages has not received the same priority as in Australia there is encouragement for schools to offer a range of languages from the Form 1 level, though this falls short of making such language learning compulsory. Recent initiatives involve the drafting of curriculum guidelines for languages such as Chinese and Spanish and the planning of unit standards for community languages and international languages that will fit into the new qualifications framework being introduced into schools.

Further advances are also occurring in the area of distance education. In Australia and New Zealand there is a trend towards use of distance education technologies to enable schools to share resources. This may involve a system, as in Victoria, where schools are grouped in clusters making it possible for a specialist teacher in one school to conduct lessons for small classes in other schools through telecommunication links. Use of computer networks and interactive multimedia is becoming more widespread in distance education delivery systems in the region.

In other countries in the South Pacific bilingual programs involving English as a second language and local vernaculars also continue to show a steady increase (see the review by Lotherington in Volume 5). The Tongan Curriculum Development Unit, for example, has published a large number of books in Tongan and English to support its new bilingual, whole-language oriented curriculum. An alternative approach has been the development of 'hand-crafted' books prepared by teachers at regional writing workshops (Moore, 1994). The Institute of Education of the University of the South Pacific is playing a major role in literacy development in both English and vernacular languages through its Literacy Centre and its involvement in the Primary Reading and HOLEA (Whole Language Approach to Teaching English) Projects which have included the trialling of a story-book based English as a second language curriculum in Fiji, Kiribati, the Marshall Islands, Tonga, Tuvalu, Western Samoa and Vanuatu (Moore & Lumelume, 1991). The Institute of Education *Waka* series which had its origins in regional UNESCO book production workshops in the 1970s now includes a large number of English and vernacular titles which are distributed throughout the region. The *Vanua Readers* (Vanuatu: English and French) and the *Nguzu Nguzu* series (Solomon Islands: English only) are other significant local responses for the need for books.

Perhaps one of the most important developments in the South Pacific region is the reform of elementary education in Papua New Guinea. This follows on from the vernacular pre-school program (*Tok Ples Pri Skul*) which had been established in several provinces in the 1980s, to enable children to commence development of literacy skills in their own language before transition to English-medium schooling in Grade 3. This ambitious undertaking poses significant challenges for a country with over 800 languages and has major implications for teacher recruitment and training as well as vernacular materials development (Olsson, 1987; Siegel, 1996).

PROBLEMS AND DIFFICULTIES

A common problem which affects the degree to which innovative programmes can be mounted to meet learner needs in countries in the region is teacher supply. The expansion of LOTEs in Australia has created shortages of language teachers (Djité, 1994). In New Zealand there is also a lack of teachers of Maori as well as of other languages in demand, particularly Asian languages. In addition, there is a need for increasing numbers of suitably qualified ESOL teachers to provide English language support across the curriculum. Similar problems in recruiting and training teachers are found in many Pacific Island countries (Tavola, 1991; Mosely, 1994; Siegel, 1996).

Apart from qualified and experienced teachers additional resources are required in most countries in the region to meet the needs of second language learners. For many small Pacific Island countries there are major problems in the costs involved in production of locally designed textbooks and other curriculum materials. However, even in Australia and New Zealand there are examples of shortages of suitable materials. A case in point is the need in New Zealand for Maori teaching materials that relate to different curriculum areas for use in immersion classes.

A further matter of concern is the organisation of the instruction that language learners receive. In many cases effective linkage between institutions is lacking with the result that second language learning initiated in primary schools is inadequately followed up and consolidated at more advanced levels. Failure to build upon students' previous experience in the language may well contribute towards high attrition rates in language study. Outdated language syllabuses and curricula also compound problems for students and make it more difficult for students to make progressive advancement towards communicative competence in the target language. For instance, the South Pacific Commission Oral English Course has received major criticism for its audio-lingual methodology but still remains in use in a number of South Pacific countries.

FUTURE DIRECTIONS

The slow and steady rise in the status of vernacular languages is likely to continue in the South Pacific. It is also probable that pressure to give greater recognition of the rights of indigenous peoples will intensify. In education this will result in increasing the role given to languages such as Maori in New Zealand and Aboriginal and Torres Strait Islander languages in Australia. Nevertheless, there is also little doubt that countries in the region will continue to place high importance on learners developing competence in English (and French in New Caledonia, Vanuatu and French Polynesia) as media of instruction and languages of administration and commerce. As a result, increased attention will need to be paid to following appropriate models of bilingual education to ensure that the learning of English or French is an additive bilingual experience for students not a subtractive one.

Demands to offer a wider range of languages are likely to increase in response to developing trade and political links with countries in regions such as Asia, South America, the Middle East and the African continent (National Languages and Literacy Institute of Australia, 1991). This will require development of a range of strategies to overcome shortages of teachers in languages in demand and to develop locally-produced resources tailored to the interests and needs of learners in the region.

To allow further time for students to progress towards higher levels of competence, particularly in languages which are linguistically very different to the native language of the learners, greater emphasis will need to be placed on commencing language study at the primary level and careful co-ordination of primary and secondary programs to ensure that there is continuity between the two levels.

These developments will inevitably place extra strain on already over-stretched resources and may encourage countries in the region to co-ordinate programs more effectively and share expertise. This applies not only at the national level but also at the regional level. Consequently, one might envisage greater pooling of resources and increased participation in regionally-based projects targeted at discovering ways of meeting more effectively the particular needs of second language learners in the region.

Massey University, New Zealand

REFERENCES

Baldauf, R.B.: 1990, 'Education and language planning in the Samoas', in R.B. Baldauf & A. Luke (eds.), *Language Planning and Education in Australasia and the South Pacific*, Multilingual Matters, Clevedon, Avon, 259–276.

Benton, R.A.: 1979, *Who Speaks Maori in New Zealand?*, New Zealand Council for Educational Research, Wellington.

Benton, R.A.: 1981, *The Flight of the Amokura: Oceanic Languages and Formal Education in the South Pacific*, New Zealand Council for Educational Research, Wellington.

Berthold, M. (ed.): 1995, *Rising to the Bilingual Challenge: Ten Years of Queensland Secondary School Immersion*, National Languages and Literacy Institute of Australia, Canberra.

Cazden, C.B.: 1989, 'Richmond road: A multilingual/multicultural primary school in Auckland, New Zealand', *Language and Education* 3, 143–166.

Clay, M.: 1985, *The Early Detection of Reading Difficulties* (third edition), Heinemann, Auckland.

Clyne, M.: 1991, *Community Languages: The Australian Experience*, Cambridge University Press, Cambridge.

Clyne, M., Jenkins, C., Chen, I.M., Tasokalidou, R. & Wallner, T.: 1995, *Developing Second Language from Primary School: Models and Outcomes*, National Languages and Literacy Institute of Australia, Deakin.

Cunningham, D.: 1992, 'Languages and distance education technology in Australia', *Babel* 27, 10–15.

De'Ath, P.R.T.: 1980, 'The shared book experience and ESL', *Directions* 4, 13–22.

Djité, P.: 1994, *From language policy to language planning: An overview of languages other than English in Australian education*, National Languages and Literacy Institute of Australia, Deakin.

Elley, W.B. & Mangubhai, F.: 1983, 'The impact of reading on second language learning, *Reading Research Quarterly* 19, 53–67.

Gale, M.A.: 1990, 'A review of bilingual education in aboriginal Australia', *Australian Review of Applied Linguistics* 13, 40–80.

Government Review Team: 1988, *Government Review of Te Kohanga Reo*, Te Kohanga Reo National Trust, Wellington.

Lo Bianco, J.: 1987, *National Policy on Languages*, Australian Government Publishing Service, Canberra.

Marriott, H., Neustupny, J.V. & Spence-Brown, R.: 1993, *Unlocking Australia's Language Potential: Profiles of 9 Key Languages in Australia*, Vol. 7 – Japanese, National Languages and Literacy Institute of Australia, Deakin.

Matthewson, C.: 1994, 'Distance beyond measure: A view from and of the Pacific', *Directions* 16, 29–35.

McConnochie, K.: 1982, 'Aborigines and Australian education: Historical perspectives', in J. Sherwood (ed.), *Aboriginal Education: Issues and Innovations*, Creative Research, Perth, 17–32.

McKay, P.: 1994, *ESL Development: Languages and Literacy in Schools, Volume 1: Teachers' Manual* (second edition), National Languages and Literacy Institute of Australia, Deakin.

Mills, J.: 1982, *Bilingual Education in Australian Schools*, Australian Council for Educational Research, Hawthorn, Victoria.

Moore, B.: 1994, 'Handmade books', *Pacific Curriculum Network* 3, 22–24.

Moore, B. & Lumelume, S.: 1991, 'Ready to read in the South Pacific', *Directions* 13, 54–64.

Moseley, L.: 1994, 'Language, aid and literacy: An outline of activities in the Solomon Islands', *Language and Education* 8, 41–45.

National Languages and Literacy Institute of Australia: 1991, *Language is Good Business Conference Proceedings: The Role of Language in Australia's Economic Future*, National Languages and Literacy Institute of Australia, Melbourne.

Olsson, M.: 1987, 'Language and education in Papua New Guinea', *Papua New Guinea Journal of Education* 23, 119–148.

Rado, M.: 1991, 'Bilingual education', in A.J. Liddicoat (ed.), *Bilingualism and Bilingual Education*, National Languages Institute of Australia, Melbourne, 141–197.

Siegel, J.: 1996, *Vernacular Education in the South Pacific* (International Development Issues No. 45), Australian Agency for International Development, Canberra.

Stanley, J., Ingram, D. & Chittick, G.: 1990, *The Relationship between International Trade and Linguistic Competence: Report to the Australian Advisory Council on Languages and Multicultural Education*, Australian Government Publishing Service, Canberra.

Tavola, H.: 1991, *Secondary Education in Fiji: A Key to the Future*, Institute of Pacific Studies, University of the South Pacific, Suva.

Willmett, K.: 1993, 'Differing approaches to education policy by aboriginal communities: Case study of Yirrkala and Yipirinya', *Access: Critical Perspectives on Education Policy* 11, 114–130.

Watts, N.: 1974, 'George Hogben – Language teacher', *Education* 13, 26–28.

SUBJECT INDEX

NAME INDEX

TABLE OF CONTENTS

VOLUME 1: LANGUAGE POLICY AND POLITICAL ISSUES IN EDUCATION

TABLE OF CONTENTS

Section 4: Practical and Empirical Issues

TABLE OF CONTENTS

VOLUME 2: LITERACY

TABLE OF CONTENTS

Section 3: Focus on the Social Context of Literacy

Section 4: Focus on Selected Regions

TABLE OF CONTENTS

VOLUME 3: ORAL DISCOURSE AND EDUCATION

TABLE OF CONTENTS

TABLE OF CONTENTS

VOLUME 5: BILINGUAL EDUCATION

TABLE OF CONTENTS

TABLE OF CONTENTS

VOLUME 6: KNOWLEDGE ABOUT LANGUAGE

TABLE OF CONTENTS

TABLE OF CONTENTS

VOLUME 7: LANGUAGE TESTING AND ASSESSMENT

TABLE OF CONTENTS

TABLE OF CONTENTS

VOLUME 8: RESEARCH METHODS IN LANGUAGE AND EDUCATION

TABLE OF CONTENTS

Encyclopedia of Language and Education

Set ISBN Hb 0-7923-4596-7; Pb 0-7923-4936-9

1. R. Wodak and D. Corson (eds.): *Language Policy and Political Issues in Education.* 1997

   ISBN Hb 0-7923-4713-7
   ISBN Pb 0-7923-4928-8

2. V. Edwards and D. Corson (eds.): *Literacy.* 1997

   ISBN Hb 0-7923-4595-0
   ISBN Pb 0-7923-4929-6

3. B. Davies and D. Corson (eds.): *Oral Discourse and Education.* 1997

   ISBN Hb 0-7923-4639-4
   ISBN Pb 0-7923-4930-X

4. G.R. Tucker and D. Corson (eds.): *Second Language Education.* 1997

   ISBN Hb 0-7923-4640-8
   ISBN Pb 0-7923-4931-8

5. J. Cummins and D. Corson (eds.): *Bilingual Education.* 1997

   ISBN Hb 0-7923-4806-0
   ISBN Pb 0-7923-4932-6

6. L. van Lier and D. Corson (eds.): *Knowledge about Language.* 1997

   ISBN Hb 0-7923-4641-6
   ISBN Pb 0-7923-4933-4

7. C. Clapham and D. Corson (eds.): *Language Testing and Assessment.* 1997

   ISBN Hb 0-7923-4702-1
   ISBN Pb 0-7923-4934-2

8. N.H. Hornberger and D. Corson (eds.): *Research Methods in Language and Education.* 1997

   ISBN Hb 0-7923-4642-4
   ISBN Pb 0-7923-4935-0

KLUWER ACADEMIC PUBLISHERS – DORDRECHT / BOSTON / LONDON

FEIWEL AND FRIENDS
NEW YORK

An imprint of Macmillan Publishing Group, LLC
175 Fifth Avenue, New York, NY 10010
fiercereads.com

Our books may be purchased in bulk for promotional, educational, or business use. Please contact your local bookseller or the Macmillan Corporate and Premium Sales Department at (800) 221-7945 ext. 5442 or by e-mail at MacmillanSpecialMarkets@macmillan.com.

Library of Congress Control Number: 2016953574

ISBN 978-1-250-15868-0 (paperback)   ISBN 978-1-250-12340-4 (ebook)

Endpaper credits: Eye photographs © JR-ART.net; illustrations © James Manning; brick wall © Shutterstock/Dan Kosmayer

Originally published in the United States by Feiwel and Friends
First Square Fish edition, 2018
Book designed by Liz Dresner and Sophie Erb
Square Fish logo designed by Filomena Tuosto

10   9   8   7   6   5   4   3   2   1